That's Me, Groucho!

# That's Me, Groucho!

## The Solo Career of Groucho Marx

MATTHEW CONIAM

*Foreword by* Frank Ferrante

McFarland & Company, Inc., Publishers

*Jefferson, North Carolina*

ALSO BY MATTHEW CONIAM

*The Annotated Marx Brothers: A Filmgoer's Guide to
In-Jokes, Obscure References and Sly Details* (McFarland, 2015)

**ISBN** (print) 978-1-4766-6373-9
**ISBN** (ebook) 978-1-4766-2597-3

LIBRARY OF CONGRESS CATALOGUING DATA ARE AVAILABLE

British Library cataloguing data are available

Front cover artwork © 2016 Stuart Troxel

Printed in the United States of America

*McFarland & Company, Inc., Publishers
Box 611, Jefferson, North Carolina 28640
www.mcfarlandpub.com*

For George Bettinger, who gave me the napkins.
And for Don Whearty, who drew them.
And for Frank.
And for Miriam.

# Contents

# Foreword

## *by Frank Ferrante*

And here he is … the one, the only … *Groucho*!

An unholy trinity, those Brothers Marx. They remain an eternally sublime trio, forever linked as arguably the funniest, most original comedy team of the past century.

However, middle brother Julius Henry Marx, a.k.a. Groucho, debuted as a single act, persevered on stage for a remarkable 71 years and bookended his career solo. At 15, Julius toured the vaudeville circuit as a boy soprano and on his first contract was abandoned and left penniless by an unscrupulous actor/manager. At 85, Groucho trouped and wheezed renditions of "Show Me a Rose" for throngs of young fans like yours truly. And even then there was the sense that Groucho was alone. "Show me a rose … or leave me alone."

Those of us who venerate Groucho Marx relate to the loner. He is often the lone wolf within the context of the three Brothers' stage and film shenanigans. Chico and Harpo individually and in tandem often conned and plotted against him—an outsider within his own tribe. (Recall Dr. Hackenbush's "tootsie frootsie-ing" in *A Day at the Races* and S. Quentin Quale's pickpocketing in *Go West*.) Asked by Dick Cavett to which brother he was closest, Groucho's response was "Gummo," with whom he shared hotel rooms while zigzagging throughout the country in vaudeville. Perhaps, in terms of the fraternal dynamic, art imitated life. And yet the Brothers' bond is undeniable. Groucho's son Arthur Marx who co-wrote "Groucho: A Life in Revue," in which I portrayed our hero, mentioned to me that Groucho spoke to his brothers daily, even if the conversations consisted of "How are you, Chic." "I'm fine, Grouch."

I've had the furtive delight of listening to Richard J. Anobile's 1973 Groucho interviews, which comprise the core of *The Marx Brothers Scrapbook*. The seeming harshness of his responses on the printed page belies the surprisingly tender timbre of Groucho's staccato delivery. Sprinkled throughout those exchanges with Anobile: "I loved my brothers." "I loved Chico."

He became famous as one of four performing brothers, but according to son Arthur and daughter Miriam, Groucho never felt like a star. After over 25 years as a Marx Brother, he was primed to strike out on his own. When the Marxes disbanded in 1941, Groucho lamented his subsequent radio failures and insecurities to Miriam in letters she generously shared in her published collection *Love, Groucho*.

In his fifties, Groucho struggled with a sense of failure. Arthur confided to me that his father, often morose and solitary, planned for his demise from age fifty. The elder Marx, who never made it past the sixth grade, took solace in his solitude and intellectual pursuits. He spent incalculable hours reading while smoking his pipe and the occasional Dunhill cigar. Henry James, Somerset Maugham and Ring Lardner lined his shelves, as did *The Best Plays* volumes 1921 through 1944. Groucho subscribed to multiple periodicals and kept a dictionary in his car glove compartment. He composed thousands of letters, of which there are two published volumes—*The Groucho Letters* and Miriam's memoir. A dedicated guitarist, Groucho strummed along to Gilbert and Sullivan operettas, reveled in classical music and that of his contemporaries—Berlin, Gershwin and Porter.

All of this fed Groucho's comic mind, spirit and art, and he was well oiled when *You Bet Your Life* appeared on the horizon. The quiz show, sans his brothers, generated hundreds of hours of entertainment. Contemporary and fluid, Groucho's wit was transcendent, gleeful and refreshingly honest. Tempered contempt, juxtaposed with a certain warmth, exuded from the kindly old quizmaster. Groucho the soloist was born, and King Leer reigned supreme.

Groucho never devised a solo act for Las Vegas, the performing arts center circuit or concert halls, like peers Jack Benny, George Burns and Red Skelton. The consummate wordsmith did not consider his comic style suited for Vegas or Friars Club roasts, and on Cavett's program he lambasted "dirty entertainment." Words were not necessary when eyebrows conveyed volumes. In the twelfth hour of his career, despite obvious fragility, he forged on with his *An Evening with Groucho* live performance—in true vaudevillian fashion, premiering it out of town, in Ames, Iowa. A subsequent album from his Carnegie Hall show was released and, like many of my peers, I wore out the grooves of that sacred disc. From his "First, I'd like to take a bow for Harpo and Chico" to the rapturous applause capping "Lydia, the Tattooed Lady," Groucho elicits goose bumps. The great man's highly anticipated performance is moving, funny, exhilarating and sad— and I was left imagining the possibilities if Groucho had taken his act on the road decades prior.

What if Groucho Marx had performed a one-man show in 1934 between filming *Duck Soup* and *A Night at the Opera*, instead of the summer stock production of *Twentieth Century* in Skowhegan, Maine? For the past 30 years, I have performed my show, *An Evening With Groucho*, with that premise in mind. With the benefit of hindsight and Groucho's inspiring legacy, I mix his interrogative conversational banter from *You Bet Your Life* with the attack of his brasher, younger stage and film persona, breaking the fourth wall so today's audience can experience a taste of Groucho up close. It is my fantasy, my homage, and one that I hope Mr. Marx would appreciate.

Matthew Coniam's homage here is a welcome and long overdue addition to the Marx literary canon. Mr. Coniam is a Marxist of the highest caliber. The sheer amount of performance, entertainment, laughter and joy conjured by Groucho Marx over his lifetime and beyond is immeasurable. But Mr. Coniam, a dedicated devotee and chronicler, reveals the expanse of the great man's solo contributions and lasting influence. Groucho Marx would love this book.

In Groucho's final years, he transitioned from quizzer to quizee on the talk show circuit. These interviews read as solo performances, displaying the breadth of Groucho's intellect and humor—gold nuggets from his enduring comic mind. Live appearances were few, but I was privileged at 13 to attend one of his last. Just short of 86, Groucho appeared at the Ambassador Hotel in Los Angeles. With trademark beret and thick glasses, he shuffled to the podium. I followed my hero like a duckling and sat patiently at his feet. Groucho mumbled inaudibly to a concerned, packed room. The tension felt by hundreds of expectant admirers was palpable. Finally someone asked, "Groucho, are you making any new Marx Brothers movies?"

He paused. "No," he growled. "I'm answering silly questions."

*Actor, writer and producer Frank Ferrante was named "the greatest living interpreter of Groucho Marx's material" by the* New York Times. *He has portrayed Groucho on three continents in more than 400 cities, including New York and London, where he was nominated for a Laurence Olivier Award.*

# Preface

"Do you realize there are *twelve* books out on the Marx Brothers, not counting the ones *we* wrote?" an incredulous Groucho once asked Roger Ebert.[1] "We're getting to be like Abraham Lincoln. But a lot of these books, I've looked at them, they're crap."

That's as close as the man himself is going to come to bidding you welcome to my second addition to the crap pile. My first, *The Annotated Marx Brothers*, was in a sense the repayment of a debt. There are many things I love and admire in life, but few prompt me to speculate as to what my life might have been like had I not encountered them. This is an acid test: what influences are so formative, so essential to one's sense of self, that to speculate on their absence is not to imagine mere loss but rather to posit a complete *revision* of self-definition? First on my list are the Marx Brothers. And it's a short list.

So my previous book was something of a thank you note. This follow-up of sorts is slightly different, in that it is designed to fill an external gap as much as meet an internal need. This is a professional life of Groucho Marx, and so far as I am aware it is the first such study of his work apart from his brothers. There are of course several lives of Groucho available, but while they will contain a few sentences on, say, *The Mikado*, among several paragraphs on what was happening in his private life at the time he made it, here that ratio is reversed.

However, while it most definitely is *not* a biography, the framework in which the material is arranged *is* biographical. This was not planned, but rather suggested itself during the writing. Sub-headings remain to indicate the arrival of a specific project, and readers are, of course, welcome to skip between these out of sequence if what they are looking for is background information on a particular production. But the dry arrangement of separate sections I had first planned seemed to call for context, and as Groucho's career choices are in themselves reflective of where he saw himself as a man and a performer at that point in time, it seemed natural to convert the material into an unfolding story.

As with *The Annotated Marx Brothers*, the aim is more to divert the confirmed enthusiast than to introduce the subject to the newcomer. Though I trust that nobody will go away confused, some may question my priorities a little. If I am guilty of marginalizing some of the better-known elements of the story in favor of dustier corners, that is because I have intended to present almost everyone with something they may not already know, and so a general awareness of Groucho and the course of his career, especially its milestones, is taken as read. The aim here, as before, is to dig beneath the surface, and see if there are any surprises hiding there. For the most part, personal detail is included only when relevant to an understanding of his career trajectory, and rarely dwelled upon—at least until his final decade, where it seemed to me unavoidable. But where psychological interpretation does intrude, as at times it must, the conclusions drawn are entirely mine, and I take full responsibility for them. Where I part from consensus it is, I hope, always in the direction of generosity.

Through the course of researching and writing, many individuals and institutions have helped me in many different ways. First and especially, there is Mr. Frank Ferrante, who not only wrote the foreword but also provided additional information, access to rare sources, previously unseen photographs and a lively correspondence. I would also like to single out Richard J. Anobile for agreeing to break a long silence and patiently return to a subject he now views as part of a previous lifetime. If, as I hope, readers find glimpses in these pages of a Groucho rather different from the one they thought they knew, it's in large part thanks to these generously provided personal perspectives, along with those of Sue Tyler Edwards, Paul Krassner, Bill Marx, Elaine Tyler May, Jack Rennert, Lucinda Irwin Smith, Steve Stoliar and Judy Tyler. It was an especial pleasure to make contact with Marie Behar (Lesley-Marie Colburn), who told me of a childhood encounter with the off-duty Groucho that was powerful enough to serve as afterword to this book. And a comparable delight to speak to the ninety-four year old Don Whearty, the cartoonist drew the Groucho novelty cocktail napkins ("nap-grins"), which I will be arguing capture and embody the moment when Groucho transformed from comedy star to eternal icon. "It's not often an old artist gets thanks for his work," Whearty told me when I made that point to him, "and it's a wonderful feeling." (He also told me not to get old. I said I'd do my best.)

The book was written and re-written in the online company of Bob Gassel, R.S.H. Tryster and Ed Watz, whose collective gifts in the fields of research, interpretation, corroboration, disputation and absurd good humor were, once again, a privilege to draw upon. I would also like to give special thanks to my splendid appendix writers, all of whom exceeded my hopes for their contributions: thank you, Noah Diamond, Jay Hopkins and Gary Westin. Noah also selflessly rationed his own archival researches to assist me with mine, and then for dessert made a major structural suggestion that completely transfigured the book. The hell with him, I say. Stuart Troxel painted the stunning cover portrait especially for the project, and so, despite the old adage, this is one book I'm more than happy for you to judge by its cover.

Among the many others who helped along the way, to be singled out are Cameron Allen, George Bettinger, John V. Brennan, Mark Brisenden, Marjie Cardwell, Jeffrey Cohen, Steve Cox, Frank Diernhammer, Ross Freedman, Andy Hollingworth, Jim Junot, Jane Margaret Laight, Frank Lazarus, Simon Louvish, David McGillivray, Glenn Mitchell, Andrea Orlando, Cinco Paul, Jim Ramsburg, Brent Reid, Scott T. Rivers, Michael Roberts, Ben Robinson, David Sabih, Scott Saternye, Maxwell Siegel, Andrew T. Smith, Colin Stanley, Roger Stevenson, Ralph Torres, Doug Tyler and Mikael Uhlin.

As always, this would all be blank pages without the encouragement and support of my wonderful family: Angela, Edward, Helen, Sanday and Sandra—respectively my wife, son, sister and parents.

And thanks, finally, to Groucho Marx, who would doubtless have told me to take a hike were he still alive, but, as he is not, proved the most unfailingly patient, courteous and helpful subject a writer could hope for. ("That's what *you* say.")

# Introduction: Subtracting Sheep

My brothers are even lazier than I. We'll never work together again. It's too bad because I just happened to think of a good line I could have used in *The Cocoanuts*, 33 years later. I played a hotel manager and had one scene where I called a guy and asked him if he had a girl in his room. I forget the line I used when he said no. Just the other day, the scene returned to me and I had the guy answering yes. I just said "Congratulations!" and hung up. It would have got a hell of a laugh in 1927.

—Groucho Marx, 1960

Journalist Barry Dillon interviewed Groucho Marx not long before his death in 1977. Dillon's article described the poignant simplicity of Groucho's daily routine, far removed from the life of comfort and distraction one might have supposed to be the lot of a living legend. His days were quiet now, very different from when, under the regime of his notoriously controlling factotum Erin Fleming, the house was filled with a steady stream of celebrity pilgrims. Occasionally, Zeppo would drop in. "The last time he was here he brought me some fish," recalled Groucho with a smile.

The highlight of his day was to be driven the ten-minute journey to a nearby park, where he sat alone with a loaf of French bread, feeding the birds and goldfish: "By the time I'm finished here I'll be responsible for breeding the biggest goldfish in captivity." His favorite film, he said, was Disney's *The Incredible Journey*. Occasionally, Dillon noted, "people would recognise the sad elderly gentleman in the deer stalker suit," but the sad elderly gentleman was usually too lost in his private thoughts to reward the acknowledgment with insult or quip. The subject of death, never raised explicitly in the interview, hovers over all. "Did you know that you can stay awake," Groucho asked suddenly in the middle of an unrelated conversation, "by subtracting sheep?"[1]

It is, of course, only to be expected that a man who helped define his century would find it especially unjust that time and fate should give no higher priority to his physical permanence than anybody else's. And yet there was an unsettled quality to Groucho's personality from the first, an underlying aura of dissatisfaction, not created but merely amplified by the unpredictability of his career and the ironies of his final years. But in what was this dissatisfaction rooted? After all, his success and acclaim were undoubted. First a quarter, then a third of the Marx Brothers, he was in reality always more than an equal share. For many if not most fans, his is the presence that defines the act, the pivot around which their plays and movies revolved, always the principal and defining character, and always receiving top, non-alphabetical billing. Few if any of us are exactly the people we want to be. Yet with Groucho we sense a greater than usual disjunction, especially in terms of professional attainment.

Certainly we should remember that any family of brothers establishes a hierarchy from the first, and it may not square with how the audience prefers to rank them. On screen, Groucho was the leader of the Marx Brothers, while his elder brother Chico found his role an ever-diminishing one. But behind the scenes Chico was their mother's favorite, a dazzling, effortless success with women, easy in company, with a superb head for business, and a man who made friends and influenced people with an enviable casualness. ("I'd always looked at Chico with a mixture of envy and exasperation," Groucho recalls in *The Groucho Phile*.) Everything came easy to Chico, even his art. As Groucho observed to Charlotte Chandler in her biography *Hello, I Must Be Going*, "Chico's idea of practicing was to dip his hands in a basin of hot water." From the inside looking out, the group dynamic may have been very different from the one we perceive.

"When we get through this present contract we'll all be through," Groucho told a reporter, on behalf of his brothers, on the set of *At the Circus* in 1939. "It will be amazing if they are not fed up with us before then."[2] The team's subsequent retirement is generally presumed a group decision, so ingrained is the popular image of Groucho as leader and spokesman. In truth, Groucho was acting unilaterally, and not, by any means, from disinterest in his career. He wasn't tired of performing, and far from presuming audiences were tired of him—he was banking on their not being. But he knew that only by disposing of the Marx Brothers would he stand a chance of being accepted as Groucho Marx, alone. "I am firm about disbanding," he wrote Arthur Sheekman, "and from now on I'm strictly on my own."

The other Marx Brothers shared none of these frustrations. It is true that Harpo was finding their workload increasingly tiring in a physical sense, but the professional angst and dissatisfaction besetting Groucho was entirely his own. (Harpo was financially able to retire and wanted to spend more time at home, so put up no opposition. "My dad was thrilled with Groucho's solo success," reflects Harpo's son, Bill. "Dad loved working, but he started to have heart problems that slowed him down somewhat, and mom had turned him into quite a family man."[3]) Chico, as usual, was the sticking point. "Why the hell should I want to quit?" Chico responded in 1942 to the *New York Post*'s Earl Wilson, when asked why the Brothers had decided to call it a day. "I hope that after Groucho lays off of that black mustache for a year or so, he'll get the urge to wear it again."

But Julius held firm, and fifteen years later it still rankled with Chico: "We just got tired of making pictures, it got boresome. Not to me, but to Groucho."[4]

The transition between the Groucho of the Marx Brothers and the solo Groucho is less disruptive than it might have been, mainly because of the accident of Irving Thalberg and MGM. The producer's recipe for reinvigorating their careers in the mid–1930s had involved a great deal of smoothing and tempering, and much of what had made the pristine Groucho so confrontational had already been neutralized by the time opportunity came for him to fly the nest. Listen, even, to his voice. The most fundamental weapon in his armory was the nasal sneer, which automatically rendered his every utterance insincere, and by which compliments were made to seem hostile, and hostility complimentary. Had he leapt from *Animal Crackers*, say, straight into *Copacabana*, the degree of domestication might have seemed intolerable. But over the course of five features for MGM, his vocal patterns had softened in tandem with his character's reduction into benign crazy—his character, in becoming less distinctive and malign, seems almost in preparation for dispersal into various solo environments. And so the transition seemed accountable, at least, if not inevitable.

The really defining difference between the Groucho of the Marx Brothers and the one who appears alone is the mustache. In daily life, the Groucho of the Marx Brothers period wore no mustache at all; the Groucho of *You Bet Your Life* and beyond had a real one. The ludicrous greasepaint smear of the archetypal Groucho, however, is both and neither: simultaneously present and absent, it is the frank acknowledgment of irrational denial. As such, it seems pregnant with intention. The odd thing is that it appears, in truth, to have been accidental (accounts of its origin vary—see Appendix II—but they usually hinge on contingency rather than inspiration). But its effect is certain. It is both a feigning and a dismissal of bourgeois propriety. Groucho's scorn for characters with facial hair is relentless in the Marx Brothers' films: he seems to take it as a certain indication of pretension. His own "mustache" is therefore a comic revenge: not a mustache at all but the pretense of one. It is the mustache equivalent of Magritte's pipe, announcing that it is not what it is, and is what it is not. Groucho's essential character in these films is that of an interloper, and his mustache seems to say, "I will adopt the standards of the world I am attempting to crash, but only in the most superficial way imaginable." It therefore signifies both ingratiation and contempt; the absurd half-heartedness of the gesture announcing its intent more forcefully than would no mustache at all. It is a badge that reads "Interloper." His power comes from his discovery that if he is bold enough, and makes himself attractive enough in some or other fraudulent way, his hosts and victims will be too spineless even to acknowledge it.

In substituting a genuine mustache, Groucho's character changes fundamentally. He is rendered not merely more realistic but also less malevolent and powerful. But he also gains a freedom denied him before. One senses that Groucho wanted to be two things: an actor and a comic personality, sufficiently unburdened by gimmicks and characteristics as to be acceptable as "normal" in the latter capacity, and free to sustain variation in the former. The Groucho of the Marx Brothers was neither: he was a comic character, with all the limitations implied by the term. In swapping the one for the other he gained in potential what he lost in uniqueness. It was a trade-off he must have been aware of, but never wavered in his desire for. And, as we shall see, he was well aware of the significance of his mustache in terms of its symbolic focus.

What should have been an easy transition was further complicated by a more fundamental if equally unforeseen side effect. A funny thing had happened to Julius: he and his character seemed to have merged, to the extent that when breaking out into other roles, the popular perception was not that one character had been abandoned for another so much as that the first one was now pretending to be the second. "Groucho" the character had become Groucho the man.

Of course, the public always likes to think that the shadows they see on screen are indistinguishable from those who cast them, but for Groucho the demands were different. All that Jimmy Stewart or Cary Grant needed to be in their old age to qualify for our adoration was alive, and nobody demanded that the elderly Harold Lloyd should still climb skyscrapers. But being Groucho wasn't so easy. The truism that the lightning-fast, rapier-sharp wit that characterized the onscreen Groucho was also innate in his off-screen namesake was not entirely true. No account of the Brothers' childhood or youth or vaudeville days recalls the younger Groucho as possessed of devastating verbal skills. We hear repeatedly of his diffidence, his introspectiveness, his bookishness. But it wasn't until *On the Mezzanine* in the early 1920s, when the "Groucho" persona as we know it began to emerge, that so did the suggestion that it was a variation of his real self. And with it came the demand that it be lived up to at all times, even in private.

From then on, confusion—sometimes productive, sometimes obfuscating—reigned. Instead of Julius Marx playing a character called Groucho, who reappears in different contexts in play after play and film after film, we have an actor called Groucho, who plays Mr. Schlemmer, Captain Spaulding, President Firefly, and so on. But that character is nonetheless also known simply as Groucho…

Every artist with a fictitious persona is essentially two people, and the biographer must be diligent not to confuse them. But with Groucho the risk is greater in that he was in effect not two men but three. There was "Groucho" of course. He was the persona: the wild, wise-cracking, loping, lecherous hero of the Marx Brothers' shows and films. Then there was Groucho, without quotes—the actor that plays "Groucho." He existed in the real world, but he's still a persona. He's the guy who hosts *You Bet Your Life*, who writes the autobiography and appears on talk shows. Then, there's the one called Julius that plays *him*. The world likes to pretend as much as possible that "Groucho" and Groucho are essentially the same; but that Groucho and Julius are the same there is no doubt. Are they, though? Only Julius would know, but it's Groucho who does the talking.

Groucho is a teller of tall tales. Charlotte Chandler once remarked to him that his stories sometime conflicted, and asked which she should believe. His reply was, "Both. I'm a liar." But this man Groucho is not really a congenital falsifier; he's just a careful builder of myth. He is an elaborator—and sometimes, when the truth feels too pressing, he is an obscurer. While "Groucho" is a fantasy and Julius a real man, Groucho is both and neither, and he has a unique license to confuse, and to construct his own legend.

So much of what we think we know about him was perfected for posterity, just as his book of letters helped cement the myth of his heroically impudent response to Warner Brothers' supposed attempt to force the Brothers to re-title *A Night in Casablanca*. (I put that one to bed in *The Annotated Marx Brothers*, but it shows no signs of sleeping just yet.) But did he really get stuck in Philly traffic dressed as Napoleon during the run of *I'll Say She Is*? Not possible, says Noah Diamond, masterly researcher (and recreator) of that chapter of Marx history.[5] Did he make the joke about taking a cigar out of his mouth on *You Bet Your Life*? Unlikely, says Gary Westin (see Appendix III). Did he and his brothers really strip naked and roast potatoes in Irving Thalberg's office? Not according to Thalberg's private secretary, who blandly informed Charlotte Chandler, "When they came in to see Mr. Thalberg they usually arrived with some gag or other—none of them were very funny or I'd have remembered them." And then, after a bit more prompting: "I do remember one time they had to wait because Mr. Thalberg was not finished with a conference—and I think it was Chico who tried to blow some smoke under the door into Mr. Thalberg's office, but it didn't work because the door was insulated."

Sometimes this legend building can have wider consequences. Groucho's account in a 1931 humorous article of the failure, abandonment and possible destruction of the Marx Brothers' first film *Humor Risk* (1921) became the standard history, convincing several successive generations that to even try to find the film would be pointless. Thus he perhaps fatally consigned to history a film that just might have been traceable had we acted faster and on sounder information.[6] He likewise convinced most subsequent chroniclers that Margaret Dumont was the mirror of her screen persona and had no understanding of his jokes—a masterly deception only now being deservedly reduced to rubble by some long overdue research that reveals a truly fascinating woman he had no business hiding from us.[7]

Any dictionary of modern quotations will include lines attributed to Groucho that were in truth uttered by "Groucho," and thus attributable to his screenwriters. That is inevitable. But what about some of the things attributed to the real Groucho? The internet abounds with misquotes, misattributed quotes and blatantly invented ones. His first known association with some of these lines can in many cases only be traced back a few years. But even correct attribution is not proof of actual authorship. Much of what was attributed to Groucho in newspaper gossip and showbiz columns during his career was the work of studio publicists.

Occasionally, if it's a good line, it will stick, and endure. Good luck finding an account of *A Day at the Races* that doesn't tell you in all certainty that Groucho responded to director Sam Wood's observation "You can't make an actor out of clay!" with a peevish "Nor a director out of Wood!" It's always presented as hard fact, and yes, he *may* have said it. But the fact that it appears in newspaper columns as a publicity squib at the time of the film's release (alongside scores of others that history has not held onto) strongly suggests it was just another good line dreamed up by MGM publicity.[8] (And the weight of meaning it is now presumed to hold, as illustration of the two men's genuine resentment and loathing of each other, is simply not there.)

With Groucho, this distinction between attribution and actual authorship takes on a unique significance. Let's go for broke and examine what is probably his most famous quote of all—"I don't want to belong to any club that would have someone like me for a member," penned in a letter of resignation he sent to a club secretary. Reams have been written, and continue to be written about it: what it means, what it doesn't mean, and what it therefore tells us about him. But before we get carried away with that lot, let's start with: is it true?

Everyone agrees he said it—but when? Where?[9] The club itself varies from telling to retelling. It's usually the Friars or the Hillcrest—if only they'd kept a copy! Still, it must be a matter of record when, or if, he resigned from their books?

And the earliest located citing of the story is as a newspaper publicity item—implying it occurred recently—from 1949.[10] This was well into the period where Groucho was saving his correspondence for posterity (he first announced *The Groucho Letters* as a forthcoming book in 1952), and he obviously liked the story enough to put it in his autobiography in 1959: so why not save the carbon? The final section of *The Groucho Letters*, titled "Short Shrift" is full of similar examples, carefully preserved, none as good as that certain classic. So all we can say for certain is that it originated as a story attributed to Groucho, and was explicitly endorsed by him later, which could well have reached the columnists from him directly, rather than a publicist. But did he really write it in a real letter that he really sent to a real club? There's really no compelling reason to think so.

Few comedians would turn down the chance to be identified with a great line, of course. But sometimes Groucho will confuse us in more intriguing ways. Until the end of his life, he proudly displayed on his wall a strange painting that was, he said, his one and only effort in that medium. It hardly seemed to be the kind of subject we might have expected of him: a garish Christmas scene, showing two angels blowing trumpets, a house made of candy canes with red stockings hanging from the chimney and, on the snowy lawn outside, a jolly snowman and two wide-eyed, blonde-haired children in banana-like clogs. The name "Groucho Marx" is signed to it, in capitals, in the bottom left corner. It is reproduced in *The Groucho Phile*, and a photograph in *Hello, I Must Be Going* shows him proudly holding it.

So where did it come from, and how and why did the master of sardonic wit come to paint anything so schmaltzy? Its origins are to be found in a 1952 Hallmark greetings cards promotion. According to their advertisement, Groucho, along with Jane Wyman, Henry Fonda and Fred MacMurray, was enlisted to produce a Christmas card design ... and so he produced the bizarre artifact and kept it framed in his house ever after.

Honesty in advertising being fluid, any number of explanations is possible for this painting, including outright deception. One could easily imagine stars being asked to put their name to a random image, for example, and thinking little of it. Or, perhaps, he might have designed it, but allowed another artist to actually create it in paint? Yet these would not square with the paternal pride he took in it, for proud he was, and insistent that the work was entirely his own.

The part of his claim that simply makes no sense is that it was his *only* painting. If he meant the only painting that ever appeared before the public that would be different, but we should then expect *some* recollection of him dabbling in the art as a hobby from friends or family. Is there even one? Harpo, certainly, was a keen amateur painter, but nobody seems ever to have recalled Groucho with a brush in his hand. Clearly, this cannot be *anybody's* first attempt at painting. It is in no way exceptional, but it betrays a casual competence in line, color, angle and perspective not to be expected of a literal first-timer. It is, at the very least, the work of a confident amateur. And so the mystery persists. Only Julius knows the truth, and he's not telling.

Perhaps strangest and most intriguing of all is the "Karloff affair." Late in life, in what may have struck him immediately as too revealing an admission, Groucho told Charlotte Chandler that, when staying in digs in his vaudeville days, he would often sleep with a bureau against the door and his trunk in front of the window because he "used to get scared at night" and "was afraid that some night I might go to the window and open it and jump out." When Chandler asked him why, he began to answer straightforwardly ("I guess it was a kind of nervous point of my life") before withdrawing from the mood of confession with a suddenness that leaps from the page and offering a glib explanation that makes no sense: "I'd seen some Boris Karloff movies."

Understandably incredulous and doubtless thinking he was joking, she pursued the matter. But he stuck to the absurd claim, despite repeated opportunities to withdraw it:

> **GM**: I saw one Boris Karloff picture, and I took sleeping pills for about a month after that, every night. It was the only way I could get to sleep.
> **CC**: But you knew they were just movies...
> **GM**: I knew it but they affected me. That sounds strange, I guess. I think a lot of people get scared when they go to a frightening movie. They frightened the hell out of me, those Boris Karloff movies. All I know is I couldn't sleep at night...
> **CC**: Which Karloff film terrified you the most?
> **GM**: Every one.
> **CC**: What did he do that scared you?
> **GM**: He looked like a monster! I think those pictures scared a lot of people. I think all people have periods in their life when they are a little nutty or think they are.

Cautious as we should always be before wading in with psychological assessment, what is happening here *seems* fairly straightforward. Having already told Chandler that he sleeps with his door locked and once consulted a psychiatrist ("because I was troubled") he makes an uncharacteristically candid admission and immediately feels he has rendered himself too vulnerable. Unable to withdraw it, he bats it away with a silly explanation to which he then sticks with a kind of desperate inflexibility. The story of him piling up trunks in front of his window to stop himself leaping out is so strange and seemingly out of character that it has the feel of truth, as especially does the line, "I think all people have periods in their life when they are a little nutty or think they are." It is the subsequent attempt at a banal rationalization that rings false.

And this is something we will often find Groucho doing, as if by making a production number out of an admission he can exorcise it without being caught in the act. The thought of the vaudeville Groucho, alone and in strange surroundings, at the mercy of compulsive fears is an intensely humanizing one: a rare glimpse of the man with his guard fully down. The idea that it might have been the result of seeing Boris Karloff films seems a plain fabrication even without taking into account the fact that Karloff began his monster movie career in 1931, when the forty-one-year-old Groucho was already in Hollywood.

Print the legend, John Ford instructed, and Groucho would have agreed. But there's a flipside to this that is more serious. The existence of this third Groucho, the man in the middle, neither fully flesh nor fully fantasy, has given armchair psychologists a seemingly unique license to interpret the real man in any way they choose. Because this frivolous fellow also writes his own history, the most dangerous myth of all has taken hold: that Groucho and Julius are one and the same, and the former can be taken at face value as a mirror of the latter.

Take this comment, so far as I know unseen since it was first published in the *Pittsburgh Post-Gazette* and elsewhere in 1962: "Women don't think once they get married. In fact, all women are crazy. The single ones have to have some sense in order to hold down a job. But once they get married the game's over."

What a gift that would be, were my aim to roll out the now commonplace portrait of Groucho as demon husband and monster father! (And what an obstacle if I dare to attempt any other course.) But who is actually saying this? It's not a line from a film—it's an interview, ergo it's the real man? Hardly. It's still a performance, conforming to a popular image: that of the cynical, acid-tongued observer of life known as Groucho (the same fellow who opines in *Memoirs of a Mangy Lover* that "the female is only about fifteen years removed from the jungle," before hastening to add that this, along with "a bulging bra," is "part of their charm"). It may have its roots in the screen persona known as "Groucho," and doubtless it echoed *somewhere* in the real man known as Julius. But the person saying this is Groucho, the intermediary who causes all the mischief and confusion. It is when we miss that distinction that the trouble starts, and a portrait of the man as misanthrope, chauvinist and tyrant emerges and solidifies in the biographical literature.

And it's in *that* light that what might have earlier seemed a somewhat pedantic, perhaps even iconoclastic dissection of apparent trivia becomes significant. We can argue into the night about whether the "club member" line should be interpreted as an expression of self-deprecation or of arrogance. But if (and I do say if) it wasn't something he actually *did*, then all that we are debating is the meaning of a joke, or at most the interpretation of a comic persona. The real man is not to be found here and, more importantly, the one we are enjoined to conjure in his stead—a man who sends cocky resignation letters to clubs—is much less interesting than one who wants us to believe he sends cocky resignation letters to clubs and yet, nonetheless, does not. It's hard not to think of W.C. Fields, another whose popular image—like Groucho's, created by his own efforts and those of studio publicists—was allowed for decades to stand in proxy for him mainly because we preferred it that way.

So ask yourself: If you were Groucho, why *wouldn't* you behave exactly as people expect? What is stopping you? There would be no detrimental consequences, surely? Perhaps, despite all efforts to appear otherwise, it was a fundamental conservatism, an unwillingness to offend, an adherence to accepted standards of civilized behavior, even shyness staying his hand … all those things we don't remotely associate with Groucho Marx. And at a stroke, surely, he becomes more interesting: a man who found uninhibitedness somewhat inhibiting.

In fact, I would go further even than this, and argue that our best way of understanding him is in light of this very conflict between the expectations created by his persona and a deep internal reticence. And from this, too, his desire to break away from the Marx Brothers mold, and from a character that, somehow, had pushed him into this limiting corner. The quieter, reserved, socially conservative Groucho is abundantly evident in many later interviews and in the letters to his children. There are also many occasions when we see him letting this reticence go and living up to his popular image, and they tend to have the same unexpected result: they backfire.

His first wife, Ruth, is typically portrayed as a deeply humorless woman who didn't get his shtick and was embarrassed by its every off-screen manifestation. Just as likely she was disturbed by the slow transformation of a man who, perhaps, kept his real and stage selves rigidly separate at first, but as the excitement of their marriage palled and his international fame solidified, began more and more to keep up the performance in real life. And the more their problems intensified, the more one can imagine him retreating further and further behind the act. The famous occasion—which does appear to be entirely true—on which he wrote "smuggler" as his occupation in a customs form, leading to his entire family being detained and (if the anecdote doesn't get *slightly* carried away with itself at this point) subjected to a time-wasting and humiliating strip search, is usually cited as evidence of both his incorrigibility and Ruth's incompatibility with such a wild spirit. I see it more as a classic example of Groucho disobeying his true instincts in front of what he may have naively believed to be "his public" and paying the consequences—and having others pay them, too.

The claim that he was so beloved that he could never genuinely insult people, even when he wanted to, is not borne out by the evidence of several more uncomfortable episodes. Harpo's wife Susan, and his TV co-host George Fenneman, among several others, recalled excruciating dinner parties and restaurant lunches in which he made a crass aside that ruffled feathers. A rare chance to actually see one of these sticky moments unfold before our eyes can be found in one of Dick Cavett's interview shows, in which he comes perilously close to causing an onscreen incident with a series of crude comments about co-interviewee Debbie Reynolds. Only Reynolds's steely bonhomie saves the moment. But tellingly, a prior engagement calls her unexpectedly away after an interview break. And let us not forget the entire saga of *The Marx Brothers Scrapbook*—when the elderly Groucho decided once and for all to throw caution to the wind, and brewed a costly and acrimonious scandal. The more I ponder these questions, the more convinced I become that the Groucho who wouldn't belong to any club that would have him as a member is a two dimensional fantasy, masking a real man who never quite defined his role, or his limits.

Of this real man, Julius, I'm afraid I have no startlingly radical conclusions to draw—unless, as may be, it is radical to conclude that he was a good man. Simon Louvish, one of our wisest as well as wittiest authorities, once told me he found himself "getting more and more angry" with Groucho as he worked on his biography of the brothers. But how heinous were his faults, really? True, he was not the easiest man to live with, to put it mildly, and it would be absurd to say he did not make people unhappy in his long lifetime. Any man who is divorced three times is, plainly, not a natural husband either. But nobody has ever seriously alleged violence, wanton infidelity, irresponsibility, neglect…. Rather we are told that he could be, on occasion, belittling or downright rude, either insufficiently outgoing (for Ruth) or too socially minded (for Kay, his second wife), withdrawn, quick to judge, stern, unwilling or incapable of articulating his deeper feelings, stingy with household money, and overly fond of Gilbert and Sullivan records.

None of these are admirable traits (though opinion differs on the latter); indeed, they are exactly the kinds of flaws we might expect of a man who had been divorced three times. But when one frequently hears them cited as evidence of actual moral disorder—proof of his dysfunctional relationship with his mother, or illustrative of misogyny, of an inability to conceive of women as human beings, or the means of his "driving" his loved ones to alcoholism—well, then it's time to throw open a few north-facing windows and breathe deeply and slowly. This is pop-psychology—a free-admission fantasy island where the marriage of symbolic cause and developmental effect is essential, immutable, and proscribed with mathematical complacency—and its century is up. That'll be a hundred dollars, please, made payable to Alfred Hitchcock and Salvador Dali.

Steve Stoliar, Groucho's last secretary and subsequent author of the memoir *Raised Eyebrows*, told me:

> I'm certain that Groucho could be a difficult spouse, with his put-downs and Victorian view of "a woman's place," but the idea that these women were happy, and mentally and emotionally healthy, until *he* came along and turned them into raging alcoholics is simplistic and unfair to Groucho. His second wife, Kay, already had a severe drinking problem before she met Groucho. Groucho chose young, attractive women .without much intellect and then proceeded to try to fill those empty vessels with an appreciation for the things he was into. It was unfair to expect those women to become something they never were, but it was also unfair of those women to marry Groucho thinking it would be a piece of cake. I would say they each made poor choices. But the simplistic armchair diagnosis that he "drove them to drink" borders on the preposterous.[11]

"Being Groucho" was a job, and note how these instances of Groucho behaving badly (especially of his rudeness) so often occur in social settings. The line between Groucho belittling his wife at a dinner party and President Firefly insulting Margaret Dumont, though definite, is nonetheless fine. The former may not be "Groucho" performing on stage, but neither is it truly Julius, at ease and being himself. It's Groucho, giving the audience what he thinks they want, and often misjudging both the occasion and the company, to say nothing of the effect his performance can have outside of the proscenium and the edge of the frame.

But very close friends *did* get to meet Julius, at least once in a while, and the difference was striking and obvious. These fortunate few recall loyalty, fairness, decency, sensitivity, keenness to help friends privately and publicly, and a natural passion for justice. Norman Krasna told Hector Arce that his gentle side was something he preferred to keep hidden: "Unless you were really close you might think he was quite selfish. He wasn't afraid to show you his intolerance. Then he would turn around and do these enormous things. What he wouldn't do for himself, he'd do for a friend."

Nat Perrin made the same observations to Charlotte Chandler:

> Groucho's exterior belies a somewhat different interior. He's a much more sentimental man than people know. He has enormous loyalties, and, for me, that's the giveaway. He has many of the old friends he's always had.... He's a different kind of person from what his brand of humor would indicate. He's always had a lot of interest in family and family ties. He was always good company, and is. He doesn't just sit back, but works hard to make things pleasant. But it's not that he's always "on." He doesn't use people as an audience.

"He's a sentimentalist, but he'd rather be found dead than have you know it," wrote his son Arthur in *Life with Groucho*. "Why he persists in this attitude is something only he can answer."

Then there is his supposed lack of concern for Chico, either from selfishness or long-delayed revenge over their mother's favoritism. Looking back at *The Annotated Marx Brothers*, I fear even I may have come down a little hard on Groucho in that regard, when documenting how his keenness not to revive the act in the 1940s and 1950s left Chico in the lurch. It would be a big mistake to think that his prioritizing of his own career meant an indifference to Chico's welfare, yet this belief seems to have got around. Here's, of all people, Harry Ritz:

> Chico was a sweet guy, but he lost all his money gambling. Well, I just say if a brother's down and out, you take care of him once in a while. Groucho made a lot of money—he's still making money with that damn TV show of his with the duck—but he never helped. He ran around with a different crowd from his brothers.[12]

In fact, he kept Chico on the payroll of that damn TV show of his with the duck and, with Harpo, did everything he could to insulate Chico from the consequences of his own reckless-ness. "The Brothers were bonded together and loyal to one another," says Bill Marx. "There was no animosity between the boys, at least none I ever experienced or felt."[13] If Groucho spoke a little too freely and cynically about Chico in later life (and there is reason to believe he may have regretted doing so) that is only because Chico the profligate gambler and wom-anizer had likewise passed beyond reality and into legend. And legends are for printing.

Part of the problem is that Groucho conforms to neither of our age's preferred models of the off-duty comedian: he was plainly not the same laugh-a-minute fellow he was when "on," but just as surely not a tormented, manic-depressive wreck. Instead he was just unspec-tacularly serious, and ordinary, and at times curt, cold and curmudgeonly. A charge of misog-yny might be our best chance of rendering him fashionably flawed, but it's still a bad fit. His view of women may have been Victorian in its lack of nuance, but it was far from disrespect-ful.

He was certainly chivalrous. (If chivalry itself offends you I can only wish you the best of luck, but let the record state that chivalrous he certainly was.) June MacCloy told her friend George Bettinger that he was anything but wolfish on the set of *Go West*, asking if she was "decent" before entering her trailer to chat and play guitar. She specifically recalled him as astute in his reading of the moods of others, and wise in his responses.[14] Gloria Jean remem-bered him taking to task the entire crew of *Copacabana* for their lewd comments and refer-ences to her sexual inexperience. ("He was really upset about this," she recalled to her biographer.[15])

Perhaps it is simply that, as leader and focal point of the Marx Brothers on screen, we expect him to be similarly dominating privately. In fact, as far as dramatic or notable personal lives go, he is effortlessly outclassed by both Chico's irresponsibility, gambling and woman-izing, and by Harpo's sweetness and devotion to his family. Neither as reprobate as the first nor as estimable as the latter, Groucho falls between stools, and it may be that the need to exaggerate his faults and over-dramatize his problems is to some degree an unconscious reflection of this seeming disparity. It just feels wrong, somehow, that Groucho, when the cameras stop rolling and real life resumes, should become the Zeppo of the act. (Even Zeppo—an interesting if largely unknown character in his own right—wasn't *that!*)

Of all sources, by far for the most useful as a window to the private man is *Love, Groucho* (1992), the compilation of letters to his eldest daughter, Miriam. *The Groucho Letters* no more reveal the inner man than do his movies, but this volume shows Groucho in all moods from puckish to despairing. It also clarifies and balances the sense of his and Miriam's relationship that we form from secondary sources. Biographies tend to play their fractious association as bordering on irreconcilable, with a tyrannical Groucho oblivious to the destructive effect his pettiness and misjudged sense of priorities are having on his daughter. (Indeed, his treatment of Miriam tends to hover around the top of the customary charge-sheet drawn up against him.) The letters, by contrast, show two things: first, that the pair were much more evenly matched than usually suggested (perhaps evenly mis-matched, rather) with Miriam very much giving as good as she gets; and second, that the bond of love between them splintered only rarely and briefly. Through most of their ups and downs it is transparent and strong, and Groucho's faults, for the greater part, are simply those of a man trying to do the best thing and not always getting it right. He shows himself to be a chronically un-astute judge of human nature at times, and there are occasions in the book where one finds oneself wanting to shake him, so blind is he to the real substance of the issue in hand. But he rarely if ever comes across as less than a caring and committed father. ("My father knew Miriam well," recalls Lucinda Irwin Smith, daughter of *You Bet Your Life* writer-director Bernie Smith. "She was very close to Groucho. I could see that Groucho tried to be a good father, though I'm sure he found it difficult, with his multiple marriages and busy career."[16]) "I have nothing but good feelings about him," is Miriam's own summation in the book's introduction.

Again, of all negative traits, what comes through strongest in Miriam's book is that troubling commodity I noted at the start of this introduction: dissatisfaction.

My aim in the pages that follow is to make a story of dissatisfaction satisfying. The fact is that, with the glorious exception of *You Bet Your Life*, Groucho's solo career brought him more frustration than reward, and those who have documented his legacy in subsequent years have tended to concur, and thus make short work of dealing with it. In making it my focus, I cannot help but recall a joke cut from an early draft of *Monkey Business*, in which Groucho attempts to convert a reluctant sucker to the advantages of his revolutionary non-burning coal: "No trouble with ashes, no lame backs from shovelling, lasts a lifetime, and best of all there's no heat." That, if we wished to be cynical, could be said to be what I am offering in dealing comprehensively with material that, by and large, even the man's biggest fans don't like very much: A subject that has never been fully analyzed before, a wealth of new stories and information, and best of all—who cares?

Certainly, if we are to examine these productions sympathetically, adjustments need be made in our expectations, compared to those with which we approach the work of the Marx Brothers. In my previous book, *The Annotated Marx Brothers*, I was able, if anything, to err on the side of critical parsimony, so profuse are the riches still offered by their baker's dozen of unique comedies. Groucho's solo movies rarely even approach such a level. But I hope I was able to show in that book that a film need not be great to be an interesting object of study, and that the behind the scenes stories of even their least celebrated works, such as *Room*

*Service* and *Love Happy*, were just as fascinating—if not more so—as those of their certain triumphs. Surely, there are tales here that merit telling.

I hope, therefore, that what follows will make that case by itself. Readers must, of course, form their own judgments. But if all else fails, try to remember Groucho's own dictum, as recalled by *You Bet Your Life* director Robert Dwan: "Always be glad you're not at the dentist."

# 1

# A sort of summer mental aberration

He was, after all, the first.

No, Groucho Marx, or Julius Henry Marx as he was known to registrars of birth, was not the first born of the Marx Brothers. But he was the first to take to the stage.

Harpo and Chico were both reluctant at first. Gummo and Zeppo were never otherwise, and engineered their escapes to normality as soon as the world permitted. But Groucho was a creature of the limelight from the beginning, and when he began performing it was alone. The idea of teamwork was an afterthought—a brother act yet more so. By the time the Marx Brothers invented themselves, he was a veteran. To the world, he was always their leader, totem, spokesman and chief asset. That, for sure, conveyed nominal superiority. But Jolson didn't need brothers. Cantor didn't need brothers. Did Groucho?

His brothers found their way to the act by a kind of inevitable magnetic pull, a mix of genetic determinism and maternal willpower (no stronger combination, as immutable natural processes go). For Chico and Harpo the business was a means to various ends, but the inevitability that consigned Groucho to the performer's life was more fundamental. Existence precedes essence, the existentialists assure us, and for the other Marx Brothers, art was existence. The family was poor, and show business the only escape route that promised not just survival but the potential for glory. Groucho, however, was never set on any other course. For Groucho, it was essence. As Harpo's son Bill puts it: "Chico didn't really care about performing, just gambling. Dad worked to support his family. Groucho worked to keep his sanity...."[1]

So when did it begin, this desire of Groucho's to prove himself a solo attraction? When was the fire lit? Perhaps from the first. Perhaps the Marx Brothers were only ever meant to be an interlude. He was an individual temporarily deposited in an aggregate that—curse his bad luck!—had the audacity to become the most innovative comedy act of the twentieth century. And so it became harder and harder to convince the world that he was, despite all evidence to the contrary, just passing through.

The interesting thing about Groucho's accounts of his beginnings on stage is that it all seems so organic, even fated. Of course, there was show business in his blood: his maternal grandparents were a magician and a harpist and his uncle, Al Shean, made it all the way to the big time. Minnie, their celebrated mother, may have lived in dreams of theatrical glory, fuelled no doubt by her brother's success, but the popular notion that the brothers were corralled from the first as part of a carefully designed stage-mother scheme is not really the case. Natural gifts notwithstanding, the boys only gradually, and individually, gravitated towards their collective destiny. And though the Minnie master plan kicked into high gear from that point on, prior to it she had been content to watch and wait—and test-run.

Groucho, from all accounts, might have seemed the least likely spearhead for any such campaign. Chico had the proven talent, with Harpo proceeding nicely behind. The former was playing piano in nickelodeons from childhood, and, if the stories are to be believed, sometimes illicitly substituting his lookalike brother, whose severely limited repertoire alone distinguished the two, so as to double the take home pay. But the Marx boys were wild, lawless spirits: if anything distinguished the quieter, owlish and more solitary Julius, it may have been that he was the easier to mold.

At first he might have seemed set to make the family's fortunes in some more socially respectable fashion: his earliest aspiration, he remembered in *The Groucho Phile*, was to be a doctor "with a beard, a little black bag and a bedside manner that would charm the most frigid female." But unlike his elder brothers he was possessed of a streak of naïve romanticism, and Uncle Al's shows, and all the sights and sounds of the acts that shared the bills with him, began to divert his aspirations: "The first real job I ever got was on Coney Island. I sang a song on a beer keg and made a dollar."

In 1905 he saw an ad in the *New York Morning World* looking for a boy singer to join a vaudeville act. "I was fifteen at the time," he would later write in his autobiography *Groucho and Me*, "and knew as much about the world as the average retarded eight year old." But Julius Marx, one third of the Leroy Trio, was now in show business, never to return.

According to anecdote the group made it as far as Colorado when the two other thirds eloped, leaving Julius stranded and Minnie forced to pay for his fare back home. Others may have viewed the episode as a warning to keep away from the stage, but a door had opened for Julius, and slammed shut behind him. He had nowhere to go but forward, and it was at this point that Minnie stepped in, convinced (in Simon Louvish's words) "of his zeal if not his sanity," and began promoting him for all her worth. This took him from "Lady Seville and Master Marx" (in which his boy tenor singing and Yiddisher impersonations filled in the costume changes between songs from English music hall artiste Lily Seville), to "Gus Edwards's Postal Telegraph Boys" (of which *Variety* opined, "Julius Marx, a youthful tenor, contributed largely to the result through singing 'Somebody's Sweetheart I Want To Be' in good voice, sounding doubly agreeable after the discordant, harsh and shrill noises of the other boys and girl who had sung before him," but added, "about all the boys in it seem to think they are comedians, whereas there is

The last three Marx Brothers, in their last known photograph together. Left to right: Zeppo, Groucho and Gummo at Groucho's 85th birthday party (courtesy Frank Diernhammer).

not one among the crowd"[2]), to his first dramatic role as Jimmy the office boy in *The Man of Her Choice* ... and all in 1906, the year he turned 16.

What this suggests is that, whatever daydreams and aspirations Minnie had been nurturing for her boys, it was as much Groucho's own determination that galvanized her resolve. She may have lassoed the other four, but at this point it was Groucho giving *her* the impetus, not vice versa.

It was in 1907, at the birth of the spuriously named "Ned Wayburn's Nightingales," that Minnie cottoned on to the value of maintaining jurisdiction over her own group rather than hiring Groucho out to other people's, and it was in support of that project—that is to say in support of Groucho—that she began tightening the strings on the other brothers, first Gummo in 1907; Harpo in 1908; Chico not until Mr. *Green's Reception* in 1912.

The Marx Brothers were never invented: they were the product of convenience, and the pivot was always Groucho. And yet such was the speed and pace of their ascent, such were the demands of it, that it would be twenty years before another window opened to re-establish him as a solo performer, and by that time, it was no longer a reversion to the natural state of things: normality had become novelty.

"I'm a serious man with a comic sense but I don't see why, if you hit one note and are successful, you must stick to that all your life," Groucho told journalist Mary Morris on the set of *A Night in Casablanca* in 1946, vowing already to retire the act that had only just reformed after five years away from movies. "I've had enough of those scenes climbing out of the window or hiding in the closet when the husband comes home and finds the girl on the bed. There are other facets to be explored."[3]

When was the fire *not* lit?

Anyone with brothers is himself a brother, on stage as in life. But maybe Groucho never reconciled himself to that. It's too easy to misread this independence—the fierceness of it, the insistence upon it—as arrogance or ingratitude. When he retired the act, he didn't want to show his siblings that they couldn't survive without him; he very much hoped that they could. I suspect that, to Groucho, the vital point was not that he was the best of the Marx Brothers, merely that he was separate, and that their union was not immutable. The challenge he spent so much of his professional life negotiating was the desire to prove to the world something that in fact the world had no difficulty believing, but simply did not want proved.

The Four Nightingales (top to bottom: Groucho, Harpo, Gummo and Lou Levy). The moment Groucho became a Marx Brother.

## Twentieth Century (1934)

By 1934 the Marx Brothers had risen steadily through Vaudeville, Broadway and Hollywood. They had made hit movies of their stage revues *The Cocoanuts* and *Animal Crackers*, and followed them with three screen originals that remain touchstones of screen comedy: *Monkey Business, Horse Feathers* and *Duck Soup*. Now, temporarily without a contract, they were for the first time at a loose end. If the stories are true, the opportunity to perform in *Twentieth Century* on stage came along by accident.[4] There will be more than enough occasions when we are obliged to raise our eyebrows at Groucho's own account of circumstances: let's just go along with this one if we can, which finds him between the end of the Paramount films and their signing by MGM, and deciding to take his wife Ruth and children Miriam (then seven) and Arthur (then twelve) on a modest, incognito holiday to Maine.

First, though, they stopped off at Wenonah, New Jersey, to visit Ruth's sister, Mrs. Lester Russell of 4, East Willow Street. The press caught up with them there and, judging from the tone of the reports that appeared in the *Evening News* and *Camden Courier-Post*, it does all seem to have been unexpected and impromptu. Groucho's conversation, nonetheless, is largely of the stage:

> The first or second time you pull something funny on the stage or screen you get some fun out of it yourself. But the worst of it in Hollywood is that when you have rehearsed until the scene is just about perfect, and you're ready to go ahead, the camera runs out of film. Ah, well, that's life. Yes, and that's also the movies.
>
> Although the movies and radio reach millions who cannot enjoy you on the stage, I prefer the stage, where you can get the immediate reaction of an audience. Do you realize that the radio and screen have produced no real comedian? Chaplin? He went to the movies from the stage.

In other comments he predicted an uncertain future for newcomers attempting to break into the profession ("Getting anywhere in this business is about 25 percent ability and 75 percent luck: if you don't get the breaks, you'll stay in *Uncle Tom's Cabin* road shows for the rest of your life") and reflected on the importance of comedy in difficult times:

> Without something to laugh at during the past two or three years, people would have committed suicide. It seems to me that comedy has a very definite place in the world today, as it always has, and that place is the stop-gap, or safety valve between a complete collapse of the nervous system and enjoyment of life.

And in response to the question of whether he tried out his gags on his wife (a more piercing enquiry than the interviewer realized, since Groucho's relentless persecution of Ruth's absent funny bone is said to have contributed materially to their break-up), a pointed "Not anymore. I once did, but I found out a paying audience was more responsive. Even a wife gets tired of a comedian's jokes. The best place and, to me, the only place to try out gags is on the stage. There you get instantaneous response."

If he knew at this point how soon he would again be treading the boards—and hard to imagine why he would be obliged to keep a lid on it, if so—he did an admirable job of keeping it hush-hush. And so, we are led back, perhaps surprised but with no fair grounds for suspicion, to the official story.

A short while after, already clearly pining for the stage and staying in a Maine cabin with his family, he learned by chance that a nearby playhouse was putting on a series of Broadway revivals. Groucho volunteered his services and personally suggested *Twentieth*

*Century* as his vehicle; thus was presented an ideal opportunity to stretch his wings, with minimal risk of embarrassment if he found himself unable to fly. In the character of egomaniac producer Oscar Jaffe, as created by Ben Hecht and Charles MacArthur, he found the perfect choice of role for the purposes of the experiment. Contemporary journalists, however, had only one thing on their minds. "Of course I'll miss them," he responded to the inevitable question, "but that does not mean any or all of us cannot work alone. You cannot work in a team as long as the four Marx brothers without missing the others when you separate temporarily."

In a long interview with E.B. White, he confirmed that they would be reuniting soon for another film, though, pre–Thalberg, all bets were off as to what it would consist of:

> When the public next beholds Groucho and the other three Marx Brothers it will be in a production called *The Sleeping Beauty*, and Groucho will be in the character of a magician and hypnotist. The story, he says, is built around Dillinger and a bank robbery. It will be a stage production, opening on Broadway in November, and the first of September will see him back in New York getting ready for it…. No less than three pictures are in sight for Groucho Marx. The book for one of them will be by Ben Hecht and Charles MacArthur, authors of the play *Twentieth Century*, just presented; one is being translated from the German and concerns counterfeiters.

While to the *Camden Courier-Post* he had predicted a less outré but more tempting bill of fare. Though already announcing the loss of Zeppo and consequent reduction of the team from four to three (before, note, the signing to MGM), he spoke confidently of a new musical opening in New York in the Fall: "Tentatively, it's called *The Marx Brothers at Palm Springs* and it's going to be all about the love side of the movies. Ah, love, love…. You must have heard of that, even in South Jersey."

In other words, nobody had the first clue. The team was very much in limbo, and his motivation in striking out alone, he suggested, was in part merely practical:

> Harpo has been over in Russia amusing the Soviets, Zeppo has turned into a theatrical agent and Chico had his private enterprise. So I thought it was time I did something on my own…. I wanted to see if I could make 'em laugh without my mustache. It was a sort of experiment. A sort of summer mental aberration you might call it.

To the journalists who waited to question him on his first day of rehearsals he was more waspish. When it was pointed out to him that Eddie Cantor was also planning to go legit—and into Shakespeare, what's more—he asked, "What's he playing, third grave digger?" and continued: "What a nightmare that will be. Cantor must have heard about me doing this show up here and is stealing my stuff. Well, see if I care. Maybe I'll do *Green Pastures* later."

Unsurprisingly the venue was well-sprinkled with what the United Press called "prominent personages" come opening night, including Kaufman and Woollcott, and Amelia Earhart, who spoke between the first and second acts. Harpo also attended later in the run. In keeping with the venture's roots as a family *jeu d'esprit*, Ruth took the role of Anita (the part played by Billie Seward in the film version) and Miriam would occasionally wander on stage and recite "Little Boy Blue" after matinee performances. (Miriam had made her stage debut even earlier, when she appeared "as from nowhere" during a performance of *Animal Crackers* in Detroit in 1929.[5] Groucho had, apparently, arranged it himself, perhaps to accustom her to the environment, an experiment he would repeat more earnestly with his second daughter, Melinda. Arthur, too, had on occasion accompanied his father on stage during Captain Spaulding's grand entrance. It didn't take there, either.)

According to Louella Parsons, at the end of the play, when Groucho was wheeled on to the stage in a chair, over-zealous assistants sent him careening over the footlights, generating such laughter that the bit was retained, to the displeasure of the authors and, we might assume, Groucho himself. That's as maybe. But he did tell White that after starting the run committed to absolute dramatic realism, he had eventually succumbed in some measure to popular demand: "I found the public wanted to laugh at me anyway and intended to do it, so I gave them something to laugh at."

What is certain beyond doubt, however, is that the experiment was unanimously judged a success. If the aim was to show that he could appear successfully in an unaccustomed role, without his mustache and without his brothers, the reviews could hardly have offered stronger confirmation. According to a syndicated United Press review: "Groucho Marx, leading gagster of the four Marx brothers, abandoned grease-paint mustache, cigar and frock coat last night to appear in his first 'straight' role—and played it straight to the delight of the audience." Either avoiding or not imagining any revelation of insecurity in Groucho's choice of venue, the review was content to add the star to "the growing list of actors and actresses who, for small pay and love of their art, are farming themselves out to summer theaters."

> He was at ease with his part. The dialog, differing from the "gag" type to which he is accustomed, came clearly and without hesitation. An occasional sly glance was the principal reminder of his familiar stage personality. Instead of quick repartee and clownish actions there was subtle comedy, satire and devastating characterization.

Asked by White how long his version might run, he replied, "That's in the lap of the Gods," but he was optimistic about the future of live theater and, by extension, his ability to find a home there:

> The stage is not dead, as some seem to believe. The public are not going to be satisfied with nothing but moving pictures. Pictures, of course, are here to stay, but there is room for both. I predict a chain of little theaters all over the country within a very few years. I do not mean the "arty" sort, but smaller theaters, which the smaller towns can afford to support. The trend toward the stage is evident in New York. There have been more hits on Broadway the past season than in five years before that.

Instead, MGM called, so Groucho dutifully came running back to Hollywood, Harpo and Chico. But the experience, at least as much as Irving Thalberg's attentions, must have contributed to the renewed energy and enthusiasm with which he approached *A Night at the Opera.*

Another reason for his perkiness was that he had also begun writing a screenplay in collaboration with Norman Krasna. They called it *Grand Passion*, but it would be two years before it reached the screen under another name. To be a writer appealed enormously to him. *Twentieth Century* had proved his range as a single performer, beyond the persona he had fallen into with his brothers. But there was also the need to prove himself *more* than just an interpreter of the material of others.

"Groucho" was an act, not a person, and it was important to the man who shared his name that it be seen not as his wraith but merely his invention. This was surely the root of his prickliness whenever he sensed too much credit being given to others, most famously to Perelman and even, on occasions, Kaufman: it was important to his self-image that he be taken as source as well as conduit. In Hollywood, he tended to gravitate not towards other stars so much as writers, and often their attitude to those for whom they wrote suggested little had changed since Doctor Johnson's famous response when told his dismissal of "players" was hurtful to his friend David Garrick: "Punch does not feel." And thus the desire to be known as a writer—accepted, perhaps, is the better word—became all-consuming.

He had striven to make his name as a humorous prose writer since the late twenties, perhaps just a little stung by the fact that it was the less articulate Harpo who had become a regular at the Algonquin Round Table—the exact cultural environment in which one might have expected Groucho to thrive. But it's worth remembering that the Marx Brothers who arrived on Broadway were still fairly gauche, and while Harpo and Chico were perceived as more instinctive personalities, Groucho's image was one of extreme sophistication, the master of all occasions, so he would not have been insulated from the need to establish himself in company as they were. (In real life, of course, it was Chico whose glib tongue and easy charm made him the master of instant ingratiation.) And Groucho had no mentor capable of overseeing a gentle submersion into the often treacherous waters of show business high society, the service Woollcott performed for Harpo.[6] Groucho's overtures to Woollcott ended sourly (in his eyes, at least: the ever-solipsistic Woollcott probably had no notion of causing any lasting animosity and simply spoken to him as he would anyone else) and the same uneasiness made the company of all the Algonquin wits difficult for him. Idolizing the Brothers as performers as they did, they would have had no idea of his jealousy of their literary reputations. In later years he would often speak witheringly of their triviality and cliquishness, as if his wounded pride still needed an occasional bathing in feigned disdain.

When he published his autobiography, *Groucho and Me*, in 1959, he took pains to point out in interviews that it was entirely his own work. His publishers went so far as to offer professional assistance with the writing, the story goes, but he turned them down by explaining: "I don't believe in ghosts, except around four in the morning."[7] Had that always been the case, though?

His first book, *Beds*, appeared in 1930. In his 1978 biography *Groucho*, Hector Arce breezily declares both it and *Many Happy Returns* (1942) were ghost-written by Groucho's friend and regular screenwriter Arthur Sheekman. Gloria Stuart, Sheekman's wife, claims likewise. There is no doubt Sheekman was paid for working on the books, but the moot question is in what capacity and to what extent.

In an anthology of Groucho's writings, *Groucho Marx and Other Short Stories and Tall Tales*, editor Robert Bader suggests that Sheekman served only as editor and sounding board on the two

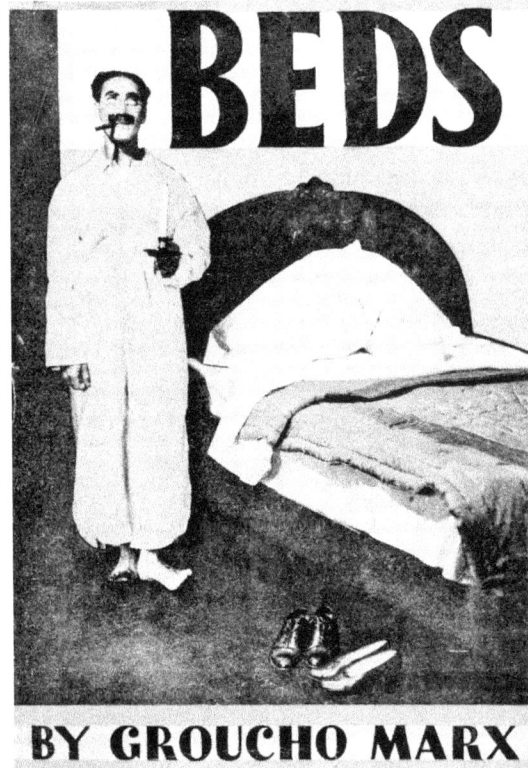

*Beds* (1930): Groucho's first book, and his last for twelve years.

books. (He does concede that several magazine pieces that were unquestionably Sheekman's own work appeared under Groucho's name in the 1940s, but reads the gesture as that of an altruistic Groucho fronting for Sheekman at a time when the latter was finding commissions hard to come by. The only trouble with this blameless account is that even as one reads it so many other more sensible courses of action leap irresistibly to mind, most obviously to simply present them as collaborations.) Steve Stoliar recalls with certainty being told by Arce that the admission of Sheekman's authorship came direct from Groucho himself, during the interviews conducted for the book, and that he saw no reason to doubt either of them.[8] Now, obviously, Groucho was not the most reliable self-chronicler by this point, but while it may be possible to imagine him claiming authorship of something he had not written, it is altogether harder to imagine him, or anyone, fraudulently or even absent-mindedly denying authorship of their own work, and giving full credit to somebody who merely assisted.

Groucho enjoyed two prolific periods of magazine writing: the 1940s, over which Sheekman's shadow hovers (albeit with nagging lack of definition), and the late 1920s and early 1930s. The picture is hazier still with regards the latter, but it is on record that Groucho employed Howard S. Benedict[9] to ghost for him in 1929, and that Benedict successfully placed material under Groucho's name in *Collier's*, *The New Yorker*, the *Saturday Evening Post* and the *New York Times*.

## "Press Agents I Have Known" (1929)

Howard Schwab Benedict (1902–1996) was well known to Hollywood in the 1930s and 40s, first as head of publicity at RKO (in which capacity he launched and promoted *Room Service*), then as a producer for RKO and Universal. But in the late 1920s he was a figure on the fringes of the New York theatrical scene. At least part of the time he was a humorous writer in his own right, but not, it seems a safely-enough established one to permit specialization. (Two of his contributions to Heywood Broun's column take the form of his self-mockingly, but no less sincerely, begging for work.) Regular wages came via his more widely recognized talent as a theatrical press agent: in the latter capacity he worked for the Shuberts, Gershwin, Noel Coward and Max Gordon among others. More than just a hack on the payroll, however, he seems to have been a popular and respected member of several inner circles, rubbing shoulders with Gordon, Kaufman and others on equal terms. One anecdote claims Gordon asked him to sit in on a rehearsal of *The Great Waltz* and lend his view of the production, to which he replied with confident audacity: "I was hired to press agent the show. There was no agreement I had to sit through it!"

As well as a keen sense of comic observation, a facility with words and a fondness for puns, Benedict possessed a highly beneficial talent for assuming the writing styles of others. A 1927 piece entitled "Sincerest Flattery," published under his own name in the *New York Sun*, is an exercise in outright pastiche, in which he shows how to ply the press agent's trade in the borrowed styles of H.L. Mencken and Scott Fitzgerald, among others. (The comic writing published under his own name strongly suggests Benedict thought being a press agent a little beneath his dignity: the inanities and duplicities of his trade are a recurring subject for his prose.) In its clever mimicking of known styles it reads as a virtual calling card for a would-be ghost, but it also shares with a number of Benedict's pieces the specific format of a single piece of information being repeated or illustrated in different ways from variant perspectives. This trick shows up often enough in his writing for us to at least provisionally claim it his defining comic technique.

A good example is still another drawing on his experience as a press agent. "Birth of a Theatrical Item," published in the *New York Sun* in December of 1926, relays the same minor news item concerning "Suzie Simper," a fictional chorus girl, first in the form that she relates it to her press agent, then as her press agent tells it to the papers, then as the papers print it.

In both subject and style these all surely sign Benedict's name to a Groucho piece, "Press Agents I Have Known," published in *The New Yorker* in 1929 (exactly when, and where, we know Benedict to be working on Groucho's behalf). As well as the theme of the wily press agent, drawing with the usual self-deprecation on its author's inside knowledge of the trade, the piece compares the manner and tactics of various kinds of agent in Benedict's usual style.

Benedict's familiarity with the world of theater made him an invaluable writer for Groucho: it would mean he could easily pen the bulk of the "reminiscence pieces," in which "Groucho" recalls his vaudeville past, while still incorporating specific nuggets supplied by Groucho. A number of the early "Groucho" articles use autobiographical material as a starting point, another reason, perhaps, why ghosting has rarely been suspected. "My Poor Wife," one of the most famous "Groucho" pieces, is an especially heretic place to discern Benedict's inky dabs, but viewed coldly, the piece plays as if several different fragments, in more than one voice, have been spliced with definite but far from invisible skill. Factual information squats within pre-formed sentences as if dropped from above. The repeated citing of "Ruth" evokes the image of a form contract with blank spaces for the names; one almost expects the typeface to give way to handwriting every time she is mentioned. A brief discussion of the private manner of other noted wits, that to a modern eye reads as if copied and pasted ("Ring Lardner, for example, is one of the wittiest men in America; certainly he is the most humorous...") suddenly rings out in Groucho's own voice. But once the wagging resumes, the tone is too alien to be easily attributed even to Groucho attempting to ape the styles of others:

> How often (I couldn't help thinking), how often she must have wished she had married a plumber or an undertaker, who, although he might talk shop at home, would hesitate to work at it after hours! I had seen my wife wince when I told the story (again) about the Scotchman who painted red stripes on his son's thumb so the child would think he had a peppermint stick....

This isn't some nascent, 1920-vintage version of Groucho supposedly writing this—this is the year the movie version of *Animal Crackers* came out. There are plenty of other examples like that throughout the early writings, and the more one attunes oneself to look for them the more they jostle to announce themselves, and the suspicion that all is not as the by-line would have us believe becomes an increasingly hard one to shake.

By whatever means, Groucho was a regular contributor to magazines and periodicals by the early 1930s. But magazine writing was by its nature ephemeral, and perceived by many as hack work. He may have viewed it primarily as a stage in a process, and as previously stated, by the middle of the decade he had decided he was ready to try original dramatic writing. Ample precedent for the leap from journalist to playwright was to be found among his wisecracking associates: why should he not join them?

For a brief moment it looked as though Zeppo, of all unlikely people, was poised to steal the lead on him in that department. In 1930 the already restless younger brother had penned a self-described "story for Slim Summerville and Zasu Pitts," to be called *Muscle-Bound*, and began shopping it around Hollywood. Judging by the treatment that survives in Groucho's papers at the Smithsonian it may perhaps best be described as "naïve." The story is a fanciful confection concerning one "Doc" Hale (pharmacist and inventor of U-Ha-Va Linament, a revolutionary tonic with near-magical powers of rejuvenation), and the adoring Dot Harty, the "most efficient soda water jerker" at the drugstore where both are employed. Though sweet on Doc, Dot is also being ardently courted by his archrival, Signor Bonita, "the world's champion six day bicycle racer." After a thrilling bike race finale, all ends happily with Doc and Dot married, and mass-producing their elixir in "a huge factory belching forth smoke."[10]

Sadly no interest was shown in the younger Marx Brother's efforts, but something of its frivolous spirit re-emerges in one of Groucho's own screenwriting efforts. *Madcap Mary Mooney* was written with Ken Englund in 1937 and conceived as a vehicle for Carole Lombard, of whom Groucho was much enamored (seemingly because rather than in spite of her disregard for what he usually considered appropriate female language and decorum). Both are somewhat in the manner of those sub–Marx oddities Paramount turned out in the 1930s, like *International House* and *Million Dollar Legs*, or for that matter *The Big Broadcast of 1937*, with which Englund made his Hollywood debut at around the same time, but like Zeppo's effort, *Mary* never made it to the screen.[11]

The draft treatment (subtitled "A Romantic Comedy for the Screen") is surely unfilmable. It would have opened with Mary parachuting from the top of the Empire State Building, landing among an excited crowd and exclaiming, "It was wonderful! I did it because I was bored." We would then learn that she is an indulged but enervated heiress, daughter of "Barton Mooney, fat, grey-haired titan of industry," and facing a loveless marriage of convenience to Joseph B. Woodbury, a corrupt senator in Mooney's pocket. As a result, she offsets ennui with daring displays of public thrill-seeking. (In synopsis, the work seems to threaten political satire in the characterization of the bumptious senator, but everything here is painted in strokes much too broad for meaningful effect.) In the next scene she steals and drives away a train, then sends her father a telegram that reads: "Dear Daddy: Let's see you get me out of this. I'm in jail in Omaha. Wish you were here."

The Grouchoesque feel extends even to the script notations ("We now get a better look at Mary, and Mary is worth looking at") and there is some promising dialog. When our hero, modest flying ace Ken Thomas, tells Mooney his daughter expressed a desire to marry him "while flying back from Omaha," the tycoon snaps back: "Nonsense, she was just killing time. She doesn't like to read."

> **Ken**: I would like to marry your daughter.
> **Mooney**: That's very unusual. I doubt if there are more than ten million men in America that want to marry my daughter. Don't you know she's engaged to Senator ... whatsisname?
> **Secretary**: Senator Joseph B. Woodbury.
> **Mooney**: Yes, Senator Newberry—a grey-haired fellow, has a bad left leg.
> **Secretary**: I beg your pardon, Mr. Mooney—it's his right leg.
> **Mooney**: It's his right leg when he's walking away from you, but when he's turned around it's his left leg.

Unlike the more realistic feel of Groucho's writing with Norman Krasna, here the situation resolves itself in purely zany fashion, with a second act in which Mary engineers a phony disappearance while on a scientific expedition to the Tropics with her sweetheart.

Also on board is an eccentric scientist who just happens to be called Julius, and who causes trouble when the time comes to return by sabotaging the plane, partly to remain with "his Polynesian sweetheart Muki" and partly "so that he could complete his lizard collection."

It's all great fun, but totally undisciplined and would have needed massive revision before any studio took it seriously. On the face of it, Englund's suggestion that it was jinxed by the death of Amelia Earhart, on the very day the script was submitted, has something of the feel of wishful thinking. Oddly, however, an unforeseen resemblance to real events had genuinely helped scupper the chances of an earlier Groucho screenplay—but after production rather than before.

## The King and the Chorus Girl (1937)

Groucho's writing alliance with Norman Krasna is best remembered for the stage play *Time for Elizabeth*, but the two first cut their teeth on a movie script written, as already noted, during the early stages of *A Night at the Opera*, while Groucho was still buzzing from his independent success in *Twentieth Century*. According to Krasna's recollections in Charlotte Chandler's *Hello, I Must Be Going*, their working method involved him sitting at the typewriter, staring at a blank wall and "twisting paper clips into Jimmy Durante's profile," while Groucho paced up and down the room and talked, "usually about other things."

*The King and the Chorus Girl* is essentially *Madcap Mary Mooney* in reverse. As the title suggests, instead of wealthy Mary attempting to marry the man she loves against customary opposition, this time around it's Joan Blondell's Dorothy, good-hearted Folies Bergère girl, who is deemed inappropriate wedding material, and the bored heiress is a bored visiting king. The king is played by Fernand Gravet, a European import the press were so unanimously certain would waltz into everyone's heart he barely stood a chance from the start. (In what was presumed to pass for a sophisticated welcome, several papers waggishly claimed that his name had been changed slightly from the original "Fernand Gravey" to avoid confusion with the ubiquitous meat sauce.[12]) But neither is he helped by the script, which for the most part is anything but madcap.

The film is unmistakably inspired by the fizzy champagne comedies that the likes of Lubitsch and Mamoulian had made for Paramount in the early 1930s, and which Groucho greatly admired. Sundry elements of these films—from the sub–Ruritanian background, to the sing-songy dialog, to Edward Everett Horton—were imported wholesale. But it's all in the handling, and this time the mixture doesn't rise. Though Blondell would later recall it as her favorite of all her movies,[13] five minutes could easily be trimmed from every successive ten, and only Horton's absurd list of titles ("...an ordinary Knight of the Bath, an average Knight of the Garter, an everyday Keeper of the Scrolls, a routine Captain of the Lancers...") and the occasional mild exchange ("How did you find Belgium?" "I didn't look for it") approach the expected breeziness of tone. Krasna told Groucho's biographer Hector Arce that the script reflected the sentimental side of Groucho's nature, no less fundamental for being usually hidden, especially in his professional life. His name—and it *was* played up in promotional materials: some of the posters went so far as to feature his face, above the legend "He Wrote It!"—can only have misled.

Under Krasna's sterner supervision there are no absurd plot twists, characters called

Julius, or gleefully wacky dialog, and the closest we get to the Marx Brothers is a singing appearance by Kenny Baker, soon to be seen in more generous quantities at the circus.

(There's also a ready-made part for Margaret Dumont here, but Mary Nash bags it.) The most interesting portion from our narrow perspective is probably the pivotal scene in which the king attends a revue show and first catches sight of his true love. Before that he watches, without enthusiasm, a cross-patter routine (delivered with clear authenticity by vaudeville double-act Al Shaw and Sam Lee). Krasna explained to Charlotte Chandler how the scene was devised:

> I said to Groucho, "We need some used jokes. Can you tell me some jokes?" Groucho said, "About what? Tell me the subject." I didn't have anything in mind, but we'd just been talking about how I'd been losing my hair, and Groucho had recommended I have some scalp massages, so I said, "The subject is hair," and he started. He said six or seven jokes in a row about hair, like "Hair today, gone tomorrow," "My hair is getting thin, so who needs fat hair," "How do you save your hair? In a box," "How do you avoid falling hair? You step aside." And he went on and reeled off just about any joke anyone ever thought of about hair. He wouldn't use any of these, of course, but I realized he had a wonderful memory, and he went on to make up his own.

**He wrote it! Warners were careful to feature Groucho prominently in the advertising for *The King and the Chorus Girl* (1937).**

Some of these ancient hair gags do indeed make it to the final cut, but on the whole Groucho was unhappy with the way the screenplay was treated by director Mervyn LeRoy (soon to be the man that brought the Marx Brothers back to MGM, after the death of Irving Thalberg and their defection to RKO). He approved the recruitment of Arthur Sheekman to polish the script (Sherman Rogers and another of Groucho's pals, Julius Epstein, also helped out), but LeRoy further added some of his own touches. For some reason, an innocuous line making reference to Coney Island earned Groucho's lasting resentment. Krasna again:

I'll never forget after the preview of *The King and the Chorus Girl* when we were walking out of the theater. Standing there was Mervyn LeRoy, the director, who said, "Did you like it?" Groucho just said "Coney Island," in a disgusted tone and walked off. He was referring to a line in the film, which meant that he hated it. Groucho wasn't afraid of anyone.

Warners were sure they had a hit on their hands and allocated the film a massive publicity budget. But in the event it came to be defined not by its own merits but by its superficial plot resemblance to recent events in Britain, where the new King Edward VIII had opted to abdicate rather than be thwarted in his wish to marry the former Mrs. Wallis Simpson. In reality, the writing had pre-dated the crisis, and the film barely resembles it in any but the broadest terms. (The original script, titled *Grand Passion*, had been completed and optioned by Paramount as early as February of 1935.) By the time it was picked up by Warners, however, the story was breaking and the similarities were at first taken as a godsend in terms of publicity. The American public was transfixed by the affair, and Joan Blondell herself deemed the unfolding saga "the most romantic thing possible, in or out of the movies."

In Britain, it was very different. Not only was the matter seen as a constitutional crisis rather than a quaint across-the-tracks soap opera, it had also been subject to a total media blackout. The first that British newspaper readers knew of the business, in those pre-global media days, came when it was already reaching its epoch-defining climax. Accordingly, it seemed shocking—even tragic—and not a subject fit for Hollywood trivialization in any degree. Kaspar Monahan's predication that the film "will probably be barred from Great Britain" proved all too accurate.

The *Spokesman-Review* assessed the matter in detail:

As soon as the picture gets under way, beginning with a grand chuckle, you say, "Aha, the duke of Windsor and his troubles," or something like that. Maybe so. But I heard that the picture was completed last October.

And more than that. The lady next to me said, "He even looks like the ex-king." And maybe he does—a brunette duke of Windsor. But the only analogy is that the hero is an ex-king who is bored to death with life, until a Follies Bergere chorus girl is brought into his life—and an American one. And then life begins at—well, possibly not forty.

At first, Warners clearly thought the coincidence the most enormous lark and a boon to publicity, but when a series of photo teasers hinting at the connection caused outrage in Britain and the commonwealth (Australia was especially incensed) the game backfired. The Hays Office issued a stern dictate that any resemblance to the real events would be hugely problematic in the U.S. also, and Warners were forced to back pedal at high speed. The hitherto endlessly repeated suggestion that Gravet was a dead ringer for the Duke was suddenly just as relentlessly denied, and Max Milder, the Warner man in England, was dragged out of the pub and into the rain to state for the record: "The film was planned out at least eighteen months before the crisis which ended in abdication, and the production was begun before King Edward abdicated." (Indeed, Blondell later recalled the shooting temporarily halting so as to hear the abdication speech on the radio.)

All forthcoming Hollywood scripts were carefully scrutinized for even inadvertently suggestive material, and if necessary pruned. One such victim of this new squeamishness, according to reports, was the Marxes' own *A Day at the Races* which, between scripting and production, lost Groucho's putdown of Harpo: "I'm afraid your brain has abdicated."[14] But the British blood had already boiled and continued to simmer. *Picturegoer* magazine published an open letter to Warners in its issue of April 3rd, 1937, declaring it "a painful shock in this year of grace 1937 to find a reputable film organisation indulging in such an outrage on good taste."[15]

When the dust settled, the receipts were good, and the critical response in America basically positive. The saturation marketing and aggressive promotion of its star in the fan papers did their job with dutiful crowds, and though it proved to be one of those films that never demanded reissue, it was by no means deemed unsuccessful. If Groucho felt any sense of personal disappointment at how it had turned out, he should still have been encouraged by the nature of the attention his involvement received. "When Mr. Marx decides at last to abandon the cork mustache and bushy eyebrows, the wolf should hold no terrors for him," claimed Harold W. Cohen. "In fact, the animal will probably be met at the Marx door by a flock of writers' agents." "I hope Groucho Marx continues to write comedies," opined the *Spokesman-Review*, "the screen needs him." "Any time that Groucho cares to sign a writer's contract with the producer Mervyn Le Roy, he'll find the papers ready for his signature," added Eileen Percy.

But the last word surely belongs to the *Sunday Morning Star*: "The name of Groucho Marx, and his face, were freely used in advertising *The King and the Chorus Girl*, which he helped write. Norman Krasna was co-author but his name was lost in the shuffle. Now he's being called Norman Zeppo Krasna."

# 2

# I wish Harpo and Chico were here

Groucho saw in the 1940s with a series of endings—a perhaps necessary precondition for a new beginning. In 1941 he retired the Marx Brothers at the end of their current MGM contract, just as he had promised to do three films back in 1939. And in 1942, he and his wife Ruth finally called time on a marriage that had been on the ropes for no small while.

If his third marriage, to Eden, was an old man's indulgence, and his second, to Kay, was a lonely man's mistake, then his 1920 union with dancer Ruth Johnson had been, perhaps, the wishful thinking of youth. Not that he was all that young—thirty is an age by which he might have been expected to have found himself a wife and started a family, and doubtless that was a factor too. True, Harpo was still resolutely determined to stay unshackled, but with Chico of all people now seemingly intent on giving domesticity a whirl, Groucho may well have decided to simply bow to the inevitable. In which case, Ruth was a natural choice: young, very attractive, blonde, unsophisticated and, as Zeppo's dancing partner, right there in front of him when the mood struck.

The problem seems to have been that which plagued all of Groucho's attempts at happy families: simple incompatibility of interests. But they were married for 22 years, produced two children, and for a long while it looked like they were solidly, if unspectacularly, matched. While in subsequent marriages Groucho had his own as an example, first time round he may have simply not seen the warning signs. While he liked to live quietly, with his books and records, and to socialize only with a select few, Ruth was a vastly more gregarious animal, who presumed that a star's wife was entitled to a share of glamour and excitement. And while Groucho was never exactly profligate, the savage losses he sustained during the Depression, as the marriage approached its first decade, turned him into a considerable skinflint, obsessed with household accounts and always on the alert for needless extravagances to complain about, like new outfits and nights out.

Ruth also felt herself hopelessly outclassed, intellectually speaking, by Groucho's erudite and cynical circle of close friends, a situation hardly helped by his tendency to cast her as Margaret Dumont in social settings. This insensitive behavior—often portrayed as deliberate cruelty in the more sensational biographical analyses—was more likely sheer thoughtlessness: Groucho needed a feed, a straight woman to keep up the act in public, and who else was there? That it was having a negative effect on the marriage may not have even occurred to him until it was too late, and Ruth, with the secretiveness of one who was increasingly finding release from boredom and insecurity in drink, may not have made her feelings plain. In any event, theirs was certainly not a dramatic split, but more a slow, sad parting of the ways, finalized with sadness and reluctance by both parties. Tellingly, Ruth cited Groucho's belittling jokes as grounds in the divorce papers.

Starting over both privately and professionally in his fifties was tough work for Groucho, especially when confronted with uncomfortable indications that the world was readying to think of him in the past tense. As often as not he found himself at a loose end, telling Sheekman in a letter that he now spent his evenings alone at the cinema "alternately smoking and sleeping. I used to sleep on Ruth's shoulder when we were married—now I don't even have that."

The kind of offers he wanted, and had expected, were not forthcoming—at least not in movies. Would he find any greater liberty to break free on stage? The moot question was how far to stray from his established persona. On film, he already had the warning example of *Room Service* (for which he had intended growing a real mustache and committing himself entirely to playing the character as written, only to revert to uneasy compromise as doubts accrued and finally overwhelmed the production). On the other hand, his 1934 repertory stint in *Twentieth Century* had been unanimously hailed a success.

Whether the problem was indecision or reluctance to commit to long runs, he seemed to turn down several stage offers that he might have leapt at had they come his way in other media.[1] There was a request from the New Opera Company in 1942 to appear in Offenbach's *La Vie Parisienne*: he was intrigued by the idea, but said no. In 1945 he told Miriam he had turned down "the new Gordon musical" because "they insisted that I sign up for two years, which means that if the show clicked, I'd eventually wind up in Toledo, Chicago." Robert Dwan says he turned down the title role of *Volpone* for the Theater Guild in 1946. The same year, Hedda Hopper has him "cooking up a musical for Broadway about Johnny Appleseed in which, if plans go thru, he'll play the lead straight." (That one's got to be my favorite.) Groucho himself wrote to the *New York Times* in June of 1945 to scotch rumors that he was planning on appearing in two plays simultaneously: "Equity would object, and the hauling charges would be prohibitive." The real question with Groucho and theater is not why he kept turning it down so much as why they bothered to keep offering.

The most tantalizing near-miss came in 1942, again from old friends: Max Gordon producing, George Kaufman directing, and Arthur Sheekman co-writing. According to George Tucker's syndicated "Man About Manhattan" column:

> Max Gordon ... plans to bring Harpo and Groucho Marx to Broadway, but in separate vehicles. Groucho he will present in *Franklin Street*, and Harpo he will turn loose in a revival of a really great play, *Yellow Jack*.

The really great play was in reality *The Yellow Jacket*, in which Harpo had appeared the year before (as "The Property Man"), in a repertory engagement in Massachusetts, alongside Woollcott and Fay Wray. He would appear in the play again in Pasadena in 1952, but for now this suggestion of a Broadway revival went no further. The plans for Groucho, however, came much closer to fruition, as columnist Ted Gill reported on July 22:

> It's a complete new comedy deal for Groucho Marx when he opens Sept. 29 in Philadelphia in George S. Kaufman's farce *Franklin Street*. That trademarked mustache which has been painted over Groucho's upper lip for every performance and every picture since he joined forces will be missing. Groucho will adopt a Vandyke. The mustache is out for good, he says.[2]

*Variety* told the same excited story, mustache and all. Sheekman and Kaufman's previous collaboration, *Mr. Big*, had opened and closed in a week in 1941, and the pair had high hopes for greater success with this adaptation of Philip Goodman's stories of his Philadelphia boyhood. But for some reason, and with a lack of professionalism that was anything but typical of him, Groucho pulled out shortly after, plunging the whole production into crisis.

There is the small possibility of a link between his mysterious exit and a largely forgotten episode in his private life. Within a week of his divorce being made official, Walter Winchell was announcing his engagement to an aspiring actress called Susan Brecker. (He calls her "a Hollywood designer," presumably Winchell-speak for someone with designs on Hollywood stardom, rather than a suggestion that she worked in any studio's design departments.) The dime-a-dozen publicity mill grinds out another: big deal, we might assume—and feel justified in so doing by the fact of her complete absence from the established record. But in fact, Brecker is also the girl referenced in a mysterious letter from July of 1942 included in *The Groucho Letters*. (She is left anonymous in the book, supposedly because neither Groucho nor Sheekman could remember her name by the time it was compiled: nonsense, since she must have been named in the letter itself before it was edited for publication).

Groucho takes pains in the letter to assure his friend that, on this occasion "Dame rumor hit the nail on the head," going on to declare Brecker "far too good for me" and himself "head over heels," despite the soon to become customary age difference (twenty-two to his ninety-seven, he claims). That he was indeed besotted may be indicated by the demeaning context of the letter—he was trying to cadge a part for her in *Franklin Street*: "The suggestion that she go into your play came from Max Gordon. He was so impressed with her looks that he asked me why I didn't consider her for a part…. I explain all this lest you think she is playing me for a part in the show. Once you've met her, I'm sure you'll realize that she doesn't go in for that sort of thing. This must sound exceedingly jerky."

The Groucho–Brecker amour, however, appears to have been over and forgotten as quickly as was Groucho's involvement with the play, and we can only speculate to what extent the course of one was dictated by the other. (Another of Gordon's casting suggestions for the play—the unknown, seventeen-year-old Lauren Bacall—provided a long and invaluable account of the production in her autobiography *By Myself*, but sadly both Groucho and Brecker had gone by the time she was appointed.)

Brecker vanishes entirely from the record more or less instantly thereafter, and without Groucho, the play never did find its feet. His role was offered to Ed Wynn, who also declined, and then to Sam Jaffe, who began rehearsing before disagreements with Kaufman over his interpretation of the role led to his mutually-approved exit also. It was then re-scheduled for October, with Reynolds Evans, who had been playing a small supporting role but was also Jaffe's understudy, upgraded to lead. But it never made it to Broadway: after ten nights in Washington it was announced the play was being withdrawn for a complete rewrite. The following year Kaufman hopefully announced plans to restage it as a musical to star Bert Lahr … and that was that. Had Groucho narrowly avoided a disaster, or had his late withdrawal helped cause one?

Kaufman, at least, had no hard feelings, because he was back in 1943, this time in collaboration with Moss Hart, with the offer to star Groucho in a parody of Sherlock Holmes.[3] Oddly, the idea had first been mooted in 1941, without Hart and Kaufman, as a vehicle for all three brothers. Announced somewhat bafflingly by the *Melbourne Argus* as a project "for stage and screen," it was supposed to star Groucho as Holmes ("a part for which his characteristic walk, it is thought, equips him admirably") Harpo as either Watson or Professor Moriarty and Chico as Inspector Lestrade. ("The Sherlock Holmes Club, under the presidency of Christopher Morley, is inclined to favor the project, as Groucho is known to have been a reverent student of Sherlock Holmes for many years," quoth the *Argus*.) Impossible to say if there was any link between this suggestion and the Kaufman and Hart proposal, but the latter was definitely a Groucho-only affair. Sadly, it too came to nothing: despite initial enthusiasm, both star and writers concluded there was not enough scope for a full-length play. Kaufman suggested mounting a revue instead (a fascinating idea at this point in both their careers), but Groucho declared himself "not much interested in high-kicking on the New York stage or any other place."

## The Hollywood Victory Caravan (1942)

The year 1942 should have been the first year of the rest of Groucho's professional life. Early signs pointed to an altogether more worrying conclusion. To set aside the divorce and the debacle of *Franklin Street*, the good news should have been the publication of his second book, *Many Happy Returns*, again with "assistance" from Arthur Sheekman. This jocular indictment of income taxes emerged in January but only scraped about 5,000 copies in sales. Just as the quiet reception of *Beds* in 1930 had been attributed by Groucho to the lack of laughing spirit in the wake of the Crash, so this time he pointed the finger of blame at the bombing of Pearl Harbor in December of 1941. A hurriedly designed cover showing a cartoon Groucho conking the heads of the axis leaders with a fairground mallet marked "Income Taxes" wasn't enough, he claimed, to offset the book's general lack of patriotic spirit.

With writing, radio and theater all seeming dead ends, Groucho began to look with deep concern at an appointments diary that seemed void of all work other than the voluntary sort. "I am up to my ears in activities that don't bring in a dime," Leo Rosten recalled him telling a friend around this time:

> Last week I did a show for the army—free. Then I auditioned for radio—no money. Then I wrote a guest column—gratis. Today I'm recording a speech for the Heart Fund in Chicago. The only thing I can get out of that is that someday I may be lucky enough to have a heart attack in the Loop.[4]

"Groucho was a performing seal," says Bill Marx, "and a dead man walking when he wasn't working."[5] So when he was asked to join a contingent of Hollywood stars touring America to perform shows in aid of Army and Navy Relief he jumped at the opportunity. His desire to contribute meaningfully to the war effort was never in doubt, but neither did he have anything much else in the offing to make the decision in any way difficult. Thus the Hollywood Victory Caravan added a Marx Brother to a team that also included Bob Hope, Desi Arnaz, Olivia De Havilland, Cary Grant, Joan Blondell, Laurel and Hardy, Claudette Colbert, Frances Langford, Charles Boyer, Frank McHugh, Fay McKenzie, James Cagney, Merle Oberon, Eleanor Powell, Pat O'Brien, Joan Bennett, Bert Lahr and Jerry Colonna, among others.[6]

To the professional eye the show was a bit of a hodgepodge, and clocked in at a numbing three and a half hours on its first night (the curtain dropped well after midnight), but it was tightened to two and a half thereafter, and the sheer weight of its star power made up for any technical rough edges. (Or, as *Variety* put it: "Twenty-two top Hollywood names on any one platform at one time, no matter what they do, is worth a healthy scoop out of anyone's poke.") But that it may not have been quite the triumph habitually recalled is suggested by this intriguingly unsentimental financial report that appeared in *Variety* on May 6th:

With approximately $218,000 grossed in its first five dates, the Hollywood Victory Caravan appears on its way to garnering a healthy chunk of coin for Army-Navy Relief, although perhaps less than the very optimistic $750,000 hoped for.... Take went over the top in Boston and Philadelphia, but was considerably less than expected in Washington, Detroit and Cleveland. In these cities, last-minute rescaling of the houses was necessary to hype sales of high-priced seats. Goal was exceeded by $3,000 in Philly. It was almost $15,000 below the $40,000 originally hoped for in Washington and $10,000 under the $42,000 sought in Cleveland.... It was originally hoped to get $123,000 in Detroit with such devices as $600 boxes. Lack of advance sales, however, brought about four rescalings until even the $50 and $25 seats were going at $10. Revised goal was $75,000, but even with the State Fair Coliseum packed with 12,000 spectators, including standees, gross hit on $53,000.

The final gross was around $600,000—decidedly not chicken feed, but, as *Variety* predicted, a ways short of the target.

Before embarking on the tour, the team were invited to a reception on the White House lawn by Eleanor Roosevelt. ("I hope they have pumpernickel," Groucho wrote to Miriam.) Here, according to *Variety*, they "drank some lightly-spiked punch and munched pastry while Groucho Marx engaged Mrs. R. in a less than erudite discussion of Jerry Colonna's mustache." The same paper elsewhere claimed Groucho arrived ahead of the rest and elected to welcome them as they arrived, explaining: "I always wanted to greet people on the White House steps." John Lahr's memoir of his father Bert, *Notes on a Cowardly Lion*, adds substantially to the store of anecdote:

> The tenor of the day was proclaimed when Marx, McHugh, and [Bert] Lahr stepped into a car driven by a well-dressed member of the American Women's Voluntary Service. "Where would you gentlemen like to go?" the lady asked in upper-class tones. "Is there a cathouse in the area?" "We were a bit uncomfortable," recalls Lahr, laughing. "But Groucho would overpower you. Maybe three or four of those jokes wouldn't hit, and then one clobbered you. He was always gagging. Groucho was never at a loss for words. He had tremendous confidence. If you weren't sure of yourself, he'd skewer you." Lahr was on his best behavior at the White House, and wishing he were not. Standing behind Groucho in the receiving line, both comedians had time to watch the attaché ask each member of the troupe his name and then announce it to Mrs. Roosevelt, who in turn would say, "It's a pleasure to have you here, Mr.———." When it came Groucho's turn, the attaché announced his name to Mrs. Roosevelt, who proceeded in her formal greeting. "I'm very happy to welcome you here, Mr. Marx." "Are we late for dinner?" Groucho said. The joke nearly reduced Lahr to tears of laughter; he cannot remember shaking hands with Mrs. Roosevelt, although he recalls biting his lip to maintain decorum in the receiving line ... "I remember a general coming up to Groucho and me and asking where Mrs. Roosevelt was. You wouldn't have believed him—medals all over him. 'She's upstairs filing her teeth,' Groucho said. The general walked away." ... "FDR wasn't there that day, and when the band began to play, Groucho turned to Mrs. Roosevelt and said, 'No wonder the old man didn't come.'"

Lahr recalled a happy, family atmosphere on the tour, the camaraderie aided as it was by much after hours lubrication. Laurel and Hardy, in particular, kept their wheels well oiled, and Groucho remembered them in *The Groucho Phile* as "pleasantly sloshed all the time I was with them." ("This, I thought, would be the leg up I'd need to outshine them. No way.")

The team set off by train from Los Angeles on April 26, arriving at Washington on the 29 for the first of three weeks of performances in thirteen cities. Groucho wasn't announced until April 22, though, according to *Variety*, as a last-minute replacement for Cary Grant who, in the event, did tag along after all. (One who did have to pull out because of inflexible commitments was Spencer Tracy, somewhat fortuitously replaced by Bing Crosby.)

The late arrival of Groucho, and—if the Grant story is true—his superfluity once contracted, may partly account for what seems to have been his rather unspectacular use in the show. According to *Variety* he appeared in a group sketch called "So Long, Sam" with Boyer, Hope, Cagney, Colbert, de Havilland, Oberon, Lahr and Colonna, and with "the entire male cast" in something called "Sweater Boy." He also did three spots of his own: the familiar radio sketch "Who's Olive?"[7] in which he appeared with Olivia de Havilland; a bit intriguingly described as "a sketch titled 'Lydia'"; and with "a chorus of nurses in the skit, 'Dr. Hacken-bush.'" A good few laughs there, one hopes, but nothing terribly fresh or stretching. "It's all right for guys like Bob Hope," he half-jokingly told reporters. "Bob has seventeen guys writing his jokes for him. But I've got to do the worrying about my material." When told that Hope was in fact travelling with only six writers, Groucho replied: "For Bob, that's practically adlib-bing."

Clearly there was a hierarchy, with some performers given greater priority than others, but just as obviously box-office drawing power could not be the sole arbiter of who did what and how much. Some of the biggest screen stars simply had no experience of live revue work, so that their presence alone could be their only attraction. Others were old hands, to be relied upon to provide the actual substance of the entertainment. Groucho had hands as old as any, and so should, in theory, have been a headliner. Yet plainly he was not, quite—were those hands perhaps just a shade *too* old?

There is a definite sense that he had been shunted somewhat to the sidelines, among the specialties. Groucho was more than capable of dominating the bill, and yet in a very real sense he was an unknown and hard-to-place commodity as a single act. In that, he must have seen on a small scale his larger predicament. While Hope was hip and omnipresent, Grou-cho—and, for that matter, Laurel and Hardy—was marginal: a novelty, not of the fabric, and somehow nostalgic. In Stan and Ollie's case, that was perhaps fair enough, but Groucho didn't feel like a comforting memory. He wanted to be contemporary. He wanted to be a radio star. He wanted, in short, to be Bob Hope.

"Fact is, it was more Hope's than Hollywood's Victory Caravan," noted *Variety*. "As long as the Pepsodent peddler was at the mike the show had zest and lift. And it was those players whose turns consisted of gagging with Hope who came out best." Groucho was not among them. Though it would indeed be gagging with Hope that later enabled him to finally make his mark in radio, leading directly to *You Bet Your Life*, the feeling here was, presumably, that their respective comic personalities were somewhat incompatible. If the wound needed fur-ther salting, *Variety* obligingly brought the condiments:

> Groucho Marx was restrained by the limitations of his old "Who's Olive?" sketch in which he worked with Olivia de Havilland. Like most of the sketches, it was much too long for the amount of humor given off. Marx followed it with his standard "Dr. Hackenbush" patter. Also sufferers from lack of material were Lau-rel and Hardy, with their simple-simon cross-talk.

That the experience prompted Groucho to ponder his professional trajectory is further suggested by a popular anecdote concerning Groucho and the Caravan, originating, according to Hector Arce, with Bob Hope's memories of the tour in 1963. According to Hope, when the cast arrived for the first show in Washington, D.C., they all filed out one at a time to a rapturous welcome. Suddenly, an anonymous figure in a bland suit emerged, to whom the crowd showed a singular lack of interest. A chastened Groucho turned on his heels, hurriedly applied a greasepaint mustache and re-emerged to a rousing cheer.

It is difficult to ascertain the extent to which he used the mustache in the show itself: there are plenty of photos of him wearing it and just as many show him without it, and a report in the *Chicago Tribune* on May 7 explicitly states that the audiences were entertained by, among other attractions, "Groucho Marx without his mustache." Judging by the pictures, it looks like he may have used it for old time's sake in the Hackenbush number, with its explicit evocation of the Brothers' act, but not (usually) in the "Who's Olive?" sketch or the finale. There is, it is true, one photo of him greasepainted with De Havilland, so it may be that he was not consistent throughout the tour. But in none of the surviving shots of him making public appearances with the cast does he seem to be wearing it.

So how suspicious should we be of Hope's anecdote? It's certainly a good story. But even if the cast weren't announced as they exited, as one might have supposed (how positively would you identify an off-duty Olivia de Havilland, even, from the thick of a crowd, a hundred feet from the action?), it is hard to imagine Groucho being either so resourceful or so desperate. His default gesture to any kind of snub was usually one of lofty resentment. The image of him doubling back and rushing to the make-up box is fanciful as well as pathetic, and unless he kept a greasepaint stick in his pocket with his spare cigars it is unlikely he would have had access to his stage kit at that point, whatever his intentions.

While the Washington crowd may well have been less enthused at his arrival, it is more likely that the diagnosis was formulated after the event as a means of tidying it up in his own mind. Perhaps he then passed this version of what happened on to Hope, who was unlikely to have been standing around scrutinizing the cast members as they exited. (It's also worth noting that Bert Lahr recalled getting the same icy reception, jokingly reporting cries of "Who's this bum?" as he emerged onto the platform.) Perhaps an unusually good-spirited Groucho might have gone into his crouch and waggled his eyebrows to make himself known. "Doesn't anybody want little old Groucho's autograph?" he supposedly asked. "You know, I'm somebody too, even if I *am* out of work." Well, maybe.

If true (or especially if false), what the story indicates is that Groucho's greasepaint mustache had become a symbolic focus of his frustrations in achieving professional independence. Hence the numerous anecdotes about it. It's a constant refrain in reports of every new project that comes his way around this time: a decisive change is indicated by the abandonment of the greasepaint. In 1944, the *Milwaukee Journal* reported on the forthcoming arrival in town of Groucho and the cast of the radio show *Pabst Blue Ribbon Town* to record a special edition of the show live from the Pabst brewery, but noted that "unless there is an unexpected and important last minute change in plans, the best known Marx since Karl will reach Milwaukee without his greasepaint mustache and eyebrows."

> Groucho's discarding of these accustomed comedy devices, which represents a determined effort on his part to break with his past as an antic buffoon, had been the subject of much discussion behind the scenes at CBS and elsewhere in Hollywood. Of all those connected with the show, including the sponsors, the advertising agency and fellow workers, no one seems happy about it but Groucho himself, and he appears more firm than pleased.[8]

But it continues:

> This recalls an incident at the premiere of a Marx brothers picture in Boston some years ago when Groucho, arriving late, tried to get through a crowd around the theater and was stopped by a cop. "But I'm Groucho Marx," explained the comedian. "A likely story, me lad," replied the law. "There's Groucho Marx on that bill-board over there. Do you mean to say you look anything like him?" Groucho could not tell the man in blue there was a close resemblance. There isn't. When he comes before his audiences in Hollywood few persons probably would recognise him but for the introduction he gets, and Groucho knows this so well he begins by telling the folks they're probably surprised to see him as he really is. In this con-

nection the comedian has made only one grudging concession to the sponsors and producers of the show. He agreed to wear his trademark make-up in all publicity photographs like the one on this page. Beyond that, he apparently refuses to budge.

Now, this cop anecdote, which could surely have come from nowhere but Groucho himself, is if anything even sillier than Hope's. While it is true that Groucho was hard to recognize without his make-up, make-up it most obviously is. No cop, even in a Lee Tracy movie, would be so stupid as to think it a real and permanent feature of the man in question. But more importantly, if the Caravan story *was* true, why—less than two years later, in an article specifically about Groucho arriving by train with a party of stars—do we get this vague anecdote about a cop in Boston at the premiere of some old Marx Brothers movie, when we could have the other, really good, up to date story? The conclusion would seem to be that these stories are largely false in detail, and change repeatedly in the telling. But in their repetition they accurately reflect a general preconception and—for Groucho—preoccupation: that a Groucho without his mustache might be something less than a functioning whole. In the focus of these anecdotes upon this problem, and in the manner in which they convert the subjective into the empirical, they recall the Boris Karloff story detailed in the introduction.

Once the Caravan had hitched up for the last time in San Francisco on May 19, it was back to business as usual for Groucho: looking for business. The most obvious outlet for his talents in the 1940s seemed to be radio, and indeed he made a popular guest star with Hope, Crosby, Jolson, Dinah Shore and just about everyone else. It was lucrative, too—to a degree he found almost baffling. "I was getting three thousand dollars a week for every appearance," he told Arce of his stint on Dinah Shore's program. "The day Roosevelt died, we didn't have a show. I got paid anyhow. They buried him the day of the next show. I got another three thousand dollars." With flawless and classically Grouchoesque logic, he concluded "there are not enough people dying."

Radio paid, but he didn't want merely what he called "the customary unfunny guest shot." Taken for granted by the networks in that capacity, it was a source of puzzlement to him that he was not in demand for a show of his own. "What's wrong with me that I can't click on radio?" he asked his son Arthur, noting the ease with which the likes of Hope and Benny had adapted to the airwaves. He had been a far bigger star on the stage than either, "yet I lose every sponsor I get."

One amusing sketch from Dinah Shore's program seems to acknowledge his own professional predicament, as he angles for a show of his own with fictitious sponsor Forbes Schneider Ink:

"Marx, I'm Mr. Forbes-Schneider, president of the Forbes-Schneider Ink Company. I just want you to remember one thing. I make fifty million gallons of ink every year."

"Well, every man is entitled to his hobby. What do you do for a living?"

"Well now, let's get one thing clear. If I give you this program are you positive that you'll be able to deliver Miss Dinah Shore?"

"Hold on, Mr. Forbes-Schneider, there are a few questions I'd like to ask. Are you saying you don't want me if I can't get Dinah for the show?"

"Yes."

"Now the next question, what about salary?"

"Well, what would you say to three thousand dollars a week?"

"I don't know. We've never been introduced. But why stand on ceremony? I'll take it."

"You'll *take* it? *You'll* take it?"

"There's still another variant of that: You'll take *it*. [subdued laughter] Well, that about washes up *that* joke…."

Groucho gets his contract and we then get to enjoy some of the shows he is given to host, including a pretentious round table discussion program, for which he adopts somber, pedantic tones ("I hate to be definite, but I can't help saying that I'm uncertain") and an inane game show, through which he yelps and laughs hysterically ("In just about five seconds we're gonna have a young married couple come out here, and now here's the fun: this couple doesn't know that you know that I know that they know that we don't know that they don't know what we know!"). But no such contract was forthcoming in reality.

Much of Groucho's work on radio in these years not only survives but is more readily available than ever, thanks to a burgeoning old time radio collectors' circuit. But even if you don't move in such circles and wouldn't know a download if you downloaded one, it's still possible to get a good taste of Groucho's guest star years, just from browsing the CD racks. A generous selection of his appearances are obtainable on compilation discs, and from these we can draw a number of conclusions.

First, he was given *a lot* of work: there are many CDs of this stuff commercially available, with little overlapping material. Second, for the most part it's pretty good. True, there is the slightly demeaning tic of everyone constantly making jokes about the sponsors, on the pretense that in so doing they're being subversive, when really they're just obediently plugging the

Radio days: Groucho, sans mustache, smiles his way through another guest spot. With Peggy Lee on the Bing Crosby Show, February 1947.

names. (This may announce itself with greater insistence to British ears, trained as they are in an essentially non-sponsored radio and TV environment, than to American ones.) But that aside, Groucho is often on form and very funny, and the material is just as often not at all bad. And when it is bad, he gets bigger laughs letting us know it than he would have with better material. And he does the Hackenbush song approximately four thousand times.

Groucho was hardly tethered in these appearances. He is allowed room to take the shows over, in generous chunks of airtime, and far from delivering a substandard approximation of the screen Groucho over and over, is given surprising comedic scope and leeway. He frequently gets to experiment with characterization, voices, even impersonation, as in his "News From Russ-ia" lecture (on the Armed Forces Radio program *Command Performance*), delivered in wicked imitation of esteemed radio commentator H.V. Kaltenborn's famously precise diction:

Good eve-e-ning, ladies and gentlemen. I was listening to the news tonight from Russ-i-a. Frankly, I don't quite understand the news tonight from Russ-i-a. However, I probably *would* understand the news from

Russ-i-a if I spoke Russ-i-an. Nevertheless, I shall continue to listen to the news from Russ-i-a. And some day it is possible I may be able to understand the news from Russ-i-a, provided they learn to speak English. However, there is a strong likelihood by that time that I will have forgotten how to speak English and will understand only Russ-i-an. In that case, I will move to Brazil. Goodnight, and nuts to you.

"I have given up on being a success on the air," he reflected in one of his letters to his daughter Miriam. "The way I figure it out, I just have too much talent for it; it requires a mediocrity that I can't acquire." His envy of many of the stars who mastered the medium was certainly informed by his sense of superiority over them. But it's not really a question of talent—more of dynamics. One of the more interesting of the available CDs ingeniously creates the illusion of presenting whole episodes of a fictitious "Groucho Marx Variety Show." The effect is sustained with cleverly interpolated intros and outros, and material carefully arranged to suggest that the stars are the guests and the guest is the star. It's a fascinating attempt to create a parallel entertainment reality, and it works well. But at the same time, it shows clearly why the absence of a Groucho show of this nature should be no surprise, either to us now, or to Groucho then.

Groucho's persona is plainly that of intruder. He disrupts. He subverts. He interrupts, changes focus, and fractures whatever gossamer pretense of "reality" the program feigns. As in the movies, Groucho only *makes sense* as a guest, not host: simply putting him in that central position changes his meaning and weakens his power. More importantly to sponsor and networks, it creates a show that doesn't make sense either; one that no audience could be expected to warm to. The host must be the core of normality, speaking to the home audience as a friend. The relationship depends on sincerity: Groucho's character is at his best when least sincere, and it's hard to imagine him even being able to fake the natural rapport that the likes of Benny or Hope enjoyed with their audiences, much less being useful or happy doing so.

The radio variety show, in effect, must be Rittenhouse Manor, and the host must be Margaret Dumont. A production that is set wherever Captain Spaulding calls home (wherever that could possibly be) would be infinitely less funny than watching him, as invited guest, exploding Mrs. Rittenhouse's weekend soiree. In a situation comedy format, such as *Flywheel, Shyster and Flywheel*, he works. As the star of the show, the balance is wrong. Indeed, the only way around the problem would be a distinctly postmodern one: a program nominally called "The Margaret Dumont Show." Every week, Dumont would come on, thank her audience graciously and give them a phony rundown of the highbrow guests and items on the show, whereupon Groucho bursts in as if unexpected the show proper begins, with Dumont supposedly straining to maintain order.

When they finally solved the problem for real, with *You Bet Your Life*, it was half invention—pitting Groucho against real members of the public in a variation on the bemused persona he displays in the movies only when dealing with Chico—and half reinvention, obliging him to become mellower and more twinkly. It worked. Audiences loved it, not least in those moments when the new Groucho couldn't resist letting the old one out of his cage. But a standard variety format under his jurisdiction would never have made sense. We've already mentioned *Pabst Blue Ribbon Town*: brother Zeppo the Hollywood agent secured him a slot as host in 1943. Within a year he had been replaced by Kenny Baker, the singing circus owner. Then there was *The Flotsam Family*. Surely that was a dead cert: a sitcom by Irving Brecher, with Groucho as a comic father in a rambunctious family. Nobody wanted to know. Brecher rewrote the character as an Irishman, changed the title to *The Life of Riley* and it took off like gangbusters—but with William Bendix in place of Groucho.

*Pabst Blue Ribbon Town* may have had no very profound effect on Groucho's career, but it did introduce him to Kay Gorcey, who in July of 1945 would become his second wife—at twenty-four, three decades his junior. It was a difficult union from the start, complicated greatly by the fact that, before falling for Groucho, Kay had struck up a fast friendship with his daughter Miriam, who then had to contend not only with the fact that her friend had suddenly become her stepmother, but also with the arrival a year later of a brand new sister, Melinda. (The correspondence between Miriam and Groucho in *Love, Groucho* is at its edgiest around this time.)

But this was far from the only problem. Along with the usual issues that dogged Groucho's marriages—differences of age and temperament, lack of common interests and an intellectual disparity that led to resentment on both sides—there was also the fact that Kay, fresh from an abusive and alcoholic marriage to Dead End Kid Leo Gorcey (also a star of the Pabst show), was somewhat unstable, volatile, and a heavy drinker. Charming company she may have been some of the time, and attractive she certainly was, but it is still difficult to imagine a man of Groucho's age and serious temperament making so plainly ill-judged a move so soon after the collapse of his first marriage. Here we must recall the testimony of virtually all his close friends: Groucho was a romantic of the most idealistic sort, and in matters of the heart as impulsive and naïve as a schoolboy. He was also profoundly lonely. Those who believe in omens might be diverted by Hedda Hopper's report of the wedding, in which she notes that Arthur Murray presented the happy couple with a pair of lovebirds: "When Groucho was putting them in the cage they fought like tigers and bit his hands severely."[9]

The strain that the marriage soon imposed on his private life only exacerbated the continuing difficulties he was experiencing professionally, but in 1946 his luck finally looked to be turning. What he had most longed for was prestige film work, with no other cast members named Marx. "It was much more trouble than getting a divorce," Groucho reflected to reporters after retiring the act for a second time, after *A Night in Casablanca*. "After all, we've been together longer than most Hollywood couples. In fact, I had to establish residence for a year on the United Artists lot."[10] The reason he was still on the United Artists lot was because he had suddenly got his wish: a solo role in a musical, co-starring with Carmen Miranda.

## *Copacabana* (1947)

History has recorded *Copacabana* as a nondescript flop, and in the years following Groucho was more than happy to collude in its depreciation. The contemporary record, however, paints a somewhat surprising "new" picture of Groucho's first starring film without his brothers.[11] True, it confirms the understood outcome—audiences were cool and the film was swiftly forgotten. But it also reveals that the filmmakers were loudly confident of smash success, and that a good many reviewers spoke of in tones of rapture.

The original idea came from Monte Proser, he being the owner of the fashionable New York nightspot in which the film is set. He thought his dive a cinch for the movies and pitched the idea to every drunken film executive that happened to show up there. (Carmen Miranda herself was a regular performer, and in a cute tie-in was due to appear the week the film opened. But in one of the project's few ill-omens she had to pull out due to gastroenteritis.) Eventually luck landed Proser in the lap of Sam Coslow, in town to sniff out the Broadway shows in the hope one might be worth turning into the screen musical he was setting up for Beacon Productions, an independent outfit releasing through United Artists. According to his autobiography, Coslow "had no immediate reaction" to Proser's pitch. But he "agreed to explore the idea" when he visited the club, saw its famous "Copa girls," and "bells suddenly began to ring inside my skull."

As a film producer he was responsible for *Pass the Biscuits, Mirandy, A Knife, a Fork and a Spoon* and *From the Indies to the Andes in His Undies,* all in 1942 alone. This was a man who was just made for the movies, as a songwriter.

Later Groucho would complain to Miriam that the film "had no story and no names and no money (this last fact I wasn't aware of until we had been shooting two weeks)." On the latter point, he may well have assumed—or been led to assume—that United Artists, who had signed to release the film, was also financing it. They were not, and Coslow had swiftly discovered how much UA's breezy assurance that "any bank would finance a picture that had a United Artists release deal" was worth in hard currency. Initial plans to shoot the film in Technicolor were first to go by the board, as Coslow scrabbled after financiers in search of funds to keep the project afloat, a task he found distasteful and for which he felt himself ill-suited. A well-placed friendship secured him the ear of the Bank of America, but their investment was contingent on the signing of bankable stars. Miranda, Coslow says, was the first and obvious choice for female lead, but finding her male counterpart was a bigger problem:

> Then one morning I got a letter from Gummo Marx. Gummo managed the Marx Brothers, and they were available for a new film. There was, of course, no way I could fit all three into the script, but something clicked in my mind. I phoned Gummo. "Groucho would be the ideal star for *Copacabana*," I ventured. "How about it?" I could hear him breathing hard over the telephone mouthpiece. There was a brief silence. Finally he spoke. "Did I hear you right? Are you telling me you'd like to break up the Marx Brothers? People have been trying to do that for the past thirty years!" He kept protesting that there was just no way, but he did agree to let Groucho read the treatment.

Forget, for a moment, the presumably embellished quotation. I've no more idea than you who these people were that had been trying to split the act for thirty years, and in any event the team had been officially (and visibly) split since 1941: the point of Gummo's communication was that he was hawking an exciting reunion. But I'm interested in the chronology here. If Gummo really did write to Coslow in 1945 to offer him the Marxes as a unit, that presumably means that they had not yet secured the involvement of producer David Loew in what would become *A Night in Casablanca.* And if Groucho is to be taken at his word when he claimed that he took *Copacabana* because it was the only thing he was offered that *wasn't* a Marx Brothers movie (there being nothing he was less willing to commit to), we are left with the proposition that the plans to star him in *Copacabana* were being drawn up at the same time as—or perhaps more likely *before*—plans for *A Night in Casablanca.* Now, if Groucho had known *Copacabana* was in the offing, is there not a strong chance he'd have scuttled *A Night in Casablanca* and taken on just the solo gig? Did Gummo, well aware of that possibility and equally beholden to his other two brothers, actually *delay* bringing the *Copacabana* offer to Groucho until he was safely signed up for *Casablanca,* thus securing his participation in both?

Fortunately for all, the Bank of America was satisfied with the choice and offered to chip in a million, provided Coslow obtain a good and reliable director. Alfred E. Green, still hot from *The Jolson Story*, was a shrewd choice, and he jumped at the chance when he heard he would be directing Groucho. (Groucho, for his part, characterized Green as "an ancient incompetent" who "lives in the past and discusses nothing that has occurred since the First World War.") This appeased the bankers and the film went into production at the end of 1946 at the Goldwyn Studios ("an extremely pleasant studio," opined Groucho, "unless one is unfortunate enough to bump into Goldwyn").

Groucho's attitude toward his co-star grew from disdain through skepticism to genuine regard. As preparation he had viewed one of Miranda's Fox vehicles and scented disaster: "In addition to looking like a dressed up bulldog, she sings each song the same as the preceding one," he told Miriam. More worryingly, he "didn't understand a goddamned word she uttered. Somebody will have to provide interpreters in each theater to keep this going." But after a few weeks of shooting he declared her "charming to work with, unspoiled and unaffected." Nonetheless, according to Coslow's autobiography, Groucho "did insist on a clause stating that he wouldn't be called on to kiss Carmen Miranda at any time. He never explained why. I think the fiery Carmen would have smacked him in the kisser had she known about the clause." (More likely than any slight aimed at Miranda, the clause was probably Groucho establishing the parameters of what his character could and could not be permitted to do to retain comic credibility in the new environment of romantic musical comedy. A seriously staged, physically romantic moment would be a change too far, even for the "new" Groucho.)

*Copacabana* (1947): **Groucho and Carmen Miranda dream of glory.**

The film casts Groucho as Carmen's agent; after the Copa initially turns her down, he has her re-apply as French chanteuse Mademoiselle Fifi, in blonde wig and veil, leading to inevitable complications when the club manager signs both Carmen and Fifi. It was a simple, decent premise for comic confusion. ("That's why I think we'll have a hit," Groucho explained. "People who wait for the start will be just as confused as those who come in in the middle.") In its emphasis on huckstering and farce, it's also rather reminiscent of *Room Service*, as was Groucho's character in the movie: Gordon Miller reborn as (the much more appropriately named) Lionel Q. Devereaux. No surprise, then, that one of the screenwriters was Allen Boretz, half of the writing team responsible for *Room Service* on Broadway. A funny scene in which Groucho has stolen a fish from a performing seal and frantically tries to hide it from the animal's trainer is a fair bet for Boretz's work. Devereaux's use of a list of racehorses for the names of the fictitious acts he is purporting to represent ("How about Silky Maiden?") also has the feel of one of Miller's desperate inspirations. The film's final act, in which Carmen calls time on the Fifi persona and Devereux ends up suspected of the murder of a woman who never existed, carries strong echoes of the earlier work, in which characters attempt to hide the evidence of an entirely phony suicide.

Describing his role as "a poor man's Ronald Colman," Groucho opted to play Devereaux with a realistic (but still unreal) mustache that gave him a dapper, almost continental look. (In his own estimation, he resembled "a cross between my father, Mephistopheles and an opium peddler on the Mexican border.") But he dismissed as "nonsense" the suggestion of reporters that this new look represented a saving of time and effort over the old make-up: "Before I'd come in and paint a little grease on my face. Now they put me in a chair and work thirty minutes on me. I feel as though they should hang me on the wall afterward."

More important to him than the change in appearance was what he perceived as the role's greater dramatic potential. "I'm more of a human being. There's even a little sympathy to it," he explained. The Marx Brothers version of "Groucho," by contrast, had long exhausted its possibilities: "I figure if I make a success of this, it will open the way to other kinds of roles. The other stuff is pretty standard and confining."

In correspondence he feigned breezy disinterest. "They have a fairly good story and I am sure it will be one of the worst pictures of the new season," he announced drily, pitching himself as "a man who ventured into this just to get a little money." But in truth, it was no trivial business. This was Groucho's first big break without his brothers and he was determined to succeed in it. "Everyone told me Groucho would be a big temperamental headache with his continual demands," Coslow wrote in his autobiography. "Actually, he was very little trouble." The only real issue was with the writers. "We have about half the script; parts of it are good and the rest is being altered to satisfy my demands," Groucho told Miriam. "I am busy bouncing writers almost daily."

In addition to Boretz there was Walter DeLeon, hotfoot from Abbott and Costello and fated to die shortly after the film was released, and László Vadnay, who also conceived the basic plot and impressed Coslow as "inventive and fast." Neither man impressed Groucho. DeLeon "talks like all the writers you read about whenever you read a funny piece about Hollywood conferences," while Vadnay, "a Hungarian named Latzo or something," "fancies himself a comedy writer, and whenever I encounter him he says, 'Here is a funny line.'" At Groucho's instigation they were joined by Howard Harris, one of his radio writers, and Charles Lederer (who "insists [Miranda] is a man dressed up in women's clothes").

Groucho also contributed material personally (as he would again, I strongly suspect on no hard evidence, for *Double Dynamite.*) "Groucho invariably took his lines and injected jokes galore," remembered Coslow. "They were all very funny, but sometimes sacrificed plot and continuity to get a laugh. Vadnay would get furious, but it was impossible to control Groucho." (I would certainly nominate in this category his response to the question of what use he could have for two wives: "It so happens I like to play three-handed pinochle.") "The script at the moment is brutal, and I have fired three of the writers and replaced them with others," he told Miriam. "I am not going to worry too much about the rest of the picture but it is terribly important that I emerge from it with honor and a few kudos from the public."

Though Groucho confessed himself "agreeably surprised" by each day's rushes, there's no question that venturing alone into screen comedy took a little adjustment. He told one paper that Harpo and Chico phoned him every evening "to see if the picture's lousy"; another made the extraordinary claim that the pair were present on set in full costume for the first day of shooting "to bolster his morale." (Absurd as it seems, this hints tantalizingly at the truth of a claim made elsewhere: that there was to have been a gag where Groucho says "I wish Harpo and Chico were here," whereupon they run across the set and out again. If the papers are to be believed, it may have even got as far as being staged—a matter to be settled by the call-sheets, if they survive.) Room was also found for Groucho's wife Kay as a cigar girl. ("I was just browsing!" says Devereaux, dropping the handful of cigars he was about to pocket, on learning they cost a dollar apiece.) According to Groucho, Kay took the role "so that she can get enough money to get her mother a new set of teeth."

As work began in earnest, newspapers whetted red-blooded appetites with the announcement that after an extensive search, twelve of the country's most gorgeous girls had been selected from over seven hundred hopefuls to bedeck the sets, each receiving screen contracts and personal appearance tours in America and Europe to promote the film. "We've got thirty pages of the script and twenty-five beautiful chorus girls. I'm memorizing my lines at home. It's too distracting on the set," added Groucho.

Fifth-billed Gloria Jean, meanwhile, inspired more paternal feelings. The former child star had been off the screen for two years when she was signed to the film (and to a five year personal contract by Coslow). The butt of constant insinuations for her relative lack of worldliness (at age twenty-one), Groucho personally complained about the lewd treatment she was receiving: "Do you realize what you're doing to this girl? Let her live her life!" he yelled to the assembled company. (Partly for that reason she later remembered Groucho with great affection, but recalled Miranda as jealously guarding her close-ups and screen-time, and as a generally bizarre presence who would consume only hard-boiled eggs and carrots.)

"I must say that in comparison with [*A Night in Casablanca*] this has been easy," Groucho told Miriam mid-production. "There has been no physical work to speak of, however, later in the picture I will do a little dancing and rehearsing but that will be much better than swinging head down from a ladder and other comical stunts that writers dream up so glibly in an office." This optimism lasted all the way to completion, when a delighted United Artists footed the bill for a lavish press party at the real Copacabana in May of 1947.

The previews seemed to confirm their expectations. Groucho declared the first preview "astonishingly good," and the second even better: "They seemed very well satisfied with it, that is the producers, and the audience loved it. *Copacabana* is no great noteworthy artistic achievement, but it will make a lot of money and is a vindication of my determination to veer slightly away from the old character," he told Miriam.

Extensive promotional hoopla then began, with newspapers in several states hosting publicity competitions with prizes of free visits to the real Copacabana (probably on a Wednesday afternoon, travelling costs not provided), and such helpful suggestions for publicity as these, from *Motion Picture Daily*:

> Set up a "Copa Derby" along the lines of the popular "soap box derbies." The idea is to have four or five attractive local girls participate in a short race on the town green, in a public park or on the walk in front of your theater. Each of the girls, riding a wooden hobby-horse on wheels, should represent a sorority, school club or local firm....
>
> Carmen Miranda is well known for her weird hats and unique hairdos. Tie in with leading milliners and offer prizes for the most original hat worn to your theater on the opening day of the picture....
>
> In cooperation with a newspaper, sponsor a "Marx–Miranda Imitation Contest." This type of contest will draw entries from both sexes and interest young and old alike....

Meanwhile, the paper reported back with no trace of ambiguity as to the film's prospects:

> Gags and girls, the way they are served up here, are a can't miss combination.... Constantly it is one laugh after another. The range is from the belly rumble to the hearty guffaw. A pair of showmen who know what the audience wants and gave it to them, director Alfred E. Green and producer Sam Coslow delivered up a potentially sock package of entertainment in *Copacabana* that was responded to all down the line, and spontaneously, by a sneak preview neighbourhood audience.... Miss Miranda and Marx are a knock-out comedy team.... Never does it have a dull moment.

Other reviews adopt this same tone, as if slightly dazed by the film's magnificence. Still more gratifyingly for Groucho was the regularity with which he was singled out for especial praise. Try the *Milwaukee Journal* for starters:

> As diverting film fare it relies on the standbys of comedy, music and girls—those well stacked Copa girls. But best of all, it's got that leering wag, Groucho Marx.... Groucho is as funny as only he himself can be. With Groucho it isn't what he says but that look in his eyes when he says it. For him alone the picture is a treat.

The review then goes on to declare a mildly amusing scene, in which Groucho details to Carmen the impossibly complex schedule she must keep to pull off the illusion of being two different performers on the same bill, as "one of the funniest we've ever seen." *Motion Picture Daily* felt the film's pretty straightforward plot to be "too funny to fully describe."

Now get a load of the *Deseret News*, leading with the declaration that "a new comedy combination is born—Groucho Marx and Carmen Miranda":

> And it would be nice to have just one penny for every laugh their hilarious antics will evoke throughout the world in this first picture and in subsequent ones which undoubtedly they will make—by public demand. For if ever two comedians seemed created for each other, Groucho and Carmen do in this entertaining picture. Frankly speaking, any teaming of two highly artistic fun-makers is somewhat of a gamble, for although they may be highly spontaneous singly, they may not hit it off together at all. However, producer Coslow and director Alfred E. Green knew from the very first shot that Groucho, away from his famous brothers for the first time in his theatrical life, and the volatile Brazilian comedienne, were as much a team as ham and eggs or Dun and Bradstreet.

The reviewer may seem idiosyncratic in his desire to lay claim to one of the world's smaller collections of pennies, but his enthusiastic prediction of further joint ventures is endorsed all over.

"Come back again, folks!" requests columnist Harold V. Cohen:

Don't look now, but the Four Marx Brothers have taken still another cut. Originally reduced from four to three a decade or so ago, they are presently down to one. That would be Groucho, and since the beetle-browed stalker with the minstrel-cork mustache has always been the funniest of the lot anyway, there will certainly be no moaning at this bar.

"This is the first time the fast-talking, be-mustached, cigar-smoking Groucho has appeared on the screen without his famous brothers," opined the *Kentucky New Era*, "but with the effervescent Brazillian comedienne playing alongside him not even Harpo and Chico can be missed."

For yet more extravagant praise, try the *Evening Independent* (italics mine):

Groucho, for the first time in his screen career, is without Harpo and Chico, and *it is an improvement.* I have always been of the opinion that Groucho was *the funny one* so I enjoyed this picture in which he and Carmen were together.

Not all the reviews are this superlative, of course, but what is clear is that there was no expectation whatever how meager public interest would prove to be. Plainly baffled (or perhaps just still dazed), *Motion Picture Daily* reported that in its first week in New York the film "got off to rather a sluggish start" with a $10,000 take; realization set in as it declared week two "mild" at $9,000; and all hope was abandoned when it predicted that it "probably will wind up its third and final week ... with a poor $7,000 gross."

This was a precipitous fall from expectation, and had an inevitable dampening effect on the film's reception nationwide and internationally. By the time it was ready to cross oceans, the wine had soured. The sturdy British *Spectator* noted not only the poor quality of the jokes but also the "ghastly pause for laughter" that followed. "A tired little script struggles for its life," opined the *Sydney Morning Herald*:

Groucho submits his brilliant comedy talent to the dreary Hollywood conformity of the script. He steals fish from seals, peanuts from monkeys, waggles his eyes at all incidental pulchritude, much bespangled, and invents an unhappy procedure whereby an audience must endure two Carmen Mirandas instead of one.

Coslow insisted the film did finally show a profit, but only when it was sold to television in 1953 and became "perhaps the most-played movie on the late shows." Noting it was showing on TV that night, a journalist asked Groucho if he remembered the picture. "Yes," he replied, "I got a lot of fan mail about it. All threatening."

Groucho also told Miriam that the re-teaming of he and Miranda that so many early reviews clamored for had indeed been proposed. "I have been offered an opportunity to do another picture with Carmen," he told Miriam, "but I don't think I will take it. To begin with, she is no particular draw any more, the bloom has worn off, she is no novelty as she was seven years ago, her singing is so stylised, and in a definite groove, and as a straight woman for me, it is frequently difficult to understand her, and this is an additional handicap for a comedian.... It is too bad; I like Carmen, she is a nice woman and very easy to work with, but I have to look out for myself." And that was that. When Charlotte Chandler asked the octogenarian Groucho to recall Miranda, he remarked only that she was very small and "wore special shoes."

Viewed today the film seems far from unpleasant, yet it's not easy to fathom *quite* what so many people seemed to see in it, and for so long. Though a fairly lavish endeavor by independent standards, for a supposedly deluxe musical extravaganza it has a noticeably pinched and harassed atmosphere (of a sort common to many United Artists releases), as if the film itself were constantly looking over its shoulder to check the money hasn't run out. The mismatched supporting cast has the feel of a package deal, with the emphasis on glib novelty, typified by the casting of columnists Earl Wilson and Louis Sobol, and *Variety* editor Abel Green, as themselves. ("Each one tried to build up his part with extra lines," recalled Coslow.) Crooner Andy Russell landed a prominent role on account of his radio celebrity, but alas, as *Film Bulletin* put it, this "darling of the radio" proved "far from photogenic." ("I don't think he will go much further than the dentist," was Groucho's prediction.) As for those lovelies picked in competition and all set for screen contracts, the only one who seems to have made an impression on anybody was Mari Blanchard. Merle McHugh, the papers' favorite before release, was signed to a ten year contract by Beacon, but after one more uncredited bit the same year she disappeared from the scene entirely.

Aside from Steve Cochran—entirely out of place and casting a sullen, brutish pall over what should be a fizzy, Melvyn Douglas kind of male lead—the film's biggest problem lies in its structure. Groucho noted that the only problem at the first preview was that "Carmen sang too often and too long, and this we are remedying for the second preview...." But even in the finished film, there are simply too many songs, too regularly spaced, so that the film feels as if it is constantly stopping and starting to accommodate them. And, notwithstanding Coslow's track record in that department, they are not all that good. (Perhaps his producer's duties distracted him.) The opening chorus number—one of those uncomfortable affairs in which struggling ingénues, desperately hoping their three seconds in the spotlight will lead to stardom, sing about being struggling ingénues desperately hoping their three seconds in the spotlight will lead to stardom—is notable only for the surprising name check it gives Leo McCarey, in a couplet about how the girls are hoping to catch the eye of a Hollywood bigwig. (Goldwyn and David O. Selznick make sense, but was McCarey really a likely third choice? An interesting snapshot of a moment in time, if so.)

Nonetheless, it is a song that is for almost all present-day audiences the film's one certain highlight. In a moment of whimsical ingenuity (of a sort that feels very much of a piece with that mysterious Harpo and Chico cameo) Devereaux presents a performance by another of his clients. It turns out to be Groucho—that is to say "Groucho"—and while Devereaux watches proudly from the side of the stage, the old Marx Brother, complete with tailcoat and greasepaint mustache, delivers a more than palatable performance of "Go West, Young Man" (a nice Kalmar and Ruby number written for their abandoned draft of *Go West* and which he had occasionally performed on his army tours). "So you see," he told Miriam, "I am now playing dual roles just like Bette Davis and other expensive thespians." Coslow confirms that the song, "a bit of tomfoolery" that cost him $2,000 in screen rights, was included at Groucho's insistence. (Some contemporary reports state that Ruby has specifically written a song for the film: a duet for Marx and Miranda. It's unclear whether this is a garbled account of this, or a reference to a second number that didn't make the cut.)

Given his desire to set himself apart from his standard characterization, one might more easily imagine it being imposed upon him. But of course this is just the latest skirmish in his continued war against destiny, audience expectation and greasepaint mustaches. As he prepared to make his major film debut without his customary trappings, the scene may have suggested itself to him as insurance against the new image not taking with the public: a "reminder" of his earlier persona, that reinforced the difference, and underlined his versatility.

It is possible that, as with the Hackenbush number on the Victory Caravan tour, he is acknowledging the fact that the song has its roots in the Brothers' act. More generally though it seems to be telling us that Groucho is changing his act by choice, not necessity. You want the old Groucho, I can give you the old Groucho … but do you, now? For viewers today, the answer to that one is likely an ironic, emphatic and unanimous "yes." But the reviewers, for all their hyperbole, were right to say that the "new" Groucho does make a good account of himself here too. "I've got an explanation for this but I don't believe it myself," he says to Car-

Fancy meeting you here! The old Groucho, complete with greasepaint, makes a surprise appearance in *Copacabana* (1947).

men after she finds him in the chorus girls' dressing room. Accused of murder, he breaks down and slumps to the floor wringing his hands: "I didn't do it, I tell you, and I'm glad! I'm glad I didn't do it! And if I had it all to do over again, I wouldn't do it all over again!" Then, interrupted mid-flow, he protests: "In a minute I might have been another Peter Lorre." And there's the moment when he attempts to scare off another agent with a gangsterish threat: "You keep out of this or I'll have the boys take care of you!" "What boys?" the rival shoots back defiantly, whereupon Groucho immediately loses all bravado and meekly replies, "Oh, just boys."

In a 1949 letter to Earl Wilson, Groucho was able to assess the episode philosophically:

> The fact of the matter is, I did very well on *Copacabana*. It gave me an opportunity to rise every morning at six o'clock, glue on a fake mustache, eat an extraordinarily bad lunch in the studio restaurant and get home in time to miss dinner. Plus all this, it gave me a chance to look at my producer fourteen hours a day.

As for that producer, *Copacabana* had been Sam Coslow's big break into major features. While it was still in production, he signed a deal with UA to make a further five musicals over the next three years, at 1.5 million dollars apiece. The first was to be titled *Champagne for Everybody*, a Mary Pickford property. But everything changed when *Copacabana* was released. He never produced a movie again.

# 3

# Howard Hughes owes me
# a trip around the world

*Copacabana* had come at the end of a long professional drought for Groucho, but his second solo movie was made amidst a cloudburst of activity. The big news, of course, was that the offer to host a radio quiz show he had accepted in desperation and, as he put it in a letter to the *New York Times*, "with all the enthusiasm of a man about to handle a dead snake," had turned out to be *You Bet Your Life*, and proved one of the most momentous turning points in his entire professional life. But while that realization was slowly announcing itself, he also kept moving on other fronts.

In the theater, *Time for Elizabeth*, the play he had co-written with Norman Krasna, was finally ready to stage. As a stage performer, however, offers that he would surely have welcomed from movie companies were still being met with uncertainty and deliberation, then rejection. Arthur Schwartz approached him in 1947 to star in his Broadway musical *Inside U.S.A.*, loosely based on John Gunther's non-fiction study, one of the big hit books of the year.[1] It opened in April of 1948, running till February the following year, but without Groucho, who professed himself flattered but determined to avoid stage musicals in general and revues in particular. Jack Haley took the role intended for him.

Movie musicals were a different matter, however. Though *Variety*'s suggestion in 1945 that he might be about to team up with the Andrews Sisters in a film called *Memphis Bound* sadly came to nothing, he was very keen to appear alongside Maurice Chevalier in a project announced to the press in April of 1947.[2] By July, however, it was all off, as Groucho explained to Miriam:

> The deal was about set when he abruptly took a run out powder and screwed back to France. He said he has a picture coming out with direction by René Clair, and before he signs a contract he would like to see how this picture is received in America. I think he is stalling to see what other offers he has before he is reduced to appearing with me. Well, I am not going to worry about it.

The Clair picture, *Le Silence est d'or* (a.k.a. *Man About Town*, 1947) did well in France, but for America it was drastically shortened and released with an experimental English sound-track comprised of a running commentary (prepared by former Marx Brothers writer Robert Pirosh), and Chevalier's voice translating the dialog in the spaces between lines, the effect supposedly intended to replicate the experience of having the film explained as it unfolded by a friend sitting next to you. Unsurprisingly, such eccentricity did not find favor, and Chevalier ducked back out of movies for another nine years.

Most of the movie action at this time was coming from producer Lester Cowan, whose sole completed association with Groucho would be the hugely compromised *Love Happy* in

1949. But Cowan had been courting Groucho since long before then. As early as 1943 he picked up the movie rights to *Heart of the City*, a hit British show about the Windmill Theater (famous for its stationary nude tableaux—the motionlessness being a successful means of circumventing censorship rules regarding stage nudity—and for the fact that it managed to offer an uninterrupted program through the entirety of the London Blitz, a distinction that served it ever after in its famous slogan, "We Never Closed"). Given its parochial nature, the show had flopped on Broadway, so Cowan grabbed it for a song and offered it to Columbia as a vehicle for Groucho and Gracie Fields. A preening Groucho told Sheekman he was prepared to contribute his "scintillating personality" to the venture, provided "the part can be sufficiently built up."

In reality Harry Cohn had been completely unimpressed with the suggestion, and unbeknownst to Groucho turned it down as soon as Cowan volunteered it. Like many another who had fallen into the producer's orbit, he was keen to lose Cowan, too. He bought him off the project (which eventually emerged with Rita Hayworth as *Tonight and Every Night* in 1945) and immediately wired his lawyers: "Advise me minute deal is concluded so we can toss that mob out of his offices and use them."[3]

Though very fond of making deals and announcing plans, Cowan was skittish, ill disciplined and too keen on spending money irrationally when time came to actually see projects through. Groucho, it seems, got his measure fairly early on, but being in demand is mighty intoxicating all the same. Cowan's plans for him—including a Honolulu musical, a series of comedy detective movies and a team-up with the great British comedian Sid Field—were certainly flattering, though many, if not all, were never more substantial than column-bait. ("Don't pay any attention to any items you read in the theatrical sheets, for they are all the imaginings of my press agent," Groucho told Miriam in September of 1947. "I am so confused by the pieces I read about myself that I have decided to fire him, for it is getting so that I don't know what my next move is.") Nonetheless, real plans were definitely being thrashed out with Cowan at this time, indeed of one, unspecified, Groucho told Miriam that "I should know something definite in a week or so."[4]

The one Cowan project that all five Marx brothers took seriously was their own biopic, to be derived from Kyle Crichton's fanciful biography. (It is to be presumed that this romanticized account of their early years and the adjacent film project were at all times perceived as tandem ventures, but only the former was realized.) According to plans the movie would feature actors playing the younger Marxes, with the real team—possibly all five of them—playing themselves in linking sections, then finishing off the film with a brand new comedy routine. (Forget your Billy Wilders: *this* is the great, lamented might-have-been.) Instead, all Cowan did for Groucho was cajole him into making a cameo appearance in *Love Happy*—supposedly as the only means of keeping the project going—and thus by stealth and manipulation turned a Harpo vehicle into another Brothers venture. Groucho did his scenes disinterestedly—partly, no doubt, from loyalty. (He may have written some of his dialog himself.) But he must have also found it gratifying to be the film's guarantor of completion, and the fee was generous. (According to *Love, Groucho*, Cowan paid for a new bar to be installed in Groucho's house, but it took a protracted lawsuit to get the agreed payment. Groucho didn't much like the bar, either.) To view the matter generously, Cowan probably did want to make the other Groucho projects he announced, but he surely knew the money was not there and probably did not make that clear to his would-be star. To the more cynically-minded, it is reasonable to view the entire charade as one big lure to draw him into *Love Happy*. Same result, either way.

In 1948, however, Groucho finally received a new, reliable offer to make a movie without his brothers, and it was an interesting coincidence that, like *Copacabana*, it came just when he capitulated to the demand for still another Marx Brothers reunion. Given the disharmony and disorganization of *Love Happy*, he was in more of a mood than ever to say yes, whatever it was. Though neither he nor audiences would get a chance to evaluate it for a further three years, this new venture was, in the words of top-billed Jane Russell, "a thing called *Double Dynamite*."[5] The film would take Groucho back to RKO, a store of doubtless bittersweet memories following the Marxes' collapsed plans to relocate there after the death of Thalberg, with an ambitious raft of projects that amounted to one compromised venture (*Room Service*) and a swift return to Mayer. But the RKO Groucho arrived at this time was undergoing massive change, having been recently purchased by maverick eccentric Howard Hughes. In the event, Groucho's association with Hughes's RKO would extend to a second collaboration, but neither escaped his customary cynicism in recollection. "Both pictures were lousy, and I never saw Hughes," he stated in 1975, claiming "one of the inducements he offered was to fly me around the world on one of his planes."[6] Sadly, the offer was not honored and, at age 85, Groucho had reached a decision on the matter: "Howard Hughes owes me a trip around the world."

## Double Dynamite (1948)

If *Double Dynamite*[7] is famous for one thing above any other, it is the inordinate amount of time that elapsed between its completion and its release, and the famously desperate measures Groucho resorted to in an effort to hurry it along. The film was completed by Christmas of 1948, yet there was still no sign of it when Groucho wrote to Hughes on January 23, 1951:

> I am not a young man any more, Mr. Hughes, and before I shuffle off this mortal coil if you could see your way clear to pry open your strong box and send this minor masterpiece whizzing through the film exchanges of America, you would not only have earned my undying gratitude but that of the United Nations, the popcorn dealers of America and three RKO stockholders who at this moment are trying to escape from the Mellon bank of Pittsburgh.

Various motives have been suggested to explain why Hughes delayed the film so long: a dislike of Sinatra, possibly because of his relationship with Ava Gardner; simply because he thought it was bad (though attempting to second-guess the man's aesthetic judgments is always risky); or perhaps it was just the indecipherable caprice that characterized his working methods. To this stew of conjecture it should be added that this was not a project he had initiated himself, perhaps accounting in part for why it was a lesser priority for him. The presence of Russell, of course, seems a sure sign of his involvement from the first; note, however, that in her autobiography she clearly recalls the assignment as a loan-out. There is confusion here: she says she was loaned to RKO before Hughes bought it, but he took control of the studio in May of 1948, and the film landed there in October. However, it had begun (as *The Pasadena Story*) back in February, and at Columbia. Presumably, therefore, what Jane was slightly misremembering was that she was already in place in this first incarnation of the film, and Hughes scooped both her and it back up when he took charge of RKO.

In its pristine form the story was a simple one: a timid bank clerk unexpectedly wins big on the horses, and cannot prove his story when a substantial sum goes missing from his place of employment. Michael Curtiz had purchased it in 1947, and announced it as a vehicle for James Stewart. Father and son team Irving Cummings (director) and Irving Cummings, Jr., (producer) then bought it from him, and set it up at Columbia. When it reached RKO, the timid bank clerk was Frank Sinatra and the title was changed (first) to *It's Only Money*, before finally becoming *Double Dynamite* on release.

Since *It's Only Money* is one of the film's Jule Styne–Sammy Cahn song numbers, it would also seem the film only became a musical after the journey to RKO and the acquisition of Sinatra. The songs feel very much grafted on, there are in any case only two (though the title number is reprised), and real and impressive effort seems to have been put into coming up with ways to avoid staging them properly. ("It's Only Money" features Groucho and Frank walking along a back-projected street, while for the entirety of "Kisses and Tears" Jane and Frank are lying in their respective beds.)

Even so, Hughes's meddling was likely kept to a minimum overall, given that Cummings and Cummings remained happily *in situ*, and brought it in with uncommon efficiency, too. Groucho told Charlotte Chandler that the mercurial mogul never showed his face on the set, or expressed any obvious interest in the production: "He was only interested in girls. He thought of the title *Double Dynamite*, which was supposed to refer to Jane Russell's knockers. It's a good thing the guy was a millionaire. Otherwise, how would he have made a living?"

Groucho, Jane and Frank reported to the RKO lot on November 19 to record the songs prior to shooting beginning on the 22nd, and the whole thing wrapped on December 18, three days ahead of schedule (a record, the press reports claimed, though without disclosing their arithmetic). As a somewhat idiosyncratic mark of his gratitude, Cummings presented the cast with gold pencils on the last day of shooting. Groucho promptly gave his to Miriam. "My guess is that it won't bring much in hock," he warned her.

Groucho plays Emile J. Keck (note the by now customary middle initial), an eccentric, poetry-spouting waiter at Frankie and Janie's local restaurant, whose wild schemes to save our two heroes only make matters worse. A smaller role than Devereaux in *Copacabana* (he's very much a supporting character, despite ending up second-billed, ahead of Sinatra), the part is nonetheless well tailored to Groucho's talents, and it's fair to say he walks off with every scene he appears in. It may, in fact, be his most enjoyable screen work as a solo performer.

Keck ("That's English for Smith!") gives audiences their last chance to see an approximation of the pure movie "Groucho." Though he is more restrained than in the Brothers' films, we do nonetheless get the full checklist of trademarks: the quipping, the lechery, the walk (simultaneously furtive and predatory), the cigar (he's never without it), the eyebrow waggle, the wire-rimmed glasses, and the black hair (side-parted and fluffy on top).

Only the greasepaint mustache was missing, though incredibly it was a decision he was still agonizing over even at this stage. RKO make-up man Mel Berns, his niece Marie Behar recalls, had to convince him that he should abandon it for good and stick to the real alternative. And he was still preoccupied with the subject when interviewed about the film by Bob Thomas: "I couldn't play with real actors when I had it on. It gave an unreal quality to any scene I would be in." As for the new, genuine model: "It might open new possibilities for me. Who knows—next season I might play Othello."

His dialog, too, has something of an authentic flourish. When Sinatra reflects on the irony of being in possession of a large sum he cannot spend without fear of arrest, Groucho sums up: "You are in a barrel of rice with your mouth sewn up—old Chinese proverb." Later, posing as a millionaire so as to deposit the money at the very bank from which he suspects it to have been stolen, he assumes the persona of the country's largest distributor of pickled pig's feet (slogan: "Wherever people eat, you'll find Keck's feet"). "Have a chair," offers the bank manager. "Is it clean?" Groucho snaps back. Worried by the profligate spending he declares essential to sustaining the illusion, Sinatra asks him how much his cigars cost. "Well, let's just say they're not what this country needs a good one of," he replies. And I'm

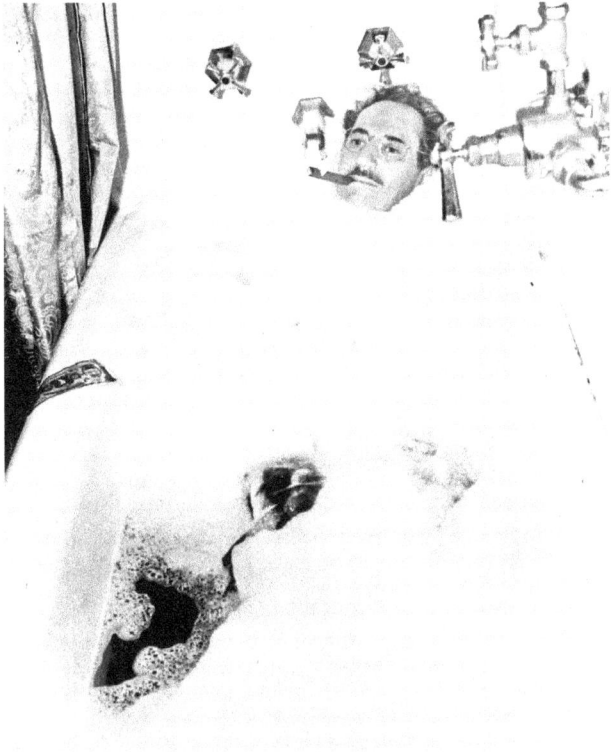

Groucho's dislike of messy physical comedy did not prevent him taking a fully-clothed bath in *Double Dynamite* (1948)— but his facial expression tells its own story.

genuinely surprised that "A woman can smell mink through six inches of lead" is not a more widely circulated Groucho-ism: doubtless it would be if it came from a more widely circulated movie.

There's also some funny physical business with Frank and Groucho trying to hide the loot in the water pipes, which (via a causal sequence it would be senseless to clarify) ends with Groucho hiding fully clothed under the foam of a bubble bath. "RKO slyly promoted the fact that there was a bubble bath sequence in the picture," he recalled in *The Groucho Phile*. "Thousands stormed the theaters around the country, assuming Jane Russell was taking the bath."

Groucho's duet with Sinatra is a definite highlight, too. "It's only money/It fluctuates" is not the kind of couplet you hear every day, and there's a whiff of Kalmar and Ruby to this:

> I love the artwork,
> The treasury sure does smart work.
> The nicest people we know
> Are the people who get their faces on dough.

It's a fun, charming sequence, not least for being manifestly shot on the cheap, against a back-projected street scene that passes by while Groucho and Sinatra pad gormlessly to nowhere on a treadmill. The dull, exhausting work took two days to complete, at the end of which Groucho estimated he had walked forty miles, though he admitted it wasn't quite the ordeal he was expecting it to be. ("Very few things are," he conceded to Miriam.) All the stranger, then, that "what little staging could be done" was nonetheless done by Stanley Donen, perhaps at the instigation of Sinatra. ("A nice guy and I think some day he will be a very good director," Groucho predicted.)

In fact, it was all rather laid back compared to the average Marx Brothers movie, he told Bob Thomas: "It's burglary. I almost feel ashamed to take the money. You're handed a script and all you have to do is read the lines." So how did that differ from a Marx Brothers movie? "They're murder. You go through a lot of strenuous physical labor and spend all your time worrying about new routines and writing half the dialog.... There will be no more Marx Brothers pictures."

Much of the original publicity centered around the idea that it would be showcasing a new, more demure Jane Russell than audiences had hitherto enjoyed, with the emphasis on her musical and comedic gifts rather than her natural ones. "Ever since the studio came out with a ruling that Jane wasn't going to be allowed to wear any low cut dresses in this one, I've been expecting to hear Father had resigned from the venture," Groucho's son Arthur told *Radio Mirror* magazine. "Possibly he's waiting around in hopes that Frank Sinatra will break a leg or something so that he can take over the romantic lead. If I were in Sinatra's shoes, I'd be on the alert for booby traps."

Jane's move into comedy had come via her co-starring stint with Bob Hope in *The Paleface*, and she credited Hope and Groucho with helping her regain interest in her own career. "Those two helped give me a perspective about my work," she told *Screenland* magazine. "After making *The Paleface* and *It's Only Money* I began to see that the work could be fun."

It is presumably not coincidental, then, that both films share Melville Shavelson as principal screenwriter, with assistance from several other hands, including—one again suspects—Groucho himself (not least when Keck refers to a Sam Schlemmer, that being the original surname of his character in *The Cocoanuts*, and to "my uncle Julius," that being, of course, the relative from whom he acquired his own real name. According to Robert Dwan, Groucho would often signal a prepared joke in *You Bet Your Life* around this time by claiming to recount an experience that had occurred to his Uncle Julius).

Harry Crane joined the writing team at Sinatra's invitation, and much to Groucho's annoyance. "Apparently he is one of the 700 screenwriters out of work and since Frankie Boy always takes care of his friends he cajoled Irving Cummings, the producer, to hire this lad," Groucho complained to Miriam shortly after shooting began. "This will be the first unpleasantness of my new chore when I tell Cummings what I think of Crane's interpolations." (He stuck around long enough to get a credit, however.)

But the most important question from our point of view is which of the various contributors is chiefly responsible for Groucho's scenes and character. The pre–RKO screenplay, credited solely to Shavelson and titled *The Pasadena Story*, is recognizably the film we now have. Keck is present and correct, and his dialog is essentially the same as in the movie.

What, then, are we to make of the peculiar screen credit: "based on a character created by Manny Manheim"? To the question "which one?" it gives no answer, but all the main characters are present in the first Shavelson draft, which means that Manheim's influence was most likely felt at the development stage.[8]

Manheim *did* write for Sinatra on radio, but since Groucho's is the only character who really *has* a character (Sinatra and Russell just play ordinary Joes and Janes) Keck has to be the likeliest guess. And Manheim was showing up a lot in Groucho's orbit around this time. He contributed some material to *Love Happy,* and co-wrote the famous 1947 radio sketch with Groucho and Bob Hope that descended into a riot of ad libs and gave John Guedel the inspiration that would eventually lead to *You Bet Your Life.* So *if* the character of Keck was Manheim's work, that would imply it was added to the concept, by a known Groucho writer, specifically as a means of working Groucho into the picture. But here's where it gets even more confusing.

Early reports on *The Pasadena Story* give original story credit to Arnold Albert and Leo Rosten (who were apparently then set to collaborate again on *The San Francisco Story,* though how far that went, and in what form, and to what extent it was associated with the first project, I do not know). The credits, however, attribute its origins solely to Rosten: Albert seems to have fallen away somewhere between the announcements and the contracts. More commonly a producer than a writer, Albert is a tantalizing loose end to leave dangling—especially since he had collaborated with Manheim *and* Sinatra on 1943's *Road to Victory*—but leave him we must, as we look further into the involvement of Leo Rosten.

Rosten (1908–1997) is one of those guys worth pressing the pause button for. Not that we should need such exercise: his name ought to trip from the tongue as easily as that of Benchley or Wodehouse or John Kennedy Toole when considering the great stylists of humorous prose. That he does not may be due simply to the confusing range and variety of his written accomplishments. Self-described on one of his book jackets as "author of *Hamlet* and other bestsellers," he was in truth a novelist, essayist, humorist, sociologist, economist and lexicographer (among quite a few other things), whose book *The Education of H\*y\*m\*a\*n K\*a\*p\*l\*a\*n* remains a milestone of American comic writing and whose observation of W.C. Fields—"Anyone who hates dogs and small children can't be all bad"—will be misattributed to its subject until the end of time.

As with best humorists, his work is often disarmingly silly, but always underpinned by intelligence and point of view, and often informed by his various specialisms. Being a linguist, he delights in syntactic eccentricity, and as a social scientist he is keenly aware of the deadening effect of cliché and rhetorical convention, which he spears with good-natured precision. (In the former, he recalls Kaufman; in the latter, Benchley, who once ended a pretentious exegesis with the qualifier: "Or do I make myself clear?") Further, he shares Groucho's comic incontinence, incapable of suppression even in contexts where it may be genuinely unwanted. There is a moment at the end of one chapter of his book *A Trumpet for Reason*—an entirely serious and impassioned examination of student rebellion—when he suddenly extracts from the heart of the comic nowhere: "Once, after long and sober research, I estimated that 23 percent of the human race are nuts. I was wrong. I am now convinced that 32 per cent are."

And nobody who loves the Marx Brothers, let alone the cultural worlds they section, should be without his two invaluable, endlessly delightful lexicons *The Joy of Yiddish* and *Hooray for Yiddish!,* stuffed to the gills as they are with information, erudition, illumination, and perhaps the best collection of Jewish jokes I've ever seen contained between four boards. Why do I now write "shnorrer" rather than "schnorrer"? Ask Rosten.

His 1971 collection *People I Have Loved, Known or Admired* is a compilation of essays whose subjects run the gamut from Leonardo, Montaigne and Churchill to such as Joseph Pellegrino, pioneer in the art of manufacturing square spaghetti (who later progressed to "quadrilateral spaghetti on wire"), and "the unknown genius" who placed an advertisement in the *Los Angeles Times* reading: LAST DAY TO SEND IN YOUR DOLLAR—BOX 153. ("Thousands of idiots sent in their dollars," Rosten informs us.) He also contributes a splendid pencil sketch of Groucho, who he describes as exuding "the ambience of a larcenous undertaker." He notes that he did not keep up a regular correspondence with Groucho because "his answers give me the feeling that I have fallen into a centrifuge," and cites in this connection a belated reply that read, "Excuse me for not answering your letter sooner, junior, but I've been so busy not answering letters that I couldn't get around to not answering yours in time." (On Groucho's 85th birthday he sent him a message that ended, "My affection for you goes back to the days I played hooky to see the immortal four at the State and Lake Theater in Chicago. Keep being an inspiration to all of us."[9])

On the matter of *Double Dynamite*, Rosten is surprisingly—and intriguingly—detailed:

> I returned to more conventional fiction and, as a freelance, wrote a story for (I hoped) a movie. I cast Groucho, in my dreams, as "Emil Keck," a flat footed waiter and shlemiel who all his life had yearned to be a swindler. Emil so passionately admired crooks, conmen, card sharps [and thus] became a walking *Who's Who* on the masters of the special arts of malfeasance. From a reverent memory he could respond ... "Green Gloves Cantrell? One of the finest scratch scribes who ever came out of the old South! Flim-flammed the yokels in St. Looey for fifty thousand bucks in 1948.... What a man! They don't make clip sticks like *that* anymore."
>
> Groucho did play the part of Emil, to my everlasting satisfaction.... [He] wedded hypocritical benevolence to subliminal derision with a nonchalance few con men could hope to match...; but Mr. Hughes decided either to sell RKO or buy Q.E.D., during which transaction, greatly complicated by Mr. Hughes' propensity for vanishing into thick air, the lovely tale of Emil Keck got lost in a publicity vacuum. It has rested there forever after.

The main point of interest here is that we have *Rosten* laying explicit claim to Keck, even by name, and coming close to suggesting he was the main figure—certainly the main point of interest—in his story. Now, it would surely be stretching probability to suggest that the property Michael Curtiz bought from him might not have had the two central figures and their plot dilemma already inserted too (unless we think it's possible Jimmy Stewart was being lined up to play Keck!) So, if the main threesome are indeed all Rosten's work, what character can Manny Manheim possibly have created for the film to claim itself based on?

My tentative and pure guess would be this: Rosten and Albert came up with the story idea, perhaps without the figure of Keck included, or developed fairly sketchily if he was there, and probably not so named. Then Rosten on his own went off and wrote a screen treatment, in which he either invented the third character or, recognizing its potential, built him up into a Groucho role and called him Emile Keck, largely justifying his solo story credit. This then formed the basis of the shooting script that Shavelson wrote and others added to. Shavelson's first draft reads as though Groucho is clearly in mind for the role from the first, suggesting, if not a massive coincidence, either that Rosten's treatment had explicitly specified the casting, or that Rosten was still attached to the project in a supervisory or consulting capacity. And so maybe at *this* point Manheim, with his proven track record as a Groucho writer, was brought in (possibly at Groucho's own urging) to authenticate the part still further. The subsequent credit "created by," then, may have been nothing more than an honestly-made error, taking his major contribution to the development of the role to be the seminal one, and Rosten either never noticed or didn't mind. No evidence for any of that, but I can construct no other course of events that even begins to make sense, and as Sherlock Holmes once said, once you have eliminated the impossible, whatever remains, however improbable, is the *Trial of Mary Dugan* with sound.

The changes subsequent to Shavelson's first draft, however, seem to have been effected with the aim of making the film less zany, and one can't help but wonder if Mr. Hughes was the architect there. The first scene, for instance, had originally called for the three main characters to be introduced in the form of wanted posters, first Frank, then Jane, then Groucho. Under Groucho's image we were to have seen the text, "WANTED FOR ROBBERY—EMIL J. KECK":

> The photograph comes to life and Emil leans out of the poster and looks down at the wording. A pleased smile crosses his face as he reads it; indeed, Emil seems quite flattered. He looks straight into camera, raises his hands over his head, and shakes them in a self-congratulatory gesture. As the picture freezes we dissolve to the credits.[10]

It's easy and amusing to imagine Groucho doing this—and strange that we have to.

Remembering the film in a cooler hour, neither Russell nor Groucho expressed much affection. Groucho, who in a private letter to Miriam spoke warmly of Sinatra as "an exceptionally nice chap," recalled in *The Groucho Phile* having to admonish him for persistent lateness on set. Sinatra's career was by this time in descent, yet Groucho recalled that he "maintained the temperament of a great star. You never know when you might need it again."

"I suspected during its making that it wouldn't reach the epic grandeur of *Gone With the Wind*" was his faux-diplomatic summation of *Double Dynamite* in *The Secret Word Is Groucho*. And Russell, for her part, remembered the film in her autobiography as "a big nothing": "All in all, it was sickening. Everyone was carefully polite to everyone else, and no one got to know anyone. Not many laughs on that set."

"**Not many laughs on that set.**" Groucho and Jane Russell in *Double Dynamite* (1948).

Indeed, judging from the press reports, it does seem to have been one of those films on which nothing much funny or remarkable happened at all: everyone simply hunkered down and got the job done. The closest we get to a humorous anecdote is the claim that in one scene in which Russell was supposed to slap Sinatra on the back, "Frankie boy's knees almost buckled" and "Groucho laughed so hard he almost swallowed his famous cigar." (Jane and Frank are sweet enough in the leads, but more than one reviewer noted her obvious physical superiority. *Modern Screen*: "She's bigger than he is, but outside of that they make a cute couple." Jane's own summing-up: "I looked as though I could throw him a few blocks.")

Then there was the one about Sinatra bringing a postcard on set that he just received from Gene Kelly in Paris, telling him: "Over here they think Sinatra is some kind of American food." The reports go on to add that "Frankie asked Groucho Marx, Jane Russell, and the crew for suggestions for a snappy comeback to toss Gene"—and then end right there, presumably because none of them could be bothered to. Still doomier was the account of the careening trailer, which uncoupled from its pilot car and smashed into Russell's car just moments after she left it in the RKO parking lot on her first day on set. She "missed possible death by a matter of seconds."

Superb poster art for *Double Dynamite* (1948) and *A Girl in Every Port* (1952). Cynics might call them preferable to the films themselves.

Simultaneously completing *Time for Elizabeth,* shooting *Love Happy* and recording his radio show, Groucho confessed exhaustion by the completion of the film. "I will never again permit myself to get involved in so many activities simultaneously," he told Miriam:

> It's just too much for me and my nature doesn't permit me to relax very much. The trouble with show business is that you are either very hot and many people bid for your services, or you are practically washed up and nobody wants you. I must concede that my position is the better one, but I am going to try to dole myself out more carefully.

## *A Girl in Every Port* (1952)

*Double Dynamite* finally got its release at the very end of 1951. *Film Bulletin* declared it "surprise of the month" and noted that "no reason has ever been given for the long delay in distributing the picture." Reviews were mixed: a few raves, some drubbings, the majority tending toward the lenient. *The Pittsburgh Post-Gazette* opined that "the picture belongs to Groucho.... There is one thing about a movie in which [he] plays a leading role—it just can't be all bad." *Modern Screen* liked it: "A delightful comedy which takes nothing seriously and brings back Groucho Marx at his best. Need I say more?" The *New York Times* was baffled: "Whatever that sizzling title is supposed to mean, this thin little comedy is strictly a wet fire-cracker." And *The Age* was positively withering:

> *Double Dynamite* ... is comedy because the credits are crazy-lettered and Groucho Marx is in it. Other resemblances are difficult to find. Frank Sinatra sings and looks sloppy and Jane Russell gets crying drunk, the humor of which is far too deep for me. Groucho Marx tries hard, but without his brothers and decent lines he does not get far.

Harpo and Chico may well have taken heart from the fact that many reviewers still insisted on noticing they weren't there, but for Groucho, far too much had happened in the gap between production and release to worry overmuch at the film's reception. On the domestic front, his marriage to Kay had ended in predictable divorce after just five years, leaving Groucho bemused and anxious, and concerned for the welfare of their daughter Melinda. And he'd made a further two movies in the interim, too: a cameo as himself in the Bing Crosby musical *Mr. Music* (1950), and a lead in a second film for Hughes, *A Girl in Every Port* (1952). Also occupying his thoughts at this time was the prospect of *The Groucho Letters,* his volume of correspondence, which proved a critical and popular hit when it was finally published in 1967. Generally forgotten now is the fact that publication was announced as early as 1951, as Groucho told reporters on the set of *A Girl in Every Port.* Selected letters were to be published in a magazine, with the full book to be released towards the end of the year. The idea, he explained, had come from several of the recipients (and their agents). "They seem to think some of them are pretty funny. I hope they're right."[11] In the event, the idea was shelved for another fifteen years.

Meanwhile, *A Girl in Every Port* proved an exhausting farce, casting him as one of a pair of deadbeat sailors (along with William Bendix) and detailing the various complications that ensue when they get landed with a lame race horse that proves to be one of a pair of identical twins. (Oddly, Groucho insisted on wearing his sailor's uniform to and from the set, presumably so as not to waste time being costumed. As he admitted, there was a downside to this: "I might be drafted while I'm on my way to work." His solution was to disguise the uniform in transit with a large camel hair overcoat.[12])

The return casting had nothing to do with his good work in *Double Dynamite*, about which Hughes's feelings were by all accounts cool. Rather, the thing that had made him so suddenly bankable again was *You Bet Your Life*, which had grown swiftly from a success to a triumph, and was now beating all rivals on television as well as radio.

In the event, *Double Dynamite* and *A Girl in Every Port* were released within a few weeks of each other, but it is obvious from the first frame of the latter that this is a *very* different Groucho from the one audiences had just seen with Sinatra and Russell—visibly older, much more relaxed and confident and no longer making much concession to his old screen persona. Emile Keck had retained the eyebrow waggle, loping walk and dyed hair of the quintessential Groucho. But ordinary seaman Benny Linn is Groucho the quizmaster in navy blues, with grey hair swept back from the temples and thinning on top, a modest mustache, ordinary glasses, and none of the tricks. He is putting less nervous energy into the role, because his confidence is all the greater: he knows that this is a film that wants him in it, not a film he wants to be in. (RKO were sensible enough to arrange a tie-up between the quiz show and the movie: as *Motion Picture Daily* noted, "mention of the film will be made on every show" and "3,000 Plymouth–DeSoto dealers … will display posters calling attention to the co-starring vehicle, with Groucho leering appropriately at his feminine lead.")

"How can you miss with Groucho Marx, Bill Bendix, Marie Wilson and Don Defore all in one show?" producer Irwin Allen wondered aloud for the benefit of journalists visiting the set, and further claimed the crew could hardly work for laughing (probably true for the rest of that day, anyway). But from the perspective of the present-day fan, *A Girl in Every Port* is difficult to assess. On the one hand it is the Groucho film that feels most like a star vehicle, is most generous with screen time and dialog, and in which he gives probably his most complete and organic comedy performance. On the other hand, judged purely as a situation comedy it will probably strike most viewers as significantly weaker than either *Copacabana* or *Double Dynamite*.

There are moments: Groucho plays his guitar; does his bogus Southern colonel act, recalling the Florida Medical Board routine from *A Day at the Races*; and the shipboard farce with the two horses takes us back, in our daydreams at least, to the Margaret Dumont medical examination in the same film. But though it begins promisingly, it tires itself, and the viewer with it, well before it takes its shore leave.

It is obvious from their first

"Tell 'em Groucho sent you": DeSoto, sponsors of *You Bet Your Life*, arranged a tie-up with *A Girl in Every Port* (1952).

scenes that Groucho and Bendix have been cast in the limiting mold of Abbott and Costello, with Groucho as Abbott—wily, conniving and not above duping his naïve, trusting partner as callously as anyone else. The services background, with the pair dressed for the early scenes in their navy uniform, increases the resemblance. Though the dynamic eventually relaxes enough to allow flashes of the authentic Groucho in spirit, the dialog only occasionally rises to the occasion, as when the pair first inspect the lame horse on which Bendix has squandered his inheritance:

**Groucho:** He can't even walk!
**Bendix:** Well, certainly he can walk. How d'you think he got here?
**Groucho:** That's encouraging. At least we won't have to carry him back. Looks like we got stuck with a pot of glue. Maybe we can sell him to the post office.
**Bendix:** Benny! Don't even say that! How would you like to be turned into a pot of glue and be pasted all over things?
**Groucho:** Make me an offer!

The film began shooting under the title *They Sell Sailors Elephants*, and was sometimes announced as *Old Sailors Love Elephants* and *They Sell Monkeys to Sailors*. But whatever working title, early reports are unanimous that it would be changed as soon as they come up with something better. (What they did come up with is little better, and had already done service as a 1928 film. The two productions were entirely unconnected, except by the odd synchronism that Howard Hawks, director of the first film, married Dee Hartford, a leading lady in the second. And then, Groucho, star of the second film, married Eden Hartford, sister of the leading lady, making him brother-in-law of the director of the first film. Got all that?) So *A Girl in Every Port* it eventually became, but "they sell elephants to sailors" remains in its dialog, and the credits still claim *They Sell Sailors Elephants* for the title of the original short story, by Frederick Hazlitt Brennan, on which the film is based. However, the original story, pub-

Left to right: William Bendix, Marie Wilson and Groucho, waiting for the muse to strike in *A Girl in Every Port* (1952).

lished in the *Saturday Evening Post* in 1933, had actually been titled *A Girl in Every Port*. If you figure that one out, you're good.

As stated, Groucho does well by both his co-stars. William Bendix, a performer with a rare gift for drama and the broadest comedy alike, is fun as his dopey friend. If there was any ill feeling over *The Life of Riley* we certainly don't sense it, and the double-act is convincing throughout. Marie Wilson is probably the best value contributor to the film, playing a cute, dumb blonde with much more charm and invention than the script calls for or deserves.[13] (She described the character a little optimistically as "just a little bit of Irma, combined with a less naïve character.") The reviewers seemed to appreciate her efforts, and were not slow to notice the "tight sweaters and shorts" that constituted the greater part of her onscreen wardrobe. Producer Irwin Allen denied that Wilson's "opera-length black stockings, short skirt and peek-a-boo neckline" had caused trouble with censors, but added: "we re-did the costumes a couple of times, if that's what you mean." "It's Groucho's doing," Marie happily told reporters. "When he worked with Jane Russell she wore highnecked gowns all though the picture. Groucho told Howard Hughes that he didn't want to make that mistake with me."

Her fun, perky performance inevitably steals the focus from the film's other female lead, fashion model Dee Hartford, making her screen debut. Reports carefully noted that she was "five feet, seven inches tall, and weighing 125 pounds" and "is said to have the perfect fashion figure." Possessed, no doubt, of something of the hauteur that comes from a life in couture, she was known on the set as "Icy Knockers," according to Groucho's ever-reliable testimony. But she thawed enough to introduce him to her two sisters, Peggy and Edna, the latter another model who professionally styled herself "Eden." (Groucho later claimed she made the name switch partly because "she thought (Eden) was fancier" and partly to avoid confusion, because the man she was going with at the time was also called Edna.) Ever the pragmatist, Groucho asked Dee which sister, if either, wasn't married. Eden, it transpired, was the lucky one, and Groucho asked if she would like to meet for dinner once shooting was completed. (But not before, he stressed, making a bizarre point about mixing business with pleasure.) Before long Groucho had embarked upon his final stint at matrimony, repeating exactly the pattern that had already failed twice: marrying a younger, beautiful woman with whom he had next to nothing in common. Charlotte Chandler recalled Eden telling her of a typical occasion on which she and Dee accompanied Groucho on a visit to George S. Kaufman:

> Kaufman and Groucho would converse intently, and after a long period of time would remember the presence of Eden and Dee and acknowledge their presence by directing some conversation toward these young, beautiful girls, who would answer, "Yes, oh yes." Then Kaufman and Groucho would go back into their world and become oblivious of the respectful girls until, remembering them, another "Oh yes" was called for. They spent a few hours saying very little "in the presence of the great men." As they were leaving in the elevator, Dee commented to Eden, "We're just the Greek chorus."

Dee would go on to provide glamorous backdrop for Groucho as a confident straight woman in the Dr. Hackenbush sketch in a 1964 edition of *Hollywood Palace*, but behind the scenes Icy Knockers was becoming increasingly frosty, and it has been said that her dislike of Groucho led her to strongly influence Eden to end the marriage in 1969.

But that's to jump ahead: let me instead drag you back to these various sailors, horses and elephants. On the remote chance that anyone needs to know, the horses' real names were Smoky and Silhouette, gelding and mare thoroughbreds, whose burgeoning fondness for each other led them to enthusiastically forget the script's demand that they be restrained twins. ("And they call horses dumb animals!" observed Groucho to reporters.) Tim Holt, western star—and, when in the mood, superb actor for Orson Welles and John Huston— frequented the set as a volunteer handler to the lovesick prancers. "Marie Wilson wasn't rehearsing," Groucho explained, ruling out the most likely contingency, "and Tim didn't come to see Bendix or me. It must have been the horses."

Another who took a keen interest in the horses was humorist S.J. Perelman. The venerable wag dropped in on the set for a day, and wrote up his experiences in a famous if largely fanciful essay called "I'll Always Call You Schnorrer, My African Explorer." Though the bulk of the piece is given over to plainly fabricated conversations with the star, the following, at least, borders on the authentic:

> A hush fell over the turbulent sound stage, technicians exchanged a last crisp monosyllable, and the transparency screen behind us lit up to reveal half a dozen racehorses plunging toward us. In front of them, in jockey's silks, sat Marx and Bendix on two amazingly lifelike steeds molded of rubber. As the machinery underneath them began churning, the horses came alive; their necks elongated, manes and tails streamed in the breeze, muscles rippled in their flanks and bellies. The riders plied their mounts with whip and endearments, straining forward into the camera to steal the scene from each other.
>
> "Cost twenty-five grand to build those bang-tails," the producer confided to me in the darkness. "We rent the pair of 'em for five hundred a day. But it's worth it. When they go to see the picture, 'they'll swear it's a real horse race.'"
>
> "What happens if they don't go to see the picture?" I asked, fascinated.[14]

For the most part the pair are indeed riding (pretty convincing) rubber horses, though in just a couple of shots we do see Groucho confidently atop a real nag. True, it's not galloping anywhere, but there's something so incongruous about the idea of Groucho on a horse— especially at that point of his career—and he does look very relaxed about it. (It will be recalled that, of the brothers, only Harpo actually makes contact with hide in *Go West*.)

To reporters on set, Groucho displayed his customary attitude of weariness towards the chore of film-making. This time, however, it was from the perspective of one who has found something much more satisfactory with which to compare it. He was now a television superstar, and TV was, he opined, "the only thing in my life that's easy."

> For a lazy man's life give me television every time. How anyone can ever say that a weekly television show is tougher than filmmaking is beyond me. Maybe I'm fortunate because I happened to strike a pattern for my program that requires no long rehearsals, whereas this business of getting ready for a movie scene is a lot more strenuous. I had a call to report here at 9:30. I inquired of the unit manager just what would happen in I came in at 9:45 instead. I was warned that this would be impossible, unthinkable. It would hold up everything. So, I get down here at 9:30, right on time, and what happens? It's three o'clock now and I'm still waiting to do my first scene.

The *Albany Democrat-Herald*, on the other hand, caught him in higher spirits, perhaps after a visit from his accountant: "Here I am in RKO's *A Girl in Every Port*. And what do I have to do? Say one line, that's all. Just one line. A couple dozen words and what do they pay me for this? Five thousand bucks."

All a far cry, he explained, from when the Marx Brothers played vaudeville "for thirty bucks a week … and all four of us crowded into a ratty little dressing room. Plus Harpo's harp. Plus a pot-bellied stove that burned the seat of your pants if you bent over."

A running theme of the reviews was that Groucho, though always welcome, may perhaps be getting a little old for broad clowning and leering both. Accordingly, he was somewhat defensive on the subject: "This is the age of the octogenarians," he told Bob Thomas:

> A lot of my contemporaries sometimes sit around and moan about the future of comedy. Most of them are middle-aged and they wonder where the new comedians are coming from. I tell them that as long as the money is good, new comedians will come along. Sure, they don't have vaudeville to give them experience, as we did. But they'll come from nightclubs; they'll even crawl out of the woodwork. Come to think of it, some of them have.

Calling the film a "bumpy, far from humorously rewarding ride," the *Philadelphia Enquirer* may have been the bluntest of the reviewers, but spoke for the majority all the same:

> Hopelessly handicapped by a witless script and equally uninspired direction, Groucho Marx and William Bendix fight their way through 86 muddled minutes.... The boys try, goodness knows, but they never have a chance involved with a twin pair of race horses, a brace of saboteurs, a parcel of gangsters and Marie Wilson, car-hop, who wears gloves and seems to be falling out of her clothes most of the time.... The film is more an endurance marathon than the zany comedy it obviously set out to be. And obvious is the word. For every move, every gag, every complication is telegraphed far in advance, leaving the stars little to do but mark time and make faces.

It was the same with the *New York Times* (though the reviewer liked Groucho, and noted that Wilson's "physical charms are not hidden"), while the *Sunday Herald* of Bridgeport, Connecticut, called it "a waste of talent" in which Groucho looks "every minute as if he would be happier back of a microphone giving money away to contestants." (They'd have got no argument from him on that one.) *Film Bulletin*, also receptive to Wilson's "pleasing pulchritude," felt Groucho to be "handicapped by the lack of punchy lines and strong comedy sequences," and depressingly recapped the general mood in summary: "Not even Groucho Marx's current wave of popularity was able to keep this RKO production afloat in the opinion of most New York newspaper critics when it opened at the Paramount. With one exception, they tagged *A Girl in Every Port* as a film which just didn't have the material."

The final verdict came from Groucho himself, who subjected the film to what might be considered the acid test, and reported back to Miriam in a letter from October of 1954:

> I tried running it the other night for Melinda. After two reels I had to shut it off. I couldn't watch it and Melinda left the room. There's an old saying, "Let the dead past bury its dead," and I am a firm believer in never looking backward. There are too many horrifying things lurking there.

We needn't disagree with any of that, but let us at least acknowledge in the interest of fair play the forgotten fact that the original audiences came out in gratifying numbers, and seemed to go away smiling. Despite being released alongside big-hitters *Quo Vadis* and *The Greatest Show on Earth* (and in what the trades all agree was dauntingly unseasonal opening weekend weather) it more than held its own, and for what it's worth whupped critics' darling *Zorba the Greek* at the box office. *Motion Picture Daily* recorded "a healthy $63,000" for its opening week, and "an excellent $64,000" for its second: twice what the Hellenic chap took home.

A measure of its success was the swift announcement that it would be followed by a sequel, to be titled *A Guy in Every Port*. "In this one," Hedda Hopper tells us, "three girls, including Marie Wilson and Margaret Sheridan, join the waves to see the world, especially the male part of it. Groucho Marx is again to play the sailor who shies away from girls, having been frightened by one in his youth." (*Hollywood Reporter* added Brad Dexter to the prospective cast.). Had it gone ahead, the chances of it being with Groucho aboard ship feel slim to me. By that time, he no longer had much need of movies.

# 4

# I hate work

Let's rewind, briefly, to 1947, and imagine ourselves Groucho Marx on the morning of October 29.

We're eagerly opening our copy of *Variety*, as he must have done, to see what they made of *You Bet Your Life*, the new radio quiz show he had reluctantly agreed to host in a last-ditch effort to see if he had any chance whatever of forging a career in radio. ("I wasn't particularly proud of doing a quiz show," he recalled in the 1976 retrospective *The Secret Word Is Groucho*. "It was like slumming.") Sure enough, there it is: "Groucho Marx, one of the genuine talents among comics in show business, came back into radio with his own show Monday, after several years of hit-and-miss whirls at guest-shot routines."

> As audience participation emcees go, the Groucho can keep up with the best of them. In fact, on Monday's premiere his banter on the adlib uptake was several notches above the level of the average quizmaster.... And unlike many of them, he has the happy faculty to extract laughter, not at the expense of the contestants, but from an off-guard zanyism that has a quality of freshness about it.[1]

Promising, very promising. But then:

> But the fact remains that *Bet Your Life* is a quiz show, and not a highly original one at that, and for the greater part of a half-hour major attention and interest is focused on a rehashed prize-winning gimmick that puts the Groucho talents at the mercies of the usual run of uninspired contestants.... At least they could have endowed him with a format that had an element of newness about it. But *Bet Your Life* is basically a reprise of *Strike It Rich*.... It's all been heard before. How to integrate the Groucho Marx comedy into radio programming is still something he boys haven't solved as yet.

Whereupon, he must have closed his paper, disappointed but hardly surprised by this final confirmation that Marx and the microphone just don't mix.

But now let's leap forward again, and return to the 1950s: my, how things have changed! It's like one of those corny montages in a backstage musical, where the naïve ingénue triumphs and, in forty-five seconds of teary close-ups dissolving in and out of shots of applauding audiences and spinning newspaper headlines, grows to international stardom before our eyes.

"After fourteen seasons of *You Bet Your Life*, in which I did 500-plus programs and met 2,500 contestants, I think I got the hang of it," the host noted laconically in *The Secret Word Is Groucho*, and indeed he did. The show immediately faced down the naysayers and thrived: before long it was the smash hit of its time, especially after it won the Peabody Award in 1948, then moved triumphantly to television in 1950. In a 1948 letter to his daughter Miriam, a clearly delighted Groucho struggles to account for this extraordinary turnaround in his professional fortunes:

> As you know, I was embarrassed about doing a quiz show, for it is considered the lowest form of radio life, but all of my friends, the ones who make big salaries and listen to *Information, Please* and the other erudite

programs, are nuts about this. I just don't understand it, but apparently the quality of ad-libbing on the air is so low that if anyone comes along with even a moderately fresh note he's considered practically a genius. Don't be surprised, but I think your old man has finally arrived in radio. You could knock me over with a microphone.

Robert Dwan, the show's director, in his memoir *As Long as They're Laughing!* recalled Groucho telling him, "The greatest man who ever lived was the man who invented sitting down," and *You Bet Your Life* gave lucrative returns on what seemed to Groucho a meager investment of time and effort. Groucho was a man of sedentary habits and a love of routine, and film-making had in truth never been something he actually enjoyed. ("He was never very happy when he was making a picture," wrote Arthur in *Life with Groucho*.) Entering his sixties in 1950, he no longer felt nor looked young (and according to a letter to Harry Kurnitz that year, the closest he now got to a sex life was regular correspondence from an elderly lesbian who wanted to borrow money). Here, at last, was an outlet for his talents entirely suited to his habits and tastes.

A valuable commodity once more, wooed by potential employers "like a dame hot out of Vassar," he could again afford to be discriminating. After the two Howard Hughes projects, he took no more starring roles in films. "As far as I'm concerned, movies are ancient history," he told journalists during a visit to Paris in 1954. "I went to see *Animal Crackers* on the Champs-Elysees the other night, and it was like digging up my own coffin. My first love now is television."[2]

When not turning down movies, he was turning down plays, perhaps the most enticing of which was proposed in 1955: a life of Benjamin Disraeli on Broadway. Groucho had a genuine fascination for Disraeli, reminiscent of Chaplin's infatuation with Napoleon. In *The Groucho Phile*, he recalled reading about him at school and thinking "if he could become a

At MGM, Groucho's sour-faced reluctance to take part in frivolous photograph sessions became legendary, but by the time of *You Bet Your Life* he was much more playful.

Jewish Prime Minister, what was to stop me from becoming the first Jewish President?" Both men were noted for their cynical wit, and according to Charlotte Chandler, Groucho and Erin Fleming would occasionally play-act the roles of Disraeli and Queen Victoria for their own amusement. She further recalls an occasion when the question of who he would have liked to have been was met not with his habitual "Groucho Marx" but rather an unqualified and emphatic "Disraeli."

Written by Noel Coward, the play was planned with Groucho as the lead, opposite Helen Hayes.[3] The announcement reached sources as widely-spaced as *Punch* in England and Hedda Hopper in Hollywood. Hopper reported Groucho visiting Coward in Jamaica to discuss the project and give his verdict on what had been written so far: he returned with a definite thumbs up for the first act and plans to hook up with Coward again a few weeks later when Coward was set to arrive in America to fulfill a Vegas engagement. The *Punch* article was accompanied by a superb cartoon by Will Elder (still occasionally reproduced, but with context neither presented nor presumed). Groucho, in traditional costume, is making a lunge at a buxom maid while Queen Victoria—looking suspiciously like Margaret Dumont—sits in an undignified heap on the floor. Meanwhile, an opportunistic Harpo has shown up at the door, and Chico leans through a broken window to switch the sheet music on the piano from "Mozart Sonata" to "Yer Nothin' but a Shveinhunt."

No more was heard, and the same fate befell a 1958 offer from Rudolph Bing, general manager of the Metropolitan Opera, to appear in the speaking role of Frosch the jailer in *Die Fledermaus*. Despite the promise of a limited engagement of just five or six performances, Groucho told him he'd "have to wait until I get bounced off television."[4]

Instead of the movie leads he once craved, surprise cameos, where the point of the character is the actor playing it, now became his specialty. Accordingly, all of his remaining feature film appearances from the 1950s are cameos. In *Mr. Music* he guests as himself; his last minute intervention in *Will Success Spoil Rock Hunter?* is uncredited (and was kept a surprise in pre-release publicity); and in *The Story of Mankind* he plays an historical character quite deliberately in his own modern manner. An additional factor in accepting these assignments was that they came as direct invitations from friends. *Mr. Music* was written by Arthur Sheekman. *Will Success Spoil Rock Hunter?* was directed by Frank Tashlin, one of the more useful contributors to the last two Marx Brothers movies. Irwin Allen, producer-director of *The Story of Mankind*, had become a personal friend since their collaboration on the two pictures for Hughes.

And there was almost another title to add to that list, this time for the benefit of Norman Krasna. Groucho's friend and collaborator on *Time for Elizabeth* and *The King and the Chorus Girl* had formed Wald-Krasna Productions with Jerry Wald in 1950. They had big plans and big intentions—but they also had RKO attached from the first, in a twelve-picture production deal. Disenchantment set in early owing to Howard Hughes's insistence on creative interference: by the following year Wald had bought a grateful, frustrated Krasna out of the partnership, with the latter vowing to stick to writing. (In his famous letter to Hughes asking for an update on the chances of *Double Dynamite* being released, Groucho had playfully attributed the mogul's inattentiveness to his "retooling for the war effort and duelling with Wald and Krasna.")

Wald-Krasna's *Behave Yourself* (1952) completed shooting on the RKO lot immediately before *A Girl in Every Port* went into production. A cheerful, dopey boy-girl comedy not a million miles from *Double Dynamite* in plot and style, it is perfectly ingratiating, and has a few nice ideas typical of Krasna (the cast are listed in the credits in the order in which their characters die). But like many another RKO comedy of the period, it somewhat lacks a sense of spontaneous fun—the inevitable legacy, perhaps, of a fraught, micro-managed production. What it could have well used is a shot of Groucho—and therein lies a brief diversion.

The film has Farley Granger, via a series of contrivances, present his young wife, played by Shelley Winters, with a cute dog that turns out to have been used as a means of communication between gangsters. The gangsters want the pooch back, Shelley wants to keep it, Farley's stuck in the middle, and anything can happen and probably doesn't). But according to originally announced plans, none less than Groucho and Oscar Levant had been signed up for a uncredited appearances. As the *Sydney Morning Herald* put it, they were to "appear briefly as two particularly unpleasant gangsters," and Groucho had even decided to report to work with three day's growth of beard, to give the role a touch of method accuracy.

Perhaps Wald and Krasna reconsidered their whimsy in a cooler hour and opted for players better able to actually deliver the material, or possibly the threat of scheduling clashes derailed the plans. Although Groucho's sailor movie began shooting just after *Behave Yourself* wrapped, it had in fact been intended to begin shooting much earlier; but a bout of blood poisoning for Marie Wilson held up proceedings for a month. A pity: it might have been the most enjoyable of these 1950s novelty Groucho sightings.[5]

Immediately prior to the first of them, 1950's *Mr. Music*, Groucho appeared on the radio show of its star, Bing Crosby. According to Earl Wilson, who was present at the recording of the show and described it in his syndicated column, "They had about five minutes of extra laughs that they had to throw out, most of them from Groucho, some of them a little blue."[6] Groucho and Bing perform a charming duet of Irving Berlin's "Play a Simple Melody," later to become standard in the repertoire of Groucho and Melinda, but the program is most notable for the section where Bing performs the song "The Look In Your Eyes." This was obviously through Groucho's own engineering, since the number was written by Groucho's wife Kay in collaboration with Harry Ruby (the team-up presumably also a result of Groucho's engineering). A long comedy dialog sequence beforehand contrives to repeatedly state the fact of Kay's authorship, and throughout the show, there is the touching sense of a man going out of his way, in his own showcase, to promote the efforts of his wife. But was this a purely altruistic gesture or, perhaps, a conciliatory one? Regardless, the fates insisted on their sport. Shortly after, Groucho's and Kay's marriage was officially over, with Groucho telling reporters, "We're just plain unhappy."[7] He notified Miriam in a bewildered letter that began: "There's a song in the Bing Crosby picture called 'Life Is So Peculiar' ..."

## *Mr. Music* (1950)

Bing Crosby and Groucho Marx are teamed as song-and-dancers in a vaudeville act. It's an added scene for Paramount's *Mr. Music*. Dressed in sports clothes and straw hats, they do some steps, then Groucho kneels on one knee, Crosby sits on his other.

"Listen, son," says Groucho, "and I'll tell you the facts of life."

"Yes, daddy," Bing replies in falsetto.

"If you're ever standing on a street corner and a gorgeous gal comes by..." the moustachioed comic goes on.

"Yes, daddy," Bing interrupts.

"Well, if she asks you for a match and then discusses the weather and then invites you home for dinner...."

"Yes, daddy?"

"And if she suggests you see her etchings—don't go, son."

"No, daddy?"

"No!" and Groucho removes the cigar from his mouth and rolls his eyes.

"No! Just phone me quick and I'll go in your place."

"Cut!" yells director Richard Haydn. "What a scream!"

Everybody roared around the set but the theater audiences will never see this scene. After speaking his first few words, Groucho forgot his lines. Then the two proceeded to ad lib for several minutes. After Haydn and his crew recovered, the bona fide dialogue was soundtracked—and Haydn added the discarded hilarity to his stock of "blow-ups," shown only at private parties around Hollywood.[8]

The above was reported by Harold Hefferman in a syndicated column from March of 1950. It's a pity he spends so long telling us the bits of the scene that are meant to be there but gives us no idea of the ad libs that supposedly ended up on Haydn's stag reel. Oh, well—something to keep your eyes peeled for when you're down in the vaults looking for out-takes from *Horse Feathers.*

*Mr. Music* is a dullish musical drama, much too long, written by Groucho's pal and collaborator Arthur Sheekman. His scenes were shot over a rainy week at the end of January and the beginning of February 1950, and Groucho noted in a letter to Miriam that he was looking to need "a good deal of rehearsing."

He stars as himself, and comes on only for the finale, interacting with his pal Bing (although Bing does not play himself) and delivering a few backstage quips, before joining him onstage for their duet of "Life is So Peculiar." (Sadly, when Crosby came to record the number it was with the Andrews Sisters.)

An hour and three quarters is a long time to wait for three minutes of Groucho, but their duet, once we get to it, is a truly charming film moment, probably as cherishable as anything we have of Groucho without his brothers. A delightful air of nostalgia, and therefore of summation, permeates it, and not just because it marks his return to the Paramount mountain for the first time since *Duck Soup*. It seems

*Mr. Music* (1950): Bing Crosby (left) and Groucho exercise their hooves.

to transport him back to his vaudeville past, allowing him almost to assume again the mantle of Julius the Nightingale. He looks great keeping step with Bing in straw hat and two-tone brogues (and seeing the two men side by side also gives us a rare and endearing sense of Groucho's comparative shortness of stature).

At the end Groucho leaves the stage in his boater, returns in a top hat, then hastily leaves again and returns in a pith helmet, which he retains to complete the number. Whether an intended salute to Captain Spaulding or not, it's a real treat.

Groucho himself was pleased with the end results—something that only happened once in a rare while—and saw only one problem with the footage. "It was embarrassing," he explained, "because I sing better than Bing.... I usually wait until he gets off the set before I start singing, because I don't want to embarrass him. We appear as a couple of ancient vaude-villains. I require very little make-up."[9]

What the scene most recalls is one of those moments in the Bing Crosby and Bob Hope *Road* comedies, where the pair are seen on stage putting over a hokey vaudeville song, especially the "Good Time Charlie" number from *Road to Utopia*, with its spoken sections. And it's hard to stop the mind wandering further having once entertained that thought!

In my first Marx Brothers book, I cited *Road to Utopia* as the perfect example of what had superseded the Marx style of comedy in the 1940s, making films like *The Big Store* seem so passé. But while it is true the Marxes were too well established to have adapted to this new style, there's no reason why the new, footloose and fancy free Groucho might not have fitted in—and it could easily have happened.

The new comedy style drew extensively on radio—its rhythms and its personnel. And radio, however uncertainly, *was* Groucho's new home. He needn't have become a solo radio star, just fractionally surer a success in the guest spots he had been filling. Say he had made a name for himself as a semi-regular on Hope's show, or Crosby's. How easily then might he have fitted into the *Road* line-up as featured support—perhaps a wily conman type—essentially the same character each time out, but with a different name, popping up on each journey, much like Dorothy Lamour. Bing, Bob and Dottie, of course, were not a team as such, just a temporary conglomeration, so Groucho would have had no fear of being consumed within another team: he would still have been a featured single act, but under the umbrella of the hippest new comedy aggregate around. It's easy to imagine! The *Road* trio might have easily become an unofficial quartet, and we would associate Groucho not with one screen comedy team, but two!

Well, it never happened, so let us leave this parallel comic universe before we get carried away. The fact was that against all the odds, Groucho did make it big on radio in his own show.

## *You Bet Your Life* (1947–61)

"It's true," Groucho wrote to Earl Wilson in 1955, "I was extremely reluctant to do the quiz show."

> There were hundreds of [shows] and they all revolted me. [The hosts were all] joy boys who either yocked it up or gave it the religious "deeply concerned about you" attitude. I told them I would not go for any of this nonsense. That I would neither laugh it up hysterically nor wax deeply sentimental. They would have to take me as I actually was. And, since they couldn't get anything cheaper, they signed me.

> The show is a breeze. I meet with the director every Tuesday for two hours—and that's it. Other than that, I go to the Derby on Wednesday night at 7, enter the theater at 8, get pancake slapped on my kisser by a makeup man, warm up the audience with a firebrand and some elderly jokes, do the show, discard the pancake and—unless I pick up a dame on Sunset Blvd.—I'm back home at 10.[10]

Whatever stage or screen opportunities came his way through the 1950s, *You Bet Your Life* offered him too much to swap: success, vindication and a means of combining productive employment with an ordered, domestic existence. It also made him more *widely* famous (in both geographic and demographic senses) than ever before. As Wilson noted in one of his columns from January of 1950, Groucho "is becoming more and more popular. He has adult fan groups everywhere."

> I went to Groucho's CBS studio to see him transcribe his own show. He roamed around the stage with his coat in his hands, looking for a place to hang it. "Is there a coat hanger in the audience?" he called out. Then came the contestants, one a New Yorker, born near Fulton Fish market. "How long did you flounder around there?" Groucho asked him. A chiropodist came next. "By the way, doc, my wife's foot hurt this morning," Groucho said. "Well," the doc said, "If you could tell me where it hurt…." "It hurt in the seat of my pants," Groucho said. Groucho then got to the hard questions. "How much is one and one?" One silly contestant replied, "Two." "Wrong. Fourteen," said Groucho. "I was thinking of one and one rabbits." Backstage later I talked to Groucho. His voice was low and husky by this time and he was tired, and serious, and ready to go home. "You know," he said, "it's hard to be funny every week."[11]

On television, the show further benefited from the physical interplay between Groucho, his co-host and their guests, and also from the seemingly arbitrary addition of the duck—a large toy fowl with Groucho glasses and mustache, that descended from the ceiling whenever the contestant said the secret word. It became a visual icon, associated with Groucho ever after.

The team behind the program prided themselves on the eclectic range of contestants. Groucho enumerated them in *The Secret Word Is Groucho*: "We have had scientists, musicians, singers, acrobats, an elevator jockey who sang three songs in Sanskrit, a woman who ran a hotel for cats, a man who blew up a large inner tube and then fainted just as the quiz started, an Italian widow whom we deliberately kept on for three successive weeks in hopes that she could snare a husband, and a woman who swam to Catalina and back without stopping." Others who linger in the memory of this viewer: a man who had lived in the wild for twenty years eating acorns and grass but had now married and become a singing fruit seller; "Fifi the Sheep-headed Girl," an ordinary-looking woman until she takes her hat off; and best of all, the wild-eyed and terrifying Albert Hall, who pulls off the rare feat of making even Groucho nervous with his manic stare and pedantic diction (he had worked at the *Seattle Times* "in the com-

**Bernie Smith's daughter Lucinda tempted the original *You Bet Your Life* duck out of retirement in 2009 to celebrate his co-starring appearance on a commemorative stamp (courtesy Lucinda Irwin Smith).**

*po*-sing room!" but came to Hollywood to "find out how they make *mon*-ey!") Audiences found the sheer unpredictability of the show delicious.

There were also plenty of celebrities looking in, including Harpo, on one memorable occasion. (Chico can also be glimpsed from time to time in the studio audience, seemingly enjoying himself immensely, as well he might, since Groucho had him on the show's payroll.) One who got away was Margaret Dumont. Sadly, she never appeared but did receive an offer; according to Groucho in 1960, "She said she would only come on the show if we paid her price. I told her she would get only what she won as a contestant. She refused to go on."[12]

To the end of his life Groucho remained as proud of this amusing, unassuming program as of any of the magnificently crafted movies he appeared in with his brothers, routinely excusing himself early from social gatherings at his house so as to watch the reruns on his bedroom television. The reason for his pride was obvious: he had done it, finally—and had done it on his own. What's more he had done it as himself—no greasepaint mustaches, or claw-hammer coats. (The refusal to wear the old garb, even for publicity shots, he had insisted upon from the start: an interesting reflection of how far he was and wasn't prepared to go, even at his most professionally desperate. Robert Dwan recalled him announcing his resolve on the matter at their first meeting. Gummo, in the capacity of agent, urged caution and reminded him the network executives might look on the decision unfavorably. "Fuck 'em," replied Groucho.)

And yet even here, and from the start, we sense the old insecurities in his obsession with disproving the suggestion, which he of course knew to be partially true, that his ad lib conversations with the show's contestants were more pre-planned than they seemed. It was never true that the conversations were scripted and rehearsed, but his reluctance to concede that the contestants *were* interviewed in advance (in his absence), and that he was then primed with jokes and questions to use if need arose, inadvertently allowed more absurd rumors to persist and magnify. (There is a strange, uncomfortable passage in his *Person to Person* interview with Ed Murrow where he sets out to demonstrate to the doubters that he can ad lib a funny conversation out of the blue, electing Murrow as his subject. The conversation almost immediately goes nowhere—much more the oaken Murrow's fault than Groucho's, admittedly—leaving both men struggling to get the interview back on track.) Son Arthur explained the exact procedure in 1954—it was never a secret—and stressed that the prepared jokes were basically a kind of insurance: "If, for example, a prize-fighter is going to be on the program, father will have a few prize-fighter jokes written into his notebook alongside the regular interview questions. He doesn't like to rely on prepared jokes, because almost always the real ad libs get the biggest laughs."[13] In *The Secret Word Is Groucho* John Guedel, the program's executive producer, likened the prepared material to the scaffolding needed to build a wall: the "wall" was the unpredictable combustion between Groucho and his guests on the night, but the "scaffolding" was there to give it shape and stability. "Then you put up the wall, and then often you tear down the scaffolding," Guedel observed: a very good description of the Groucho technique.

If anything was played down in these accounts of the show's methods, it was the fact that these jokes were not just acquired casually from whoever happened to think of them: the show employed a team of writers specifically to furnish Groucho with material. The assembled group must have been the closest thing Groucho had to a dedicated gang of gag-smiths since the great Paramount days, when he was catered for by the likes of Perelman and

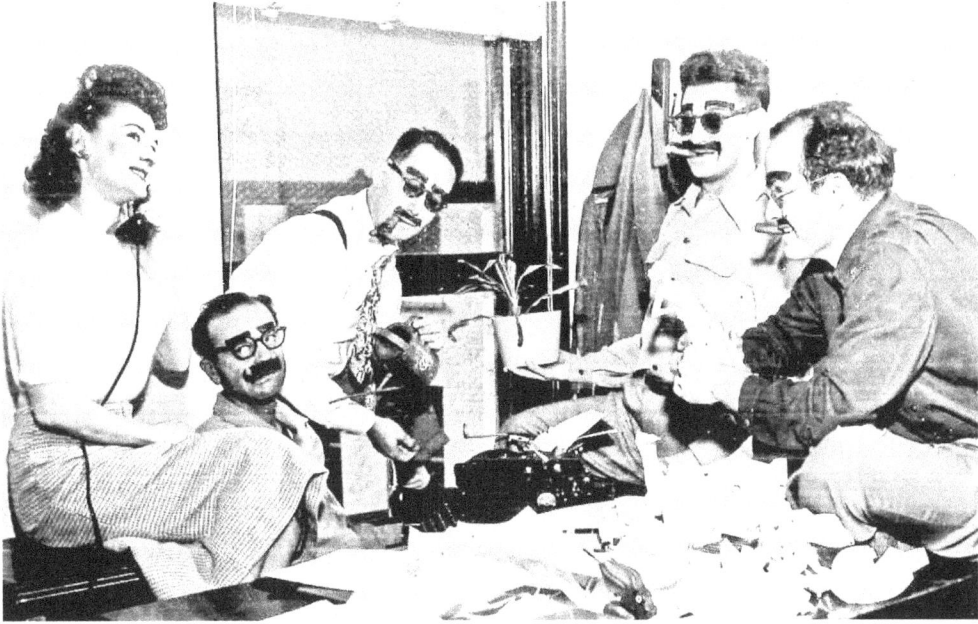

A typical *You Bet Your Life* script conference. Left to right: Dorothy Nye, Bernie Smith, Doc Tyler, Hy Freedman, Eddie Mills (courtesy Elaine Tyler May).

Johnstone and Sheekman and Perrin and Kalmar and Ruby in unruly union. This time, under the overall supervision of Bernie Smith, there was a pool of wits and wags that included: Hy Freedman, late of *Duffy's Tavern*; Howard Harris, the only of the team with previous experience of writing for Groucho, who contributed material uncredited to *A Night in Casablanca* and *Copacabana*; Ed "Doc" Tyler, a practicing fertility specialist who just happened to have a gift for writing jokes; and briefly Elroy Schwartz, a licensed hypnotherapist specializing in past life regression and, by extension, a joke writer for Bob Hope. Keeping order, when there were photographers around at least, was Dorothy Nye (Guedel's secretary and "Groucho's very ogle-able script girl," to quote the Spring 1949 issue of *Radio Album* magazine).

There are photographs of the gang goofing about together that are simply delightful, but understandably, for the sake of the show, their function usually remained somewhat shaded to the public at large. Groucho himself may have taken a while to warm to the whole idea, reluctant as he was to admit to the need for professional assistance. Sue Tyler Edwards, eldest daughter of Ed Tyler, recalls a distinct chill in his attitude towards the team that seems to have thawed as time went on (Tyler left the show after the 1953/54 season):

> Groucho kept his distance from the writers, as he wanted his fans to think he ad libbed all his lines. I only saw him once or twice when my Dad took me to the show's set, but my impression of him was that he was kind of sour and unpleasant—not funny, and not interested in socializing with the adults and certainly not with the kids.[14]

Later, however, Bernie Smith's daughter, writer Lucinda Irwin Smith, remembers her father and the full contingent of writers attending weekly meetings at Groucho's house to discuss the show together. "Groucho was absolutely more than just a work colleague," she recalls. "My father was very fond of him and absolutely loved working with him."[15]

As was ever the way with Marxian humor, which operates at best on the snowball prin-

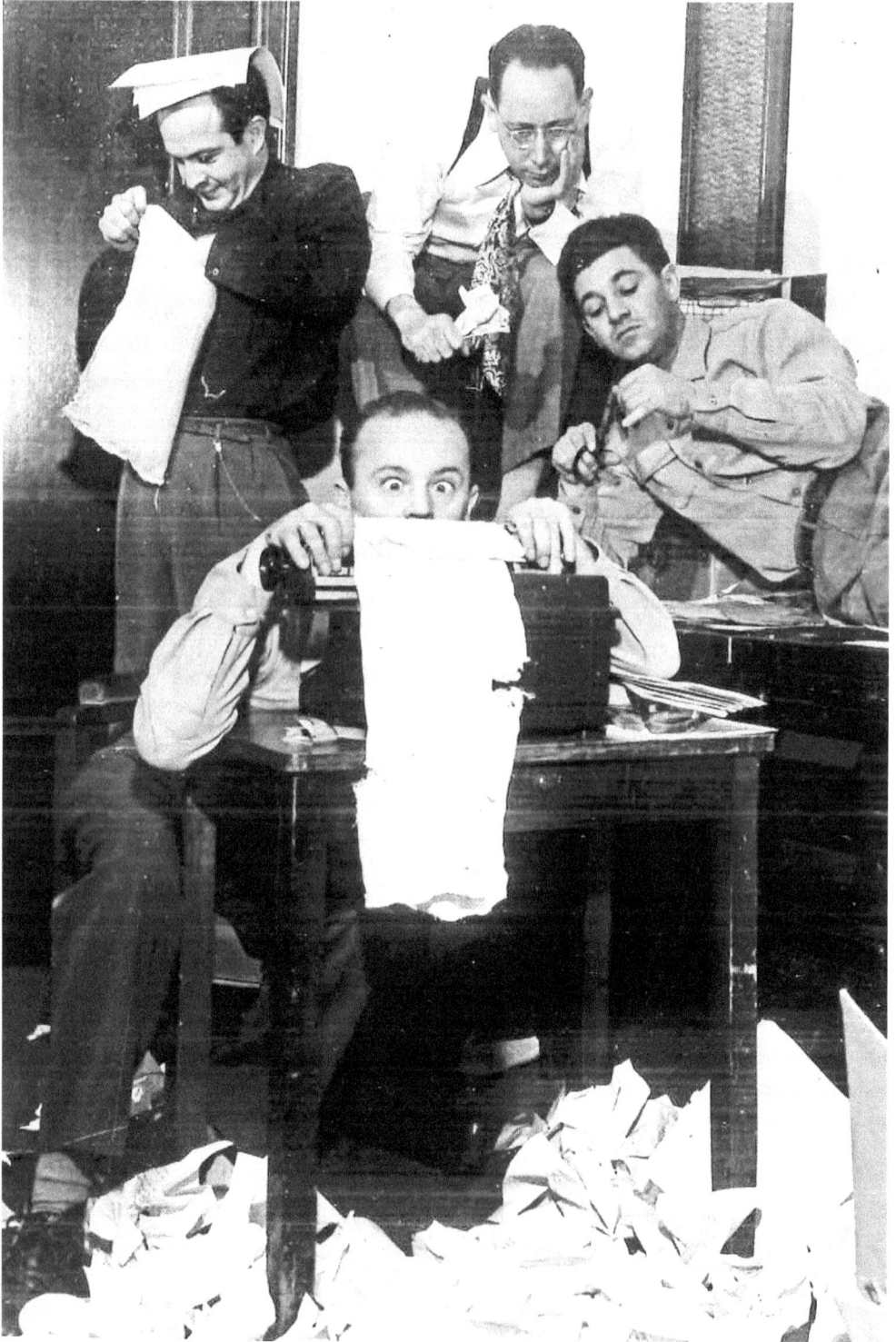

*You Bet Your Life* writers hard at work. Clockwise from left: Eddie Mills, Doc Tyler, Hy Freedman, Bernie Smith (courtesy Elaine Tyler May).

ciple, with each laugh building upon and topping the one before, collaboration is of the essence. Sue Tyler Edwards again:

> My father and Hy Freedman usually worked together on Sunday. They would hole up in my Dad's den, away from all the distractions, and create the scripts. If I came in the house and passed by the den I often heard them laughing. I think they had a lot of fun writing together. Then Dad would continue to work on the script drafts during the week, after dinner and often late into the night. I remember lying in bed and hearing his rapid pecking on the Smith Corona typewriter that we still have and treasure. It never occurred to me that it must have been difficult, stressful and exhausting, to meet the considerable demands of his medical practice and at the same time write those scripts and complete them on deadline. I guess I must have known that my Dad really enjoyed writing for the show. I never thought that he considered it a burden. I never saw him work with anyone other than Hy, though I know that he met regularly with the other writers. He mentioned them by name frequently.[16]

The mix of genuine spontaneity and cleverly scripted asides played near to seamlessly at the time, but the moments of transition between the two are fairly obvious to our more cynical eyes today. The biggest attraction to modern connoisseurs of the show, in fact, more than the laconic disdain Groucho extends to the contestants, may well be the rapport between the star and his studio announcer.

George Fenneman was employed to sell the sponsor's products, bring on the contestants and read out the scores, but he soon mutated from the anonymous man in a smart suit into one of the great straight men of all time. The interplay between Groucho and George is at times so sublime one yearns to see them together in the movies. Fenneman is an unusual foil to Groucho in that he is neither officious nor grand—indeed he is uncommonly agreeable and charming—so we should theoretically resent the manner in which Groucho summons him from his hiding place behind the studio curtains to needle and torment him. That we don't call foul is mainly down to the endearing tolerance and good sportsmanship conveyed by Fenneman, and by the pair's plainly conveyed mutual affection. "He soon became my Mrs. Dumont, and I valued his contributions greatly," Groucho recalled in *Secret Word*. "For there was never a comedian who was any good unless he had a good straight man. And George was straight on all four sides."

As a result many of their exchanges are recognized classics, and among our fondest and most instant memories of the show may be such moments as Groucho forcing a reluctant Fenneman to inhale helium, hang by his waist from a wire suspended from the studio ceiling, join him in an impromptu duet of

George Fenneman was Groucho's finest straight man since Margaret Dumont (Stephen Cox collection).

"Hooray for Captain Spaulding," or submit to an innuendo-laden interrogation as to how he recruited a pair of attractive young female contestants. (The latter sequence might be my favorite of all: when one of the girls innocently mispronounces his name as "Fitterman," Groucho accuses him of using an alias to pick up women.)

"Groucho shocked me a lot of times," George recalled, also in *The Secret Word Is Groucho*:

> Very often I would be standing backstage and I'd hear him say, "Fenneman, come out here." I'd know I was in trouble of some kind…. It was very funny, but my discomfiture was genuine. Like with the strong woman. She was a very good looking woman, but very strong. Groucho said, "Pick up Fenneman." And she picked me up around the knees. This woman had my knees in her bosom, in front of all these people and she wouldn't put me down. Here you are, a grown man with children at home, and this woman is holding you in the air. Or the guys with the whips … twins. I had just come out of the hospital with a double hernia operation. I was still a little bent over, you know, and every time I moved I could feel it. I still had the stitches. And I had to stand there while they flicked things out of my mouth or whatever.

Central to the popularity of the show even at the time—and this is the vital point that first *Variety* reviewer could not have been expected to cotton onto—was the recognition that the actual quiz elements were, if not quite irrelevant, then certainly little more than an excuse to justify the preamble. Audiences didn't tune in to learn their capital cities, or to match famous song writers to famous songs, but to see members of the public bantering with Groucho Marx, both with a seeming freshness and lack of preparation distinct from the repartee of other television shows of the time. The importance of the quiz to the show's structure should not be underestimated, however. The simple fact of its being there gave *You Bet Your Life* a coherent shape, and the essential illusion of purpose, as well as a curious kind of tension that charged and animated the conversations with the guests.

A harder sell for us today, perhaps, than the routine quiz sections are the concessions to the show's sponsors. Groucho and his team rightly noted that what enabled him to click after so many failed attempts at success as a solo personality were the subtle changes to his established persona: he was still witty, deprecating and rakish, but no longer anti-logical or destructive and, where possible, he was able to act as proxy for the home audience, assuming the attitude of a bemused ordinary fellow when faced with his contestants' eccentricity (the Groucho of the Groucho-Chico duologues). In short, he was humanized without being emasculated. ("Corny as it may seem," his son Arthur wrote in 1954, "the lack of heart or warmth or whatever you want to call it in father's comedy was probably one of the main reasons that he was never able to capture a mass radio audience before.") It still seemed a leap too far, however, when the great iconoclast perched himself behind the wheel of a DeSoto automobile in a jaunty hat, to tell us how their revolutionary air conditioning system keeps the atmosphere fresh when you fill the car with cigar smoke, or even sang of the vehicle's virtues in animated cartoon form.

Groucho's advice to purchasers, to rush to their nearest dealers and "tell 'em Groucho sent you," became an enduring catchphrase, but there's something dubious about seeing the man, however tamed, in this simultaneously subservient and bullying position. He was certainly not unaware of how problematic it was, responding to an observation (presumably) along those lines from Miriam in a letter from April 1953:

> It's true what you write about me seeming insincere in the commercials. Actually I am, but they feel that it has an extra value over Fenneman's mouthing this drivel so I am obliged to do it. I do it willingly but badly and, as you say, I guess it's pretty evident on the screen.[17]

## "That's me, Groucho!" (1954)

One signifier of the level of fame the series brought to Groucho is the fact that it was at this point that his name and image began to be systematically exploited for merchandising purposes. It marked a specific transition between celebrity and commodity that is itself a product of the television age, and for Groucho himself must have served as a reinforcement of the unprecedented levels of fame and recognition he was now enjoying. If they meant nothing more to him, the glasses with attached mustache and plastic cigar that now came with his licensed face on the packaging must surely have served as the ultimate exorcism of any lingering sense of incompleteness in the absence of his brothers. They also proved that he was now officially a favorite of all ages, including the very youngest. A series of print ads from around this time even co-starred him with Kellogg's cereal mascot Tony the Tiger, above the caption "You bet your life they're Gr-r-reat!"

Our temptation may have been to date this transformation from man into saleable icon (as with so many other innovations) to the era of Erin Fleming in the 1970s, with its "Tell 'Em Groucho Sent You" t-shirts and wristwatches. In fact, it began in the 1950s, with such glorious ephemera as the 1955 board game that "gives you and your friends the opportunity of playing Groucho's *You Bet Your Life* in your own living room." It could be argued that anyone could play *You Bet Your Life* in their own living room and didn't need to buy a board game to do so. But that would be to do without the mechanical countdown timer, trivia cards and cardboard letter tiles, with which this artifact came complete. According to the rules, players "make points not only for answering the question correctly, but also for spelling the answer in the allotted timeframe." Groucho would surely have approved of that.

Groucho the commodity: the TV star endorses breakfast cereal and his own line of napkins.

If that was the sweetest manifestation of Groucho-for-sale, the oddest were surely the sets of novelty cocktail napkins—known in the trade as "napgrins"—that Groucho endorsed and starred in in 1954. The concept had been pioneered by a San Francisco novelty company called Monogram, whose other sets included "Shakespeare Howls" (For example, three attractive derrieres perched pertly on drugstore stools above the line "There's a divinity that shapes our ends"), and a pair titled—with faux–Kinsey-esque sobriety—"Sexual Misbehavior in the Human Female" and "Sexual Misbehavior in the Human Male," that offered a series of ribald case-studies accompanied with phoney statistics. They proved a major hit with the swingier hosts and hostesses of the cocktail party era, and Groucho—as a comic character—must have been an obvious suggestion for follow-up. Thus the initial set of "That's Me, Groucho!" cocktail napkins sold so well that a second series was rushed into production the same year.

In delightful branded packaging, each set of 36 napkins contained a different cartoon featuring Groucho, drawn by artist Don Whearty, a contract artist who did a lot of work for the company, with gags written by staffers from *You Bet Your Life*. "I am sending you some unfunny napkins with smart cracks written by a couple of boys on the show," Groucho explained when sending a box to Miriam. "Apparently there's a market for this sort of backyard humor, and since everyone else is cashing in on it I thought I might just as well."

The reference to "backyard humor" is an acknowledgment that the napkins are, in many cases, considerably more risqué than anything permissible on either large or small screen at the time, occasionally to a degree that surprises, even today, considering the breezy manner with which Groucho and Fenneman plugged them on the show, and gave away boxes free to contestants. ("Each one has a cartoon and a joke about me on it—they're pretty clever!" was his officially-offered judgment.) Given the new-found breadth of his appeal, many younger and older fans may have bought them on the assumption they would be considerably more innocent than they proved. One shows him lasciviously eyeing two girls—one flat-chested, the other generously endowed—and asking their prim mother, "Are you sure they're identical twins?" Another casts him as an over-zealous customs official, forcing a woman to strip to her black lingerie while two women exclaim, "She must be a spy—this is the fourth time he's searched her." A third shows him at the receiving end of an indignant slap from a woman in a bowling alley whose imposingly spherical breasts he has grabbed on the pretense of mistaking them for bowling balls. Others are just pleasingly daft: Groucho in Harpo-mode chasing a Hawaiian girl in a grass skirt with a predatory lawnmower; as a fireman arriving at the window of a burning building with a sausage on a fork and requesting mustard from the woman trapped inside (shades of the lost finale from *Horse Feathers*); or as a plumber wading through the waist-deep water of a flooded kitchen and asking, "What seems to be the trouble?" One of them doesn't show Groucho at all, merely his office door, from which a salesman is being violently ejected, head first. "But all I said was that this machine would replace his secretary!" he exclaims in confusion to the sexy girl outside. Perhaps the most deft mingling of his contemporary celebrity and traditional persona shows him sat eagerly on a sofa with a buxom blonde, excitedly informing her: "You just said the secret word!" Above them, the *You Bet Your Life* duck is descending with a card reading: "YES."

Whearty, still in Hollywood and ninety-four at time of writing, was especially pleased to be handed the Groucho assignment, telling me: "I watched his movies to try to get his style. He was sarcastic and he kind of *looked* sarcastic; there was a sarcastic quality to his poses and facial expressions. I tried to get that in the drawings." That he was largely successful

"......YOU JUST SAID THE SECRET WORD ! "

**Groucho the napkin star—ephemera with a touch of the eternal (cartoon by Don Whearty).**

accounts in large measure for the fact that the napkins remain so appealing: as representations of Groucho they are superbly rendered.

Though the star affected an only casual or mercenary interest in the end product, he was a more active participant behind the scenes. Each individual cartoon had to be okayed by him before it could be added to the collection, though Whearty recalled that of all of them, he rejected only one: "I don't remember the joke now, but he ruled it out. I just remember that he felt it portrayed him in a bad light."[18] As so often, the pose of Groucho the disinterested bystander peels back to reveal the micro-manager within!

Groucho also promoted the napkins in magazine and newspaper ads, showing him with boxes of them under his arms and balanced on his head; one declares them "Timely as the H-Bomb." Their purpose was of course entirely ephemeral—they were meant to be used and thrown away, perhaps without ever being looked at at all. But the product's ephemerality should not be mistaken as reflective of its star: Groucho was now officially a graven image, and a character with folkloric resonance: what the napkins show us is the final and complete severing of Groucho the man and Groucho the icon. The latter, thus freed, can live forever, and while the napkins themselves may end up in the trash the morning after the night before, their star—that crouched, dark-suited satyr with identifying mustache and cigar—is deathless and eternal. In a funny sort of way, it was via these napkins and similar merchandised representations, more than the transitory fame and haphazard preservation of film and TV, that Groucho finally secured that immortality he so envied in Chaplin: the ability to be instantly conveyed by a handful of defining features. Those "unfunny napkins" were an unmistakable sign he was, at last, exactly where he had always wanted to be.

## *Will Success Spoil Rock Hunter?* (1957)

Groucho returned to the big screen in 1957, more than four years after he signed off from *A Girl in Every Port*. And like the proverbial buses, after a seemingly interminable wait, two Groucho appearances came along at the same time.

The first to arrive had in fact been the second to shoot. *Will Success Spoil Rock Hunter?* was a typical scattershot satire from director Frank Tashlin, and a superb showcase for the deceptively skilled Jayne Mansfield. Smoking a truly enormous cigar (sometimes a cigar is just a cigar—but maybe not on this occasion), Groucho appears in a joke-walk-on at the end, as George Schmidlap, Jayne's long-lost, much-mentioned first love. "You know you never even tried to kiss me?" she reminisces. "I never could get that close," he replies.

The cameo had in fact been intended for Tashlin's frequent collaborator Jerry Lewis, but Paramount had peevishly refused to free him from exclusive contract; if Groucho knew he was second choice he never let on, and it certainly doesn't seem to dampen his enthusiasm on screen. He is also clearly the superior choice: though Lewis was the hipper star, Groucho makes for a far funnier surprise identity for Schmidlap.

There is little reason to presume he gave much consideration to the nature of the piece itself when deciding to accept the role. As stated, he knew Tashlin, and the flattering nature of the role, short shooting schedule and Cinemascope-sized fee were doubtless the main attractions. (The film's voiceover narration also contrives to plug *You Bet Your Life* by name.) Perhaps needless to add, he enjoyed working with Mansfield, who reappeared and reminisced with him on his 1962 TV series *Tell It to Groucho*.

Groucho with Jayne Mansfield in *Will Success Spoil Rock Hunter?* (1957).

But while Groucho may not have given much thought to the project, and may not have read (or even seen) the entire script, had he done so it is likely the basic idea would have pleased him, all the same. Essentially a satire on television advertising, it takes wide but certain pot shots at the absurdity of TV sponsorship and the insincere ad spots that accompanied hit shows, and this, as we have seen, was something of a bête noire of Groucho's, and the aspect of his television success he least enjoyed. ("It's wonderful to be in love, and it's even more wonderful to be on a TV show without any commercials!" Schmidlap tells us.) It is also, in a wider sense, about the commodification of celebrity, and the new kind of household intimacy that stars were expected to accede to, and even collude in. Groucho must have noted, in this age of the "That's Me—Groucho!" napkins, that he was now a star of a very different sort than he had been on Broadway in the 1920s and in movies in the 1930s. Fame now meant being part of the audience's extended family, with no aspect of one's life too trivial to be of interest or a matter of public record; the indignities and absurdities of this redefined stardom are parodied by Tashlin with a tangy mix of cartoonishness and bile. The film, in these and other respects, was a good place for Groucho to be seen: a high profile comedy, modish, spiky, and just a touch daring.

## The Story of Mankind (1957)

*The Story of Mankind*, by contrast, made for a more inscrutable choice.[19] It's a film the badness of which has been massively overstated: very little of it is truly awful, because none of its eccentricities—the outlandish premise, the bizarre casting, the odd lurches between po-faced drama and silly comedy—is unintentional. But because it is silly just when you think it's decided to be serious, and then vice versa again, it's a hard film to get a handle on or maintain interest in. (It also rather cheekily sells itself as an epic, when really it is made somewhat on the cheap, and peopled almost entirely with character actors, some of whom hadn't been seen on the screen in years.) Like Woody Allen's *Everything You Always Wanted to Know About Sex* (1972), the film is episodic, faux-factual and nominally based on a best-selling non-fiction book, which it credits by name but does not so much adapt as riff on with complete indifference to its letter and spirit. And while the older film does not actually *parody* its supposed source in the way that Woody does, neither does it take it remotely seriously. This is best evidenced by the decision to have the Marx Brothers portray notable figures in world history.

Groucho told journalist Joe Hyams that he was doing the film "as a favor to Irwin Allen. He's a crook." Though it hardly makes the casting any less quixotic, Groucho had nevertheless been Allen's good friend since their collaboration on the two films for RKO, and they would remain so for the rest of Groucho's life. According to Groucho, the writer-producer-director was very much the Renaissance man on set: "He carries scenery around, too, opens the studio at 6 a.m., and writes dialog. You might call him the Orson Welles of Burbank. In fact you *should* call him that."

Any hopes that the film would provide the long awaited Marx Brothers screen reunion are swiftly and bizarrely dashed. All three appear separately, and while Harpo is amusing as a harp-playing Isaac Newton, Chico is easily missed as a monk briefly to be heard advising Christopher Columbus (with whom his father, of course, had been partners). As Peter Minuit, however, Groucho is given a generous window (a four-minute sketch, as opposed to a two-minute one for Harpo, and forty-five seconds in someone else's for Chico). More importantly (and fatally for the film itself) he's playing it very much as himself, not just in his usual style, but with wry asides to camera, anachronistic jokes, eyebrow waggles, and his 1957 glasses. There's even a reference to *You Bet Your Life* ("One answer between the two of you!").

When Hyams asked him if he would be using an accent for the role, Groucho replied, "Just my usual Dutch accent," and continued:

> Peter Minuit bought Manhattan Island from the Indians for $24, and if the market keeps dropping, I'll sell it back for less.... Peter Minuit was a Dutchman, you know. That's why they have those telephone exchanges in New York like Schuyler and Vanderbilt. There are no numbers like Goldberg or O'Brien.

For most Marx fans, the apartheid casting has left Allen the target of not always well-meant derision, but the charge is unfair on a number of counts. In the first place, and most obviously, the screenplay gave no opportunity for a trio of characters, let alone one of them mute. And given each scene was based around a known episode from human history, there was no scope to write one from scratch. Second, we simply have no evidence (apart from an ambiguous comment in the ghosted *Groucho Phile*) that the decision *was* Allen's, and much evidence (in the form of repeated emphatic refusals to countenance a reteaming, and a long list of stymied reunion projects) to suggest that Groucho would never have countenanced such a notion.

**The poster for *The Story of Mankind* (1957) seems to want to imply a traditional Marx Brothers reappearance, judging by the choice of photographs. Consensus has blamed Irwin Allen for any subsequent disappointment, but there may be another likely culprit.**

Despite the brevity of his engagement, Groucho *did* manage to find roles for his wife Eden ("an Indian chief's daughter and she's very good; she ought to get a lot of offers from Indians") and his daughter Melinda, in a separate scene, as an early Christian ("an early Christian is a Jew who gets up at 5 a.m."). Is Gummo in the picture, Hyams asked? "Sure," replied Groucho. "He's in for 10 per cent of my salary." Even Harry Ruby wound up on board, as an Indian chief, following a successful appearance on *You Bet Your Life.* "I told Harry ten years ago he should be an actor," Groucho had told Earl Wilson in June of 1956. "He looks grotesque and he sings badly. He's got everything!"[20]

According to Hedda Hopper, Groucho claimed that Ruby concluded the shooting with an elaborate practical joke:

> Groucho told Ruby he was taking the train for Chicago and would fly from there to Miami for his appearance on the Como show. He did. When he got off the train at Albuquerque, there was Harry Ruby still dressed as an Indian chief to receive him—proving how far Harry will go for a gag.

Groucho's scene was in the can by the first week of 1957, but the film did not see release until November, by which time *Rock Hunter* had been and gone. He seemed relatively pleased with his contribution when it was all over, even going so far as to plug it on *You Bet Your Life* when the answer to a question, presumably not coincidentally, was Peter Minuit.

But as usual, his idea of friendly publicity on the set was to moan to journalists about the various discomforts of moviemaking when compared to TV. To Leonard Lyons he explained, "I don't want to be in any business where I have to get up at 6 a.m." The refrain was repeated with elaboration when Hyams asked him why he didn't make movies any more: "I don't want to get up at 6 a.m. and I hate work—particularly for nothing. Let them cut the taxes and I'll work." "I'm a very unusual actor," he told Earl Wilson. "I'm crazier about money than acting. This isn't the way an artist should talk, but I'm not an artist. I'm a racketeer who got into show business." Indeed, money was no longer enough, if the effort required to obtain it seemed too great. "Wonder what Metro was offering Groucho Marx $25,000 for?" asked Sheilah Graham's "Hollywood" column in December of 1955. "Whatever it was, Groucho declined."[21] No surprise there.

By the end of the 1950s, as his seventieth birthday loomed, he began to think in terms of semi-retirement. As early as 1956 he had told reporters of his desire to reduce the *You Bet Your Life* burden to a fortnightly one, or better still to relaunch it as an hour-long show transmitted once a month. "Any comedian who appears on TV thirty-nine weeks a year is a lunatic," he reasoned.[22]

As it turned out he stuck with a weekly schedule until 1961, with *Tell It to Groucho* taking over for just a year in 1962. The new format seemed to have been devised to create the maximum sense of disruption, as if what *You Bet Your Life* had needed was a course of electric shocks. Just about everything that had become a staple of the shows was jettisoned, in favor of elements that in many cases had little to offer besides novelty, as Groucho explained to columnist Vernon Scott:

> I'm doing something entirely different from the old show. We've discarded the secret word, the quiz, the duck, Grant's Tomb and Fenneman. The show is a clearing house, a sounding board for people with opinions, hare-brained schemes and troubles…. Some of the guests will be well known. For instance, Vincent Price takes part in one show discussing modern art—which to me is the biggest fake in history. Another guy is famous for painting pictures with a basket of worms. He turns the worms loose on a canvas covered with dirt and paint. Then he sells the pictures for as much as $1,000 each. Can you imagine calling something like that art?[23]

Groucho's plans to retire had been indefinitely postponed, as he told columnist Hal Humphrey:

> I thought about not working, but the show gives me the only fun I have. I tried travelling, but when I'm in Paris I sit in my room at the George V Hotel reading the *New York Times* while everybody else goes out to some night club…. I went to Jamaica, and while everybody else is skin-diving, I'm in my hotel reading the *New York Times*. Only in Jamaica you don't get the *Times* as fast as you do in Paris.[24]

The failure of the latter show to click as its predecessor had done may simply indicate that audiences had temporarily stalled on Groucho in any format. However, it did, in addition, make two specific and crucial mistakes. First, so pervasive was the assumption that the quiz portions of *You Bet Your Life* had become increasingly superfluous that the decision was taken to pare them down to almost nothing. As a result, that almost subliminal tension was lost, and the show seemed to meander. Oddly, Groucho saw this problem coming as early as the pre-production stage, when he told Hal Humphrey: "I know that the quiz is supposed to be incidental on my present show, but I think a lot of people may tune in just for the quiz. They like to try to guess the answers."[25]

A second mistake was to trade in Fenneman for a newer model: the more decorative but less responsive Joy Harmon, described by Groucho in a letter to Goodman Ace as "a sprightly young doll with oversized knockers who leaps around the stage with all the abandon of a young doe being pursued by an elderly banker." For these reasons and others, *Tell It to Groucho* quickly stalled.

Groucho struggles with unruly cats and an unyielding format in *Tell It to Groucho* (1962) (Stephen Cox collection).

Groucho would continue to work in the years that followed, but mainly in one-off ventures: the closest he would get to a long-term screen commitment was thirteen weeks in London on a British version of *You Bet Your Life*, called *Groucho*, undertaken mainly as an excuse to visit England in 1965. And after a decade of unaccustomed professional bonhomie, he seemed to embrace the tailing-off of his TV stardom as an excuse to reclaim some of the cynicism that had been his accustomed mode of engagement with home entertainment in the years before.

Joe Hyams recorded him in feisty mood, as if readying himself for his exit from prime time, in a profile that appeared in March of 1960:

> "I'd like to talk about the TV critics," he said. "I don't believe the taste of these people is the same as that of the audience. If TV produced shows that only appealed to the critics, there would be no TV. You don't think those people would look at television if it wasn't their job, do you? What television needs is revolving critics—a truck driver one time, a housewife another, a doctor or a railroad conductor. The people who look at television for enjoyment are the ones who should criticise it. If *they* don't like a show, it's lousy."

Did he watch much television himself?

> "No," said Groucho. "I've never seen a western to the end. I hear people talking about Marshall Dooley...."
>
> Dillon....
>
> "Dooley or Dillon, whatever it is," snapped Marx. "They shouldn't allow the westerns or murder shows on television before 10 p.m. when the children are safely tucked away. Now I read in the newspapers they are going to have 30 minutes of intellectual stuff on television every Monday from 7:30 to 8. They're going to educate America. They couldn't educate America if they started at 6.30....
>
> "They can't stop me from talking publicly," said Groucho, "and I must say that in all the years I've been on television I've never met sponsor or network interference on my show.... Most of the old-line comics are so fat and rich, they don't dare jeopardise anything by speaking out publicly or privately. This fright pervades everything ... but I'm not afraid. I've saved my money. If I get fired, I'll put a feather in my cap, buy some short leather pants and go to Switzerland and play tennis with Charlie Chaplin."[26]

# 5

# A comparatively easy racket

"Groucho Marx, burned by an article urging old comics to retire in favor of younger ones, vows he'll do just that after the next season," reported James Bacon of the Associated Press in July 1960:

> By then I'll have 14 years on my quiz show on TV and radio and the public should be sick of me by then…. Maybe that will make the jerk happy who wrote the article and the magazine that was jerky enough to print it. Probably paid him $500 for dreaming up such a phony angle. Since when have I or Jack Benny or Red Skelton ever stopped any comic from working? Have I ever said to Mort Sahl: "Mort, you can't work"? The public keeps anybody working in this rat race. When the public drops you, you're through whether you're 19 or 69."[1]

Yet his decision to retire from television had nothing to do the public growing sick of him, much less stepping aside to make way for the vanguard of comedy. "I've been in show business 50 years and I'm basically lazy," he told Bacon. "Money means nothing anymore…. I've got a nice home in Beverly Hills, a pretty wife, lots of good books to read and a couple of television sets. What am I trying to prove?"

What indeed? Perhaps the only thing he had left to prove was how wide his range: he fancied himself master of a far wider span of entertainment than he had as yet been able to demonstrate. The trouble was that the offers to do so never came from film producers but always from the stage, which meant long runs that were not only nerve-wracking and tiring, but conflicted with his TV work.

Now that he was winding down his quiz show, however, a new opportunity arose in TV itself. Unlike the movies, where the financial risks were too great to permit such tomfoolery, TV producers delighted in casting comedians in unconventional settings. In the first half of the 1960s, therefore, Groucho got the oppor-

**Groucho served as narrator and host for "Merrily We Roll Along," a 1961 episode of the *DuPont Show of the Week*. The subject was the rise of the automobile (Stephen Cox collection).**

88

tunity to do probably the three things he most wanted at this point in his professional career: to film for posterity his play *Time for Elizabeth*, to take a straight role in a drama production, and to appear in a Gilbert and Sullivan operetta. Modern audiences tend to be lukewarm about all three, but for Groucho himself, each was a triumph and a vindication.

## The Mikado (1960)

"I needed the challenge of something new, and I found it in something deliciously old," Groucho said years later in *The Secret Word Is Groucho* of the experience of playing Ko-Ko in a television production of *The Mikado*. "I loved the experience, and if it made new fans for Gilbert and Sullivan, that was ample reward." As he put it to Norman Krasna in a 1960 letter, this new experience would be "screwing up *The Mikado* for the Bell Telephone Company." It was, he explained, "my revenge for the lousy phone service they've given me over the years."

Groucho's admiration for Gilbert and Sullivan was well known, so it is unlikely the idea was a happy coincidence, and, indeed, something similar had been on the cards many times in the past. In 1953 there were reports of an offer for him to do thirteen half-hour TV shows based on the operettas, and back in 1949 he had been asked to do *The Mikado* for radio. Strangest offer of all was the suggestion he might do a short version of it as part of *Your Show of Shows* in 1953.[2] The structural and lyrical similarities between their work and several of the Kalmar and Ruby numbers Groucho sang in the movies had also long been noted, including by Groucho himself. When all finally fell into place, then, it was no big surprise, neither was the casting seen as especially radical. Groucho was, if anything, an obvious choice.

To selected friends he played the usual game of cynically predicting disaster and implying strictly mercenary motives for his involvement. To Nunnally Johnson he suggested the purpose of the Bell Telephone Company sponsoring the production was to enable "a few of the executives (to) get a chance to screw one or more of the Three Little Maids from School" and predicted that "thousands of people will not only have their telephones disconnected permanently, but will also have their TV sets removed."[3] He continued:

> This is a foolish enterprise that I have consented to embark upon, but they're giving me so much money I didn't have the heart to turn it down. I won't get to keep much of it, but I can look at the check as it passes swiftly by me.

In reality, and as usual in direct inverse proportion to the degree to which he claimed otherwise, Groucho was thrilled by the engagement and proud to be involved, and plunged into extensive rehearsal under the supervision of British Gilbert and Sullivan expert and performing veteran Martyn Green.

Green (who adapted the piece and introduces the production on screen) was a lively character who affected a monocle that gave him a pleasantly raffish air and who, just the year before, had somehow trapped his leg in an elevator and had to have it amputated below the knee. Accordingly, his future as a performer was very much in question. In conversation with Charlotte Chandler years later, Groucho's friends Betty Comden and Adolph Green recalled the first meeting of Green and Groucho as somewhat strained:

> **Comden:** He invited us to dinner when Martyn Green was out there. Groucho was so thrilled and impressed with him—he admired him so.

Though Groucho was hugely respectful of Green, he eventually came to find his constant presence on set, in a wheelchair, somewhat inhibiting. In time Green would acquire a prosthetic limb and make a complete return to acting and directing, but for now he seemed to cast a slight pall over the set, scrutinizing all, gimlet-eyed, as the complicated settings and camera movements were blocked out. For Groucho, the experience proved a physical strain of a sort he had not experienced since his movie days, and something of the tension of working with Green can be sensed in the comment he volunteered to Hedda Hopper's column about the experience: "If my Ko-Ko is good, he'll get the credit." He then immediately changed the subject, though plugging *The Mikado* was the entire point of the exercise: "By the way, Hedda, my 13-and-a-half-year-old Melinda is having a tap dancing contest with Gene Nelson on the St. Patrick's day show."[4]

Even his own career, it sometimes seemed around this time, was not as important to Groucho as the prospect of Melinda's. Accordingly, he found her a small but featured role for her in *The Mikado*, as one of the Three Little Maids. (Groucho also wangled room for Eden, but only in the chorus.) Melinda was a TV veteran by this time—she had been popping up on *You Bet Your Life* since age eight—and her unusual charm, somehow simultaneously unaffected and over-rehearsed, had been much noted. Groucho was delighted and, assuming the mantle of mother Minnie, decided that here at last was the inheritor of the Marx talent, and its custodian for the next generation. As a result, he presumed her future lay in show business and gave little thought to any other scenario.

Groucho insisted in *The Secret Word Is Groucho* that he "didn't sense until later" that Melinda was not having as much fun before the cameras as she appeared to be, and in a 1954 letter to Miriam he claimed that his main reason for bringing her on the show was not so much to parade her talent as to soften his own image: "I think the injection of a wholesome thing in the form of a small innocent girl bleating the lyrics of Oscar Hammerstein may be helpful in letting the onlookers know that there is another side to this nauseating character." As Melinda recalled in *Secret Word*, shortly before his death:

When I was very little I had fun singing and dancing and I would have done it in an alley. But I quickly became aware of tremendous pressure. During later times it became very intense and uncomfortable and something I didn't want to do at all. Groucho has his own fantasy about it, which is fine, but he never asked me if I enjoyed it or wanted it. He'll deny that he was a stage mother, but I'm afraid it's true.

When asked by Bob Thomas in 1964 if his promotion of Melinda constituted nepotism, he replied, "Nepotism is when your relatives have no talent."[5] But at the root of his exaggerated aspirations was an entirely genuine adoration. Arthur and Miriam, the children of his first marriage, were in or approaching their twenties when she was born in 1946, and he may well have been guilty of assuming they needed nothing more from him in terms of emotional security; certainly he doted on Melinda with an intensity more typical of the father of a first and only child. Bernie Smith's daughter Lucinda noted the extent of his devotion during the *You Bet Your Life* years, even though a child herself:

My fondest memories are of the times my Dad, Groucho and Melinda would go someplace together. I especially remember a trip to Pacific Ocean Park, a theme park in Santa Monica which is no longer there. Groucho was very quiet in person and he wouldn't attempt to attract attention to himself, though I know we received special service. My father drove us and Groucho and Melinda sat in the back. He really cared deeply about Melinda. I absolutely sensed it the times we were together, and my Dad felt the same.[6]

As Peep-Bo in *The Mikado* Melinda is, as expected, very likeable but decidedly inorganic, and while it is a small enough part (especially in this truncated version), it's reasonable to suppose the clash of style would stand out even to an audience member with no idea of who she was. Groucho, however, was predictably oblivious, telling Krasna: "At a moment's notice she will sing you all the parts—Poo-Bah's, Yum-Yum's, Nanki-Poo's and Ko-Ko's. I only wish I knew my part as well as she does."

Groucho had these and other production shots from *The Mikado* (1960) carefully bound in a special album, a mark of the pride he took in the venture (Frank Ferrante Collection).

Various factors have conspired to make *The Mikado* harder for us to judge than it should be. In the first place, unlike the other TV specials in this chapter, it was shot on video rather than 35mm film. Worse, it survives only as a fuzzy, black and white kinescope, rather than in the doubtless eye-popping color in which it was originally transmitted. (Tempting pre-production stills exist showing the vivid costumes and sets, as well as the bizarre make-up decision to give the Three Little Maids false eyebrows an inch above their plainly visible real ones, wisely countermanded before shooting began.) Further it is made *as* a piece of television, shot as live in gliding single takes on overlit, echoing hardboard sets. It's all some distance from *Time for Elizabeth*, which is shot with cinematic resource and materials, on solid sets and locations. As a result it is a production that, today at least, keeps us somewhat at arm's length.

As an adaptation of the original, still more as an introduction to it, it suffers most from its draconian editing.[7] The biggest casualties are the absent chorus numbers, and some of the most appealingly melodic portions of the score are lost if they do not advance the plot or display the individual characters. In the main, however, rather than only use a few, it opts to retain most of the songs, but in a drastically abridged form (as well as ensuring they rattle along at express-train pace): a source of disappointment to fans and bemusement to new-comers. (Perhaps most incomprehensible is the curtailment of Groucho's beloved "Tit Willow.")

As Ko-Ko, Lord High Executioner, Groucho delivers a performance that sharply divides opinion: this viewer's, for what it is worth, is that it is excellent, given the limitations of the production and of commercial television generally. Ko-Ko is traditionally played by the principal comedian of the company, most famously George Grossmith for the D'Oyly Carte company, and this taster makes one mourn the loss of a full production in which Groucho might have found more opportunity to shine and develop the role. He is suitably lively, his singing is adequate, and his voice and mannerisms are as distinctive as ever. His energetic Charleston during "There is Beauty in the Bellow of the Blast" is certainly impressive, and when he breaks his fan in "Here's a How-de-do," it's hard to say if it is deliberate or not, but it's a lovely moment. He spars well with Helen Traubel's excellent Katisha: her similarity to Margaret Dumont has been much noted, including by Groucho himself, and adds greatly to the enjoyment.

The big question mark hangs over whether there is too much Groucho in Ko-Ko or not enough. It's clearly a

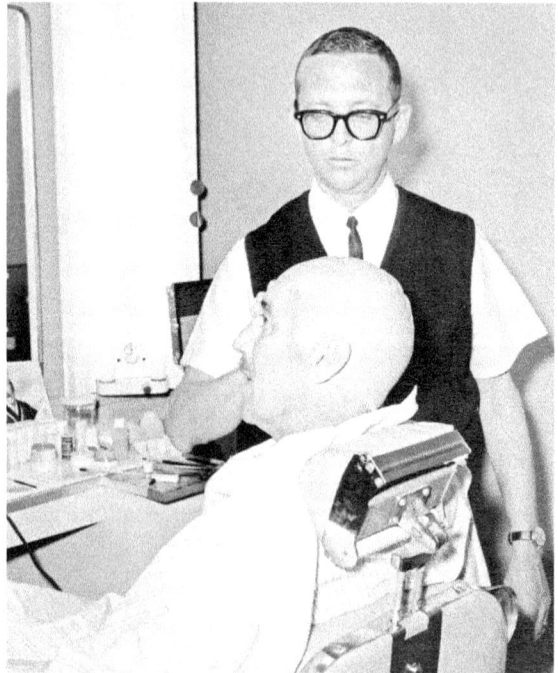

Groucho being made up for his appearance in *The Mikado* (1960) (Frank Ferrante Collection).

question that has been considered and the decision, I think, is the correct one: without compromising or trampling the original this is, essentially, the Groucho we know and—surely—were in almost every case hoping for. But he never breaks character, and while he at one point substitutes "Kansas City" for "Knightsbridge," the production does not conform to the tradition of topically rewriting "As Some Day It May Happen" (a.k.a. "I've Got a Little List," and so delightfully similar to President Firefly's "The Laws of My Administration"). The latter was noted by Norman Krasna in a letter after the broadcast:

> The further reviews of your performance are quite good, and indicate that you could easily have been more Groucho without being sacrilegious. I consider myself a genuine Savoyard and am one of the original booers when the Aborn company interpolated up-to-date lyrics for "I've Got Them on My List," however I would think your patented leer was made to order for Ko-Ko, and the lines and stage directions allow for it…. From a stranger they will take a stranger but from a known personality they must have some sort of a bridge. I conclude, Ko-Ko could have had more Groucho without violation of Gilbert's memory.[8]

Groucho was famously disdainful of those who did not appreciate Gilbert and Sullivan, often singing snatches of their songs on *You Bet Your Life* to better educate viewers, and, according to legend, cutting short a rendition of "Tit Willow" on Dick Cavett's show because nobody in the audience could tell him what "obdurate" meant. (According to videotape, he did no such thing.) In truth, response to the production was as favorable as anyone could surely have hoped: Groucho's ambition was saluted and those who enjoyed such things enjoyed it with only minor and inevitable reservations. But clearly, a Gilbert and Sullivan operetta was never going to be a ratings smash, or the hot topic around the water cooler next day. On its own terms it did well: Groucho was pleased to note that ratings were higher for the second half than the first, and he later told Hector Arce that the telephone people were pleased enough to offer him a return engagement the next year in *The Pirates of Penzance*. Only the critics felt the need to snip: "*Room Service* in a kimono" was *Variety*'s unintentionally fair summation.[9] As what he perceived to be the lukewarm reaction sunk in, Groucho wrote to Hedda Hopper in an attempt to correct the imbalance:

> Either you saw *The Mikado* and didn't like it, or didn't see it and didn't like it. Anyhow, I thought the enclosed telegram from Ed Morris in Huntington, N.Y., might amuse you: "As a Gilbert and Sullivan expert, I consider your performance the best since DeWolf Hopper."[10]

Groucho never quite seemed to accept that the pair's works were a minority taste: if people didn't like them, they just weren't trying hard enough. "I got rid of my first wife with Gilbert and Sullivan," Groucho told Charlotte Chandler near the end of his life. "She didn't quite understand it, and I kept playing it." By that time, however, he seemed to be suggesting, he too had lost his passion for their work:

> I played so much Gilbert and Sullivan at one period in my life, that then I sort of stopped listening to it. It was just too much…. I was crazy about Gilbert and Sullivan and I read everything I could. There are things that are important for a while, and then one day they aren't important. You don't want the same things your whole life. My opinions change. I used to be against capital punishment.

## The Hold Out (1962)

Groucho had been itching to try straight drama, to the extent even of considering an offer from the western series *Wagon Train* before turning it down, on account of his usual aversion to location work too far from his home comforts.[11] But he jumped at the chance to appear in *The Hold Out*, an episode of the anthology series *General Electric Theater*. In it he plays John Graham, a middle-aged father whose seventeen-year old daughter announces her decision to marry her boyfriend and settle down with him while completing their college courses. Graham believes that it would be wrong to financially support them, and risks alienating his daughter permanently when they decide to disobey him. (It is, you will sense, something of a period piece.)

"I always thought acting was a racket and now I'm sure of it," he told columnist Vernon Scott:

> I deliberately looked for a serious acting role to prove one of my own theories. My thought has always been that there are thousands and thousands of good straight actors and only fifty good comedians. When I say that I'm being generous. Actually there are many fewer than fifty good comics around…. Acting is easy compared to comedy. In a drama you aren't being tested on every line. You can talk for fifteen minutes with no reaction from the audience and nobody gets critical. But a comedian has to get a laugh every forty seconds or he's in trouble. I've come to a point in life when I can afford to gamble with my career. I don't have to worry about money anymore. From here on the things I do will be for fun.[12]

"This is the first time in my career I've ever played a serious role, unless you count that last comedy I made," he told Bob Thomas. "They took away all my trademarks. I can't even smoke a cigar. I can't go like this (waggling his eyebrows). Once I went like this (waggling his eyebrows) and the director said 'cut!' He told me not to do it."[13] Groucho does indeed smoke a pipe instead of cigars through the production (he wondered to Nunnally Johnson if the edict was intended "to cripple Castro and the Cuban cigar industry"[14]), wears a dowdy cardigan, and gets just one comic line. (When another character says he was so annoyed he hit the ceiling, Graham replies: "You must have a pretty low ceiling. I told you not to buy that modern house.") But he had more than just professional reasons for accepting the role, he explained to Thomas:

> I think this show has something to say. Too many kids nowadays expect to get married in a hurry and have the way paved for them. I've got a daughter, fifteen and a half. In another couple of years she might run off with some gas station attendant and find out she's living a lot differently from how she did before.

The reference to Melinda was no idle association: following their work together on *You Bet Your Life* and *The Mikado*, the original idea had been for the two to co-star as father and daughter. The idea got as far as a screen test, and it's hard not to be excited by *that* prospect: unfortunately, however, fifteen-year-old Melinda tested as young as she was. (Twenty-four year-old Brooke Hayward got the part.)[15]

It was in many ways a role tailor-made for Groucho. Even if you haven't seen it, you can surely hear him delivering lines like: "Marriage is a very serious thing. It means a home, family, children. It's not just a long football weekend, you know." Indeed, the dialog throughout almost sounds as if Groucho had written it, or as if we were eavesdropping at his own home, so in tune is it with the kind of pronouncements he made whenever an interviewer caught him in a non-iconoclastic mood. It's also highly reminiscent of the occasions he uses his serious tone in his correspondence with Miriam. Take for example this exchange between Mr. Graham and his would-be son-in-law (played by a young Dennis Hopper):

> **Graham:** Fred, the basis of a good marriage is independence. A man and wife have to make their own way. Solve their own problems. You can't be subsidised by your parents without a certain amount of well-meant interference. You won't be able to avoid it. And it'll wreck your marriage before it starts.

**Fred:** Well the thing is it's fine to wait for independence if there's time.

**Graham:** Time? You're only nineteen.

**Fred:** Well, the way the world is today, it's liable to blow up at any moment.

**Graham:** Please, spare me the world crisis! For my father it was a war. For me it was a war and a depression. For you it's the bomb. For your son, it'll be something else.

**Fred:** If he survives the strontium-90 in his milk.

**Graham:** Fred, death is the common hazard and common fate of everything alive. You didn't just discover it.

Groucho told Johnson that he had "tried to play the part in the tradition of Lewis Stone and C. Aubrey Smith, who are both dead, and this may do for me what it did for them." But the performance he gave was never less than adequate, and in moments rather effective. He manages a degree of real poignancy as his family turn against him, leaving him isolated and ridiculous but still determined to do what he sees to be right. The highlight is a sequence where he meets Fred's father for lunch, expecting solidarity and commiseration; instead the two men only just avoid coming to blows. Both Groucho and Fred Clark give it their all here, and the scene is compelling.

The situation is never truly resolved, however, because in having Fred change his mind himself and decide to wait, all the characters go away happy without any having to back down or reconsider their positions. That, if nothing else, reminds you that this is, ultimately, U.S. TV drama. Still, for all that, it takes an unusual subject, casts it bravely, and manages to give opportunities to all. It's not bad—and that's not so much damning with faint praise as praising with due caution.

Groucho hoped the production would spark debate and be controversial; he also, of course, wanted to be admired as a straight actor. Reaction was generally around the cooler side of median, with little evidence of either rapture or fury, though he told journalist Charles Witbeck he had received "a blast from one local critic and a good friend," over the production, but was remaining sanguine. Not everyone felt the production beneath him, however. "I received many letters of encouragement from priests and rabbis. I'll only do a show I feel strongly about and this is one point I'm a bear on—children getting married without any income. I'll fight it." As to his performance, he was content to please some of the people some of the time:

The strength of the amusement world is the divergence of opinion. This is great. That's why I never get angry if people don't like something I've done. It's hard on the actor if he takes it too seriously. You're throwing a stiletto into his ego. On TV, though, it's a little different. It's completely forgotten the next day. To me this is wonderful. You don't have to take it too seriously.[16]

"Acting is easy compared to comedy." Groucho with Brooke Hayward in *The Hold Out* (1962).

Another admirer who was neither priest nor rabbi was Jerry Lewis, who proved sufficiently impressed by Groucho's work to pick up his pen and say so. In a letter dated January 14th, 1962, he told Groucho:

> I derived a double pleasure from watching it—one, your performance, naturally ... two, the delight and surprise that came over the guests in my home, and listening to comments such as, "He's very good as an actor," or "Isn't he believable?" or "I never knew he could be serious." Well, it wasn't any surprise to me, nor do I think to anyone who does comedy, or for that matter, anyone who does anything in our business. It really was a beautiful show, and I was completely enthralled with your warm and tender approach.[17]

In his reply, Groucho said that "the big surprise of my performance ... was that it created so much surprise, despite the fact that good dramatic performances have been delivered by Cantor, Benny, Wynn, Berle and, of course, you."

> One elderly member of Hillcrest stopped me the other day, shook a quivering finger in my face, and in a voice choked with emotion said, "That's the first time you've ever been any good!" I think that dramatic acting is a comparatively easy racket, and I only wish I had discovered this twenty years ago.

## *Time for Elizabeth* (1964)

Few of Groucho's solo projects had as long and convoluted a history as that of *Time for Elizabeth*. It is by any measure a slight work, and yet, when one considers the years over which it was a live project in Groucho's professional career, the time he spent writing it and the time in which spent performing it—a span of some twenty-five years—one could be forgiven for thinking it the most important, personal, significant work of his life. The story of *Time for Elizabeth* is not so much the one that unfolds on stage and screen as the story of its author, and of his obsession with proving critics and audiences wrong and his own estimate of his writing's worth correct.

*Time for Elizabeth* was Groucho's second writing collaboration with Norman Krasna, following their popular but compromised screenplay for *The King and the Chorus Girl*. He explained its origins to journalist Charles Witbeck in 1964:

> Norman Krasna and I were loafing in Ensenada, Mexico. I was leafing through a magazine when my eye fell on an ad picturing a 60-year-old man and a young wife standing in front of a $50,000 cruiser. The caption ran: "You too can do this on $200 a month." I showed the ad to Krasna and said, "If I ever had an idea for a play this is it."[18]

But from the first, the play needed to overcome two formidable obstacles: its hero was middle-aged, with the play's comic observation tailored to the same demographic, and its take-home message is that freedom and relaxation are all very well for a while, but what a man really wants is an office job.

The hero is Ed Davis, the General Manager of a washing machine company, wearying of the obligation and stress of business life. A retiring colleague tells him that he has decided to leave and move to Elizabeth, New Jersey, with his wife: they had long intended to, and recently decided that it was "time for Elizabeth." This sets Ed to thinking; he throws it all in and moves to Florida with his wife (interestingly named Kay), but financial problems and boredom make him realize the grass is not greener on the other side, and after various comic frustrations (his long dreamed-of fishing trip makes him seasick, days on the golf course are spent mostly in sand traps, and the neighbors with whom they hope to enjoy a regular bridge evening don't know the first thing about the game), he maneuvers himself back where he started.

For so slender a piece, it had a fairly tortured birth. "*Time for Elizabeth* was written over a number of years," Krasna told Charlotte Chandler. "Neither Groucho nor I was in any special hurry." When they started it, under the title *Middle Ages*, it was presumed Groucho would be playing the lead role, and Davis's dialog seems at times plainly written with his delivery in mind. Hedda Hopper is certain he will be taking the lead in 1946, when the play was going under the working title of *Garden of Eden*. In *The Groucho Phile*, Groucho blamed "other commitments" for his decision to pull out, and in 1964 he told Charles Witbeck, "It was written for me, but by the time it was ready for New York I was committed to my TV show." But he told Miriam in a letter that he had already decided against it by late 1946–more than two years before curtain up.

In 1947 he tells her that Melvyn Douglas had agreed to take it on: "He seems to be a very nice fellow and I think we will get along swimmingly." Exit Melvyn Douglas. Fredric March was also mooted for a while, and then in 1948 it was announced, now under the title *April Fool*, with Paul Lukas. It finally opened in September of that year, with its more familiar title and the role of Davis in the hands of Otto Kruger.

Major rewrites had been constant: in 1947 Groucho told Miriam he and Krasna had "thrown out practically the whole second act and have started from scratch again." It was, he said, "the fourth time we have done this play, and it's now been ten years since we started it." In February of 1948 he was still telling her the same story:

After his pipe-smoking role in *The Hold Out*, Groucho looks relieved to get his stogey back in this shot from the TV version of *Time for Elizabeth* (1964) (Stephen Cox collection).

> Over and over and over we keep writing this turkey of ours. Tomorrow I start again. We have again rewritten the first two acts and are now off in a cloud of uncertainty on the third…. My feeling about the play now is that it will be a relief to have it open even if it closes the following night. At least I won't have the nightmare of writing facing me anymore.

Then again in June, a week before rehearsals began:

> We have found flaws in our second act and … we thought we had better try to plug up the leaks. It will even be a relief if the show opens and closes. Eleven years is too long to work on a play. It's astonishing how many people dislike this play, but Krasna and I are putting our own money in it as a gesture of thumb-nosing and defiance.

And not small change, either. Each author threw in $13,000—not a sum to be written off with a shrug. But disaster, oblivious to Groucho's playful courting of it, really did strike.

While the play defied Groucho's gloomiest prediction and did not close after one performance, it only lasted eight.

The only issue with the play itself was that it contained few surprises: the idea was perfectly likeable but developed without especial verve, and the ending felt contrived. It was "strictly magazine-fiction stuff," as the *Daily News* put it.[19] (Stefan Kanfer calls it "suggestive of the rigged dialog and pink-ribbon finales of television half-hour comedy.") The *big* problem was the simple fact that Groucho wasn't in it. Whether he had ducked out of the lead at first from his usual reluctance to commit himself to long theatrical runs as claimed, or because he wanted to test his skill as a writer without the safety measure of a personal appearance, it was instantly obvious that casting Kruger had not been a wise decision. As Groucho would eventually prove, with himself in the lead role he could fudge it, and make ordinary lines sparkle with his practiced tricks of delivery. Otto Kruger had not that option. In 1964 Groucho stressed to Krasna that Kruger's performance had been good. "However, the role calls for a comedian, a Jackie Gleason or a Jack Benny or me…. I really think if I had opened in the play we would have been a hit."[20]

Though Groucho had jocularly predicted disaster, as if to muffle the embarrassment should the worse actually happen ("you'll probably be at the birth-place of America's biggest flop," he suggested to Miriam), when the reviews did come in they were so universally bad, and so often singled him out for specific censure, that he lost all composure. What seemed especially unfair to him was not their judgment that he had failed to change streams effectively but their refusal to even let him try. Most reviewers of *The King and the Chorus Girl* had echoed Harold W. Cohen's assurance that "the wolf should hold no terrors" for Groucho if he were to permanently "abandon the cork mustache" and turn to writing. Now they were rallying around Brooks Atkinson in the *New York Times*: "Mr. Marx has everyone's permission to throw down the pen and put back the moustachio any time he pleases."

Groucho was as furious as he would ever be, at least in his working life. One after another he fired off virtually identical, uncharacteristically splenetic letters to Miriam, his friends and the press. All repeat the same refrain in more or less the same language: he was no longer going to set himself up for such treatment, and he had plenty of other ways of making a living. "Let younger fellows takes the whippings," he howled to Miriam, describing the critics as "unfair bigoted bastards."

He granted critics the right to dislike the play—just—but bridled at their reasons. As enumerated in a letter to *Variety* editor Abel Green, these included "because I had co-authored a play that wasn't sardonic, sarcastic or bitter" and "for departing from the character I always portrayed on the screen and stage." The critic who complained that the show contained not one authentic laugh, he suggested either "was stewed, or he neglected to turn on his hearing apparatus."[21]

A play that folds in a week is usually never heard of again, but *Time for Elizabeth*, despite the flimsiness of the material and the savagery of its initial reception, never quite went away. It wasn't so much that Groucho had undying faith in it so much as that he had invested too much (personally and financially) to simply let it vanish overnight. Sheer resentment compelled him to keep it alive, and so he remained committed to it out of all proportion to its certain but slender merits.

One unlikely possibility assiduously pursued was to get it accepted as a movie. Warner Brothers had provisionally bought the rights pre-production for $500,000, but the play's fate poured ice water on that option. The authors persevered, however. When Krasna and Jerry Wald became the darlings of RKO in 1950 (see chapter 4) it was immediately slipped in among the first twenty prospective titles on their production schedule. The title was changed to *Story For Grown Ups*, perhaps to take any residual curse off it, and Jack Benny was being suggested for the lead: he said he hoped to fit it in in the summer gap between TV and radio shows, but the right gap never opened. Groucho, however, remained so intent on big screen success that he pulled the plug late into plans for a TV version as early as 1957. (No shoestring production either: his co-star was set to be either Barbara Stanwyck or Claudette Colbert.) He was still making encouraging noises about the attentions of "two or three (movie) people around town" in a letter to Krasna as late as 1961. But as he recalled to the same recipient in 1964: "The reactions were always the same, "Yes, it's funny, but with the advent of TV, the teenagers are the ones who keep the picture houses open and they just won't go for this kind of a story."

The big news in the meantime was that, in defiance of every sane prediction, the show had come back to the stage and to considerable popular success (though only slightly tempered critical disinterest). The big differences were first: that this was no triumphant return to Broadway but a tour of small provincial theaters where audience goodwill was more or less guaranteed provided the cast showed up and the sets didn't fall down; and most importantly, the character of Ed Davis was being played by Groucho Marx.

He had tested the waters with a two-week engagement in La Jolla, California, in 1952. Stressing that it was an artistic rather than commercial gesture, he told reporters that he was earning, with deductions, $41.12 a week, while his hotel bill for the fortnight was $525. "I just cite these figures," he added, "to give you an idea of what a shrewd businessman I am, and how successful I would have been had I assaulted the world of finance." He started out playing Davis straight, but soon realized where the play's future lay, if it was to have one. "You're playing Walter Huston," Krasna told him after the opening night. "It's fine, but it's not what the audience wants."

Encouraged by the engagement, he plunged into the straw-hat circuit in the summers of 1957, '58, and '59, and cleaned up every leg of the way. Clearly, audiences were not responding to the play: it was Groucho they wanted to see, and the actual context was irrelevant. Robert Dwan, his *You Bet Your Life* director and now director of the play, marveled time and again at "the moment when Groucho walked onstage and the entire audience rose and seemed to say, 'We love you.' They were clearly paying tribute to an entire career, offering thanks for a lifetime of pleasure." As a further concession, Groucho took to following the third act curtain with an appearance on stage as himself, where he would tell a few of the usual anecdotes for twenty minutes. (He had in fact included this element as early as in the 1952 try-out at La Jolla where, he told reporters, it was "the talk of every sea shell from Malibu to Encinitas.") The *Knickerbocker News* usefully recorded the results of an engagement in the 1959 season: "The audience laughed 26 times in the first act, 63 times in the second and 39 times in the third. And never once during the show was there a pie-in-the-eye slapstick gag, or an off-color joke. One man in the audience said afterwards, 'I laughed till tears ran out of my eyes.'"

The theaters enjoyed the full houses and the full houses enjoyed the show, even if the former rarely had much profit left over after Groucho's fee had been paid, and the latter were a far cry from a Broadway crowd. "I hated the matinee audiences," Groucho told Charlotte

Chandler years later. "They were mostly women with hats eating candy." But as the *Sunday Herald* reported of the 1958 tour, there was ample compensation:

> Groucho is getting at least $5,000 a week on the road. It seems that the movie and TV stars who dropped out of the summer theater sweepstakes last year when rustic theater managers put a ceiling on salary are back in greater numbers than ever in fully-cast touring packages. The top price for a name performer is still $2000 a week plus a percentage. But if the box office is busy, which it has been with Groucho headlining in Ivoryton and Westport, the percentage is terrific.

Melinda and Eden accompanied him on the tours, recalling the family atmosphere of his equally gratifying appearance in *Twentieth Century* in 1934. As with Ruth in that play, a small part was found for Eden. She was originally cast in the featureless role of Davis's secretary, but eventually graduated to the role she recreated in the TV film, that of a seductive gold-digger who fleeces elderly Florida millionaires ("all retired, all with money, all in the frame of mind that life owes them someone like me"), who mistakes Ed for a likely catch. And just as Miriam had entertained the *Twentieth Century* audiences between acts with her recitations, so Melinda would on occasion help out as usherette.

Wyatt Cooper, who played Davis's son-in-law, observed to Charlotte Chandler how Groucho tinkered with the script over the run, ostensibly keeping it fresh to offset boredom, but always pushing it further in the direction of outright comedy:

> Groucho tells me about the loss of the money, and then he quotes his father about something, and I'm supposed to follow with, "I'll get a job." But instead Groucho started to ad-lib, and as each ad-lib got a big laugh, he kept adding to it: "I don't know why I keep quoting him. He didn't have a penny when he died." Audience laughs. "As a matter of fact, I was stuck for the funeral." Audience laughs. "I tried to write it off on my income tax, but they wouldn't let me." Audience laughs. "I tried to write it off under 'amusements.'" Audience laughs.[22]

When Cooper threatened to giggle, Groucho would needle him further. "And when I would break up, he would make some kind of personal remark about me such as, 'My daughter married a sex fiend,' which didn't help me much."

It was a Pyrrhic victory: Groucho had reversed the play's fortunes by meeting his audience's expectations, the very thing he had set out hoping not to have to do. "Yet, Groucho was more vain as an author than as an actor," Krasna told Hector Arce in his biography *Groucho*:

> He used to say "Our play is selling out." He didn't say, "Groucho is selling out," which was the actual truth. Soon he was inventing things I'd never heard of before. He once wrote me, "The rabbit scene is the best thing in the play." There wasn't a rabbit scene in the play.

Arce's biography was published in 1979, but it wasn't until the arrival of Robert Dwan's 2000 memoir *As Long As They're Laughing!* that the mystery of the "rabbit scene" was solved. There is a scene in the play (included in the TV version) where Davis balks at a meal his wife has prepared for him, saying that he doesn't like carrots. The scripted laugh comes after his response to her observation that carrots help him to see in the dark: "If I want to see in the dark, I'll eat what a cat does: mice!" Understandably, it did not bring down the house, so one night on the tour a restless Groucho opted to get up from the table while his wife is in the kitchen, and tip the plate of carrots into a dresser drawer. It was meaningless behavior for Ed Davis, but typical Groucho, and the result was instantaneous laughter. Feeling that he could top even that, Groucho asked Dwan if a live rabbit could be procured for the following day's shows. When the play was finished and Groucho was taking his curtain calls, he appeared on stage holding the rabbit, and put it in the drawer with the carrots.

Groucho brought the play out of storage one last time for the summer of 1963, but the gap of three seasons and the fact that Groucho no longer had a new TV series running affected the size of the houses, and he agreed it was time to call it a day. An offer in 1965 to revive it again in a tour of North Africa and the Middle East was, Groucho told Krasna, "funnier than anything we ever wrote." But luckily for posterity, it did receive one final outing: as an attractively made film for television that aired in 1964 as an episode of Bob Hope's *Chrysler Theater*. The attentive production and professional gloss of 35mm film certainly compensated for the indignity of the original script being reduced to 45 minutes plus commercials.

"The die is cast and the deed is done," Groucho reported to Krasna when production wrapped. "I think it's going to be good. We'll see." His public attitude remained constant, however. He told Witbeck:

> It won't be any good. You can't cut a play down to 46 minutes and expect to have anything. Garson Kanin wrote a splendid play, *Born Yesterday*, a big hit, and when it appeared in cut form on TV, Kanin said it was just awful. So I don't expect anything.

The opening section was the principal casualty of the process. In the play Davis's working life occupies all of the first act, which then closes with his being fired and leaving New York. In the TV version everything prior to the move to Florida becomes a five-minute prologue. But Groucho was unused to the similarly abbreviated shooting schedule, as he told Krasna:

> I never worked so hard in my life. We shot 62 pages in five and a half days. I remember the lush days at MGM and Paramount when we all considered the day a triumph if we had one shot in the can by noon. Revue (Studios) operates a good deal like a department store in 14th Street.

Continuity with the tour was ensured by recasting Kathy Eames as Davis's wife. Eames had received one of the oddest reviews of all time from the *Knickerbocker Times* in 1959: "Kathryn Eames, a blonde of indeterminate age, somewhere in her 30s as a guess, plays Groucho's wife. She did well, but needs new suspenders on her petticoats. In Act I the garment made an unscheduled descent of about nine inches. The curtain fell before it did." Also back from the touring cast was Eden (appearing for the first time professionally as Eden Marx, as opposed to Eden Hartford) as the Florida man-eater (a role that would probably have been removed entirely from this abbreviated version if anyone but Eden had been playing it). "Eden is very excited about the show," said Groucho. "She wants to do TV. But we have a surplus of actors in this town, so it's very tough."

Krasna had given Groucho permission

Groucho with co-star and third wife Eden Hartford in publicity for *Time for Elizabeth* (1964).

to do as he pleased with the property but came to feel the TV version was a mistake, telling Arce: "I was against him doing it on TV. He committed me to it and I was far away. Jack Benny wanted to do it. There was a time when Groucho as an author should have been happy to have another actor do it. Groucho used it up himself. It was no great tragedy." Groucho declared himself exhausted after "five and a half days in the meat grinder" but, incredibly, was *still* angling for a movie deal: "If the TV episode is very good, we may still be able to unload it on some gullible producer."

Harry Tugend, the television producer (gullible or otherwise) upon whom it just had been unloaded was, importantly for Groucho, a friend—as was Alex Gottlieb, who skillfully condensed the script. Tugend, formerly Fred Allen's radio producer had more recently produced the Marxes' swansong *The Incredible Jewel Robbery* (1959), while Gottlieb, a writer-producer with pedigree in Abbott & Costello movies and the film of *Hellzapoppin'*, was a neighbor of Groucho's in Hollywood; their 1962 exchange concerning Groucho's garden in *The Groucho Letters* reveals a lively rapport between them.

Groucho did betray one idiosyncrasy during shooting, as Tugend explained to Charlotte Chandler:

> Groucho insisted on having what we call "idiot cards" all around so he could see the lines. He was afraid he'd muck the lines! Which was ridiculous. He'd been playing the thing, besides having written it, but he's such a perfectionist. So I had to do it, and I did it until there was one speech that came along—a rather long monologue—which he delivered into a mirror speaking to himself. It was a sort of introspective thing in which he started analysing himself, and so on. I saw no reason why he should have to have the teleprompter or idiot cards for it, because he had to look into the mirror all the time. So I said, "Groucho, for heaven's sake, will you try it once without the damn idiot cards all over?" He used to make fun of idiot cards. Anyway, I said, "I'm willing to waste film. Let's try it as you wrote it and as you've done it over and over again, looking into the mirror without the damn cards." So he mumbled, swore, and did it in one take, without a single mistake. And yet, you never knew, they never knew what they would do in a play onstage. Groucho would adlib anything at all, and it could throw everyone completely off their cues.

Robert Dwan felt the reliance on cards gave Groucho's work in the film a stiffness that belied his long acquaintance with the material on tour, but Davis is a fairly stiff character anyway, and Groucho rarely betrays his technique overtly. For the most part, he seems relaxed and charming; the performance is a nice change of pace, given that the harassed Davis is pretty much the opposite of the traditional Groucho. (The role gives him a chance to show a little more of his range but without the disruptive break from type that *The Hold Out* had represented.) At the very end he looks to the camera, wiggles his eyebrows and says, "Tell 'em Groucho sent you," and it's a nice moment, almost like a little reward for us, but the rest of the way he is convincingly Ed Davis.

Some of the dialog nicely conveys the pathos of discovering that realizing one's dreams may not always work out how one expects, as in this exchange between Ed and his wife:

> **Ed:** What did you do this morning?
> **Kay:** I went down to the beach and watched the waves come in.
> **Ed:** Were there many of them? (Pause) What did you do then?
> **Kay:** Watched them go out again.
> **Ed:** Well, you came out even on the day.

And some of it is reasonably funny, like this exchange on his arrival in Florida:

> **Ed:** How far is the ocean?
> **Neighbour:** You mean the distance?

**Ed:** Well I didn't mean the width.
**Neighbour:** As the crow flies, one short mile.
**Ed:** What time does the next crow leave?

When they invite their new neighbors round to play cards and Ed offers them a drink, they request papaya juice, sauerkraut juice and prune juice. "Wouldn't anybody be interested in a little scotch?" he asks. "Scotch what?" replies a guest. "Scotch juice!" he snaps back.

This scene also contains probably the film's funniest moment, as Groucho, stood behind his guests, tries to tell his wife that she should wrap the evening up by miming throwing them out, in increasingly violent ways, as she fails to take the hint. In the event, he brings the evening to a close by saying he has to visit a dying friend. When one of the guests offers condolences, Groucho replies, "He's lucky."

Amusing though these occasional flashes of the vintage Groucho are, the overall mood is one of poignancy. It's a story about ageing, and about disillusionment, and about feeling oneself increasingly peripheral, and acknowledging that one is now preparing for the final stage of life. For Groucho himself, who wrote the play in his personal and professional prime, there must have come the realization of how much more of a fit the character of Ed Davis now was.

In his interview with Witbeck, Groucho gloomily compared his life to the misadventures of his lead character:

> My friends are too old to play golf, and I don't play cards, so I sit at home, but I wouldn't care to live in one of those senior citizens' spas. They are preludes to cemeteries. People are very much interested in dying while living, it seems. Soon there will be shopping centres for caskets. Do you know there are only four casket companies in the whole U.S.? How's that for a market? The whole funeral business is barbaric. I think it's awful. And how did we get on this ghastly subject?

It would surely have occurred to him that while he was younger than his character when writing and first considering playing it, he was now visibly older. Groucho's world seemed to be reaching its denouement just as Ed Davis's is. "Where did those last thirty years go?" Ed asks at one point. "I never had a good look at them."

It would be Groucho's lot to continue being Groucho, and Groucho he had to be, almost to the end: no time for Elizabeth for him.

# I hope God doesn't look like that

After winding down his TV series in the early 1960s, Groucho confidently expected his remaining contributions to entertainment to be minor, occasional, and probably retrospective. He'd finally got around to writing his autobiography in 1959: *Groucho and Me*, though light on history and unconcerned with analysis, was a well-written and amusing account that makes a pleasant companion volume to *Harpo Speaks*. Reviews were generally kind, though Groucho was, as usual, pre-emptively pugnacious. "I'm too old and too rich to care what anybody says about either my book or my program," he told Earl Wilson. In response to Wilson's question as to who would play him if the book was optioned for the movies, he replied, "Duke Wayne, of course. Or Helen Twelvetrees."[1]

Content to repeat himself, he recycled still another volume in 1963 from old magazine articles, old jokes and old memories. He told reporters that *Memoirs of a Mangy Lover* was "all nostalgia,"[2] but aside from its iconic title it proved the weakest of all his published works. "Sad to report, the book is an atrocity," declared the *New York Times*. "Who on earth reads books like this? Newts? Or real people?"[3] Groucho told Wilson that he had written it spasmodically: "I have a small portable electric Spasmodic I work on. I can type 122 mistakes a minute."

Finally, in 1967, the compilation of his correspondence he had been announcing as a book since the early 1950s finally appeared. Whereas his attitude to his screen work was usually wryly self-deprecating, his pride in *The Groucho Letters* (edited by Arthur Sheekman) was immoderate and insistently expressed, provoking a memorable riposte from

GROUCHO MARX
**Memoirs of a Mangy Lover**

Groucho on his adventures
and misadventures
as a demon lover,
plus opinions on everything
from polygamy to poker.

This splendidly designed edition of *Memoirs of a Mangy Lover* (1963) was issued in Britain in 1965.

Goodman Ace. "If you think that publishing a book of letters that people have written to you makes you a man of letters," he told the proud parent, "you're mistaken."[4]

Outside this general program of cataloging and summing-up, little penetrated. He agreed to take *Time for Elizabeth* out for one last canter down country lanes in 1963, but most new offers stalled at his doormat. He told Norman Krasna in letters from 1961 that he had been sent the scripts of *A Funny Thing Happened on the Way to the Forum*, "another play called *Young Enough to Know Better*" and "a play from George Axelrod which I immediately returned." (Whatever *Young Enough to Know Better* was, it appears not to have been produced, and since Axelrod had no Broadway jobs between 1960's *Goodbye, Charlie* and 1966's *Star-Spangled Girl* it's possible the latter two are one and the same.) "If I were ten years younger I might have tackled one of these assignments," he explained, "but I am old enough to know better."

Likewise many a legend circulates regarding his being offered a part in Stanley Kramer's elephantine *It's a Mad, Mad, Mad, Mad World* (1963). Several sources tell us he was offered the role of a doctor in the final scene but demanded too much money. Elsewhere you will encounter the claim (sometimes merely as a Groucho joke that got believed, sometimes served straight) that Ethel Merman's role in the film was rewritten for her after Groucho turned it down. Consensus does seem to go with the latter, at least, being a myth, and the jury is still undecided as to the former. Nonetheless, it seems inconceivable that he wouldn't have been approached in some capacity, and it could well be what he was referring to when he told Krasna, in a 1965 letter, "I keep getting offers for … what are humorously referred to as cameo parts in important pictures." The only thing harder to imagine than his accepting an offer is his not getting one.

Instead, there were more superstar cameos undertaken as favors for friends, this time on TV. As "Mr Flywheel" (his last appearance as someone other than himself) he contributed a sweet but somewhat baffling walk-on to a 1968 edition of *Julia* (the friend this time being the show's creator-producer Hal Kanter). And for Sidney Sheldon he made a last minute surprise appearance in a 1967 episode of *I Dream of Jeannie* that was somewhat reminiscent of his scene in *Will Success Spoil Rock Hunter?* Groucho didn't want to pay taxes on his fee for the appearance, so Sheldon arranged to have a state of the art color TV delivered and installed in his house. But when Groucho discovered it did not come with a remote control unit he had it shipped back.[5]

Groucho's professional life now looked set to revolve largely around personal appearances on talk shows, reminiscing and wisecracking with the host. Accordingly, he appeared on most of the hit shows of the time, usually scoring a return invitation. But this was a slightly slower, more serious and introspective Groucho than audiences had hitherto seen. Leo Rosten captured this new Groucho in a somber 1965 profile:

> He is seventy-five and frail (at least he *looks* frail) and the sardonic rasp of the crow in his throat is softer. But he is no less scornful of the inanity of most conversation, the mendacity of most mortals, the heartless slings of fortune, the deadly arrows of l'amour…. At seventy-five, Groucho shows a wistfulness that is aging's sadness. He has gone through dry and tragic seasons, and his letters reflect the long days of a wealthy man who does not like to socialize, does not play much golf, and has lost, through death, brothers Harpo and Chico and many a friend he loved: e.g., Fred Allen. He sees small justification for optimism—in the domestic, international, or geriatric universes. He lives a quiet life, venerates Gilbert and Sullivan and can sing their lyrics by the hour. He also reads more than you do.

There were other, more profound motives for slowing down and taking stock as he settled into his eighth decade. In 1961 his brilliant brother Chico had died. That his card had been marked virtually from the beginning as the one certain to go first, by one cause or another, did nothing to reduce the significance of the moment. He was 74. Asked to comment by reporters looking for a wryly poignant summation, Groucho replied only, "Please, I can't talk about it now."[6]

More of a shock had been the loss of Harpo in September of 1964. Everyone's favorite Marx Brother had failed to survive an experimental heart surgery at the age of 75, leaving a devoted wife, four children and, all concurred, not an enemy in the world. He had been busy to the end: as late as April that year Groucho was telling Bob Thomas: "He told me seven years ago he was retiring and he works harder than I do. Right now he's touring the Northwest making appearances for United Jewish Welfare. I didn't even know he was Jewish."[7] Harpo's daughter Minnie was due to be married that December: the ceremony went ahead as planned, except that it was Groucho who gave the bride away.[8]

For Groucho, these losses forced thoughts of personal mortality and stressed the unavoidable fact that, whatever remained in the future, the majority of his life and work was behind him. He was 74, soon to turn 75. Was that the age that Marx Brothers die?

Even when he made public appearances, the sense persisted that he was now a performer working in the past tense. The contemplative mood seemed to suffuse his two stints hosting the TV variety show *Hollywood Palace*, in 1964 and 1965. It was his first big hosting gig since the end of *Tell It to Groucho*, and interviewers were keen to know if it was the signal of a full-time return. "I don't miss the weekly show," he told UPI Hollywood correspondent Vernon Scott:

> You get lazy very easily. When you've been away from a series as long as I have you forget all about the rush and pace of it all. People write me a good many letters complaining that I'm not on the air. But I suppose that happens to all actors not on television. I may come back to a regular show some day. But don't hold your breath.[9]

Groucho made an amusing variety compere, never more than when the disgruntled tone he used when hawking the sponsor's product on *You Bet Your Life* seeped into his introductions: "She sings like a thrush—whatever that is," "I regret to say I'm now obliged to present a very talented comedian," and "We have a real international show for you tonight. We have all kinds of people from all over the world, all of them without talent." The first show avenged a cinematic injustice, allowing a still agile Groucho to put down a spirited rendition of the Hackenbush song, preceded by a lively sketch in which he appears with Dee Hartford, his sister-in-law and former co-star. The second, from the following year, proved to be something more extraordinary: an emotional farewell to the entire era of the Marx Brothers.

## The Hollywood Palace (1965)

The April 17, 1965, edition of *Hollywood Palace* was steeped in an atmosphere of time passing. When Groucho filmed it on February 26th, Harpo had been gone less than five months, and the episode seems to simultaneously look back and forward, to a past now lost, and a future in which he would play little part.

In the latter capacity, he presented his daughter Melinda, ready now to fly the professional nest entirely as a gamine pop poppet. She performs her single "The East Side of Town," introduced by Groucho as "my daughter the singer Melinda Marx." Afterwards, she joins Groucho for a little banter and a nostalgic duet, but she calls the shots. "I don't sing those lollipop songs anymore," she tells him. "I'm a teenager now."

Bob Thomas interviewed Melinda ahead of the performance, calling her "a brunette with the startling Italianate beauty of a petite Sophia Loren," and adding that she also has a good singing voice ("a fact that might prove a liability in today's world of non-music").[10] Melinda hastens to tell Thomas that she had obtained her record contract with no string-pulling from her father, who, in striking contrast with her later proclamations, she says "has never wanted to put himself in the position of pushing me into show business. He has never been a 'stage father.'" She also revealed something of what it was like to be the daughter of Groucho Marx:

> You realize pretty early that there is something different about your family. You have to learn to take a second look at people. There are those who want your friendship because you're Groucho Marx's daughter, and boys who want to date you for the same reason. All you can do is try to figure out which ones are really interested in you as a person. Then you have to make your own identity.

**Groucho doting on Melinda, his second daughter, born in 1946. He refused to believe she wasn't set for stardom.**

"She's wonderful," Groucho crooned to Hedda Hopper while plugging the show: "Doesn't smoke or drink; can be trusted anywhere. Trouble is she doesn't need me. I need her but some other fellow will get her."[11]

But the show's really big news came after Melinda's spot, as she returned to the stage to announce: "Many years ago, in fact long before I was born, my father did a musical number in a Broadway show called *Animal Crackers*. It became very famous, and tonight for the first time on TV he's going to do it in the Hollywood Palace. Margaret Dumont, who was in the original cast, is here tonight too...."

And so she was, gliding on stage like visiting royalty, to tumultuous applause that almost lifts her off the ground. The gal who supposedly never got the jokes then giggles,

**Bewigged, jodhpured and bewildering: Margaret Dumont re-encounters Captain Spaulding at *The Hollywood Palace* (1965) (Stephen Cox collection).**

double-takes to the audience and simpers like a schoolgirl as the company deliver an edited selection of the show's highlights: "Hello, I Must Be Going," "Hooray For Captain Spaulding" and the African lecture, spruced up with some new lines. "She was terribly nervous, but good," Groucho told Krasna afterwards.

The Captain has arrived again: the jokes still work, but the context is virtually shrouded in the mists of antiquity. Who knew in the 1960s knew who these people were? Who understood the exact milieu Mrs. Rittenhouse represents or the kind of novelty that Spaulding satirizes—the celebrity weekend houseguest, paraded symbol of his hostess's social status. Only those, like Groucho and Dumont, who were old enough to have been there. This was comic archaeology. And of course, Spaulding was the only houseguest: no butler would be announcing Harpo or Chico this time.

As for the imperishable hostess, she never saw the broadcast. Ten days after recording the show, Margaret Dumont died of a heart attack. "It is possible she wasn't well when we taped the show," Groucho told the *Deseret News*. "However, she was so delighted at the prospect of repeating the sketch, she would never let anyone know if she was ill."[12]

First Ravelli, then the Professor. Now Mrs. Rittenhouse was gone.

## *Groucho* (1965)

In his opening monologue on *Hollywood Palace*, Groucho says that he is about to leave for England to make a new television show. He was telling the truth, but what may have sounded an exciting new departure was undertaken, once again, *à la recherche du temps perdu*.

The opportunity to stage a thirteen-week revival of *You Bet Your Life* in London came about because it was British television policy not to import international quiz and game shows. We took Lucy and Jack and Bilko, and every western under the sun, but if a quiz show was felt to have potential the custom was to mount a separate domestic version. The trouble with *You Bet Your Life* was that it fell between stools. Really, of course, it was comedy, it was the Groucho Marx Show. But because it took the form of a quiz, with prizes in cute foreign currencies, it was impossible to import. The quiz itself was rightly deemed of no interest whatsoever, so there was never a British version with a British comedian as host. (A pity— I'd have loved to have seen Arthur Askey give it a whirl.) As such, insular British audiences spent the 1950s in complete ignorance of the program, and as a consequence saw very little of Groucho at all through that period. The BBC expressed an interest in borrowing Groucho for a British version as early as 1958, but as he was fully booked doing the show in the U.S. the opportunity never arose. Now that it had ended in the States, however, British commercial television stepped in and made an offer. As a result the series was made by the independent company Associated-Rediffusion. Groucho told reporters that not only did he have no idea what "Rediffusion" meant, it took him four weeks just to learn how to pronounce it.[13]

The result, simply titled *Groucho*, had been announced at a press conference in London in June of 1964. As usual, the topics under discussion rarely touched upon the matter in hand, except when opportunity arose for Groucho to repeat his now familiar mantra regarding the great advantage of TV over movies: "I wouldn't want to be the central character in a movie again. I don't want to work that hard. I don't need the money any more and besides, what I like about show business is that it's the only business where a guy can sleep until noon."

In addition, he affected to clear up any doubts as to whether he was genuinely the roué he appeared to be on screen: "Why do you think I am staying at the Savoy with all those exits? It's a great place. Fifteen exits."

And he also found time to commend his hosts on what he perceived to be recent developments in British dental technology: "You know, last time I was here nobody had any teeth. Now everybody's got teeth. This is a great advance."

The show that appeared the following year is usually written off as a flop, for various reasons. (To some American writers, unaware that British TV series were much shorter than U.S. "seasons," the fact that it lasted only 13 episodes seemed ominous in itself, and suggestive of early cancellation. In fact, that represented a complete run in British terms and, indeed, a long one: most series ran for slots of six or seven weeks: a combined run of thirteen was generally indicative of greater than usual prestige.) Some have suggested that the fact that Britain had spent the previous decade and a half innocent of *You Bet Your Life* meant that viewers were disappointed by sudden exposure to the format, and to what seemed a jarringly older and more sedate star. Groucho himself blamed culture clash, claiming that neither he nor the contestants knew what the other was talking about for the greater part of the time. (Simon Louvish has suggested that "he was too English for them," before conceding "that might be a paradox too far.")[14] Imported *You Bet Your Life* director Robert Dwan, meanwhile, felt the more refined U.S. network-style humor proved insufficiently dirty for those accustomed to the great tradition of British filth. Brad Ashton, one of the British gag writers, pointed the finger at Groucho himself: "He was just too lazy to learn his script. He read it off a big screen behind the backs of the contestants.... Lots of really good lines had to be cut out of the recordings because he loused them up."[15] And Bernie Smith—like Dwan, brought over for continuity and reassurance—blamed British audiences:

> In England there are two classes: "them that has" and "them that ain't got." "Them that has" don't watch television. Then we got down to "them that ain't got"—all they got is television. And pubs. The men go to the pubs and we're down to our audience, which is a bunch of women who don't have any idea of what's going on. All they can understand is somebody getting hit over the head with a baseball bat or being tickled with a feather.[16]

By far the most popular explanation—that it simply wasn't very good—is belied by the evidence of the surviving episode, which (to these British eyes, at least) is as hilarious as only *You Bet Your Life* at its very best had been. In particular, his supposedly leaden rapport with the British guests is sparkling: all four contestants are alert and funny, and Groucho interacts with them excellently. (Though the funniest of them all is actually an American, despite his cut-glass pronunciation and extreme diffidence: "Are you asleep?" Groucho asks at one point in the course of their exchange).

In the Associated–Rediffusion studios he spoke expansively to British historian and journalist Paul Johnson about the importance of comedy: "You know, Paul, from your own experience that a good cartoonist is worth twenty good reporters. In the movies a master of comedy is worth more than any of the straight actors, because he is much rarer." He also paid tribute to his brothers, implying that without their presence on stage he would not have amounted to as much: "On your own out there, and told 'make 'em laugh'—it's an awesome thought. I said to Louis B. Mayer when he was arguing about money, 'You try it, Mr. Mayer, just you try it for once.'"[17]

The British shows would mark the end of Groucho's association with quiz shows in general and the *You Bet Your Life* format in particular, but there was just one more near-revival. In 1971, producer Irwin Allen, Groucho's friend and oftentimes employer, attempted to resurrect the show under the aegis of Twentieth Century–Fox, again with Groucho in the lead. It's difficult to imagine the 81-year-old Groucho having the mental agility or the physical stamina to hold down the gig, and quite probably for that reason, it went no further than the initial announcement.[18]

But if Groucho deemed the British series a professional failure, he still enjoyed his long vacation. It gave him a long-anticipated chance to catch up with British literature and customs, and to meet interesting people both living and dead. (It was on this trip that he famously cracked an old vaudeville gag at T.S. Eliot's memorial service, shocking some and delighting others.) Eden and Melinda accompanied him, and the family spent many pleasant weeks living in Mayfair next door to Gregory Peck (with whom Groucho went pipe shopping). According to Groucho they were attentively catered for by a couple who kept house five days a week and then, every weekend, bought a hundred condoms and travelled to Ireland to sell them at massive profit.[19]

Of greatest interest, however, was the taste the trip gave him of a new kind of regard for him brewing among a younger wave of sophisticates and iconoclasts. Successive generations of mold-breaking post-war British comics cited him as hero and touchstone, first Spike Milligan and the Goons in the 1950s, then, in their wake, the university-educated satirists that shaped the comic landscape of the 1960s. While in America he was viewed essentially as one of the great old gang, a peer and counterpart to Hope and Benny and Burns, British enthusiasts (who, as noted, had far less awareness of his domestication by TV in the 1950s) homed specifically on the iconoclastic and absurdist elements of the earlier films, and therefore regarded him as a peerless comic radical. Interviewed on stage at the National Film Theater, he received early indication that his work was now being viewed from a purely retrospective position by a new generation, and still coming up hip. He also attended a packed screening of *Animal Crackers* and enjoyed a five minute ovation from the largely student audience—a reminder that not only was the film's long period of copyright exile an issue in America only, but also that when he attended the film's much-publicized American "re-premiere" in 1974, it was less than nine years since he had last seen it at a cinema with a young and adoring crowd.

The important point here is that the

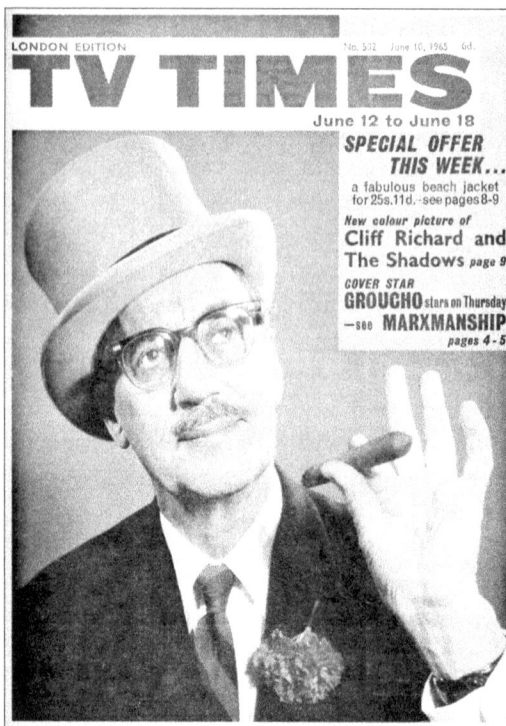

Groucho dresses like an Englishman for his British revival of the *You Bet Your Life* format, 1965 (Stephen Cox collection).

Groucho renaissance did not begin in the 1970s, and more specifically that it did not begin with Erin Fleming, whose influence on his life and career (as both manager and companion) is an inseparable part of the story of Groucho's final decade. Both Steve Stoliar in his memoir *Raised Eyebrows* and Charlotte Chandler in her biography *Hello, I Must Be Going* make the same point (albeit in support of opposite conclusions): that Erin brilliantly orchestrated the Groucho revival but did not in any way help foment it. Though not fully exploited, it was well underway when she arrived on the scene, and it began here, just when Groucho was asking himself if it really was time for Elizabeth. As the 1960s moved into their second half, as America started to drop out and London began to swing, Groucho was suddenly cool again.

He hadn't seen it coming, and for a while he didn't know quite what to do with it. In *The Annotated Marx Brothers*, I quoted an interview conducted as late as 1969 in which he opined that "kids today are detestable," "the parents are superior to the kids they're spawning," and the delinquent minority are "not a minority if they're all yours, and you have to wait for the car to get home to know your daughter hasn't got pregnant, or leprosy."[20] This is so very removed not just from the Groucho of the 1970s but even the Groucho seen elsewhere in the late 1960s that it points, I think, to a genuine chasm of indecision within him as to which of two impulses he should be obeying. ("I never thought the time would come when I'd be rooting for Nixon," he also observed, "but it's better than obliteration.") Groucho, for once rather like his familiar screen persona, seems to have wanted to be a radical in a conservative world. In a world of radicals, an equally innate conservatism came nervously to the surface. Whatever it was, he was against it?

For Groucho, the essential aimlessness of this new radicalism was nowhere more evident than in the arts. Relaxation of censorship, he felt, led to a corresponding reduction in imagination and invention (or, as he called it, "dirty plays"), and he saw little intellectual justification in the related emphasis on experiment and rule-breaking for their own sakes. What he especially deplored, he told *Variety*, were "complicated, obscure, non sequitur plays that make no sense."[21] Ditto the cinema. "Movies today, I can't follow them," he told the *New York Times* in 1970. "The Marx Brothers pictures were pretty simple, they had rudimentary plots. But that *Midnight Cowboy*.... I went to see it and you know what it's about? It's about a stud and a pimp, that's what it's about. I'll take the Marx Brothers pictures any day of the week. I *hated* that movie."[22]

In the November 1973 issue of *Gallery Magazine*, he offered his refreshingly acid take on the oft-made comparisons between the Marx Brothers and the Beatles:

> I saw all the Beatles' pictures, which I thought were bad imitations of the Marx Brothers. I was in London at the time those pictures came out, and I said, "No, these guys haven't got it." I was talking to their director, a guy named Lester, who came from Philadelphia.... I told him I thought it was a poor imitation. There was a composite something about the Marx Brothers pictures that made them so appealing, and what it was I don't know.

The last straw seemed to have broken when he attended a performance of Carl Reiner's comedy *Something Different* in 1968. The reviewers had been unkind and the auditorium was half empty; a furious Groucho rose to his feet at the end of the second act to decry indifferent audiences and pretentious critics. Despite the disruption, Reiner was unsurprisingly delighted by the impromptu soliloquy, and thanked Groucho by letter, also enclosing a recipe for cream cheese cookies "to make this a more exciting letter for you."[23] Groucho responded that the cookies had "turned out awful" despite his following the recipe religiously, "by which I mean

I wore a yarmulke while concocting the dish." On the matter at hand, however, his reply was something of an artistic *cri de coeur*:

> I regret exhibiting myself in the third row at your play. It wasn't done deliberately to attract attention, because I am more or less retired, but it made me angry to see so many empty seats. The following night I went to see *The Birthday Party* by Pinter, and made a speech to the audience denouncing them for showing up. I defied anyone in the theater to stand up and explain the plot to me. No hands were raised so I left. The only difference was the night I praised your show the curtain was up and the cast was on stage. At the Pinter play, the curtain was down so it wasn't necessary to insult the cast.
>
> There's no money in this kind of work, but I've been thinking seriously of reviewing plays from the third row of the audience—either praising them or condemning them as a sort of theatrical public defender.... With the dearth of newspapers now in New York, it seems to me there's a place for a man of my years and experience to give an opinion. At the moment, I am gainfully unemployed and all I would ask from the public is a small unfurnished room near Dinty Moore's chop house, where the Long Island flounder is superb.

For a man whose theatrical experiences were minted in vaudeville and fine-tuned on Broadway in the 1920s, the solipsism and apparent sensation-mongering of the new generation—both of which he interpreted as gestures of contempt towards paying audiences—genuinely appalled him. "I don't belong in this world," he told Dick Cavett in 1969, "I'm an incongruity."

His views on sexual permissiveness in the arts were nothing new; the only real difference was that he was being asked about them more often at this time. (Back in 1958 columnist Mike Connolly asked him if he had read *Lolita*, presumably in the expectation of a salacious comeback. Instead Groucho wittily replied that he was putting off reading it for the next six years, "until she's eighteen.")[24] His opposition to *Oh! Calcutta* (with whose creator, Kenneth Tynan, he had become vaguely acquainted in London, and whose name, for some reason, he thereafter invariably affected to recall only with difficulty) also became widely known. Groucho told Cavett in 1971 that he had been offered a ticket to see the play but had "heard it was filthy and I wouldn't go." George Oppenheimer had advised him to avoid the play in a 1969 letter, adding that "one of the sketches is a goddamn steal from *A Day at the Races*, except I can't remember whether Allan Jones and Maureen O'Sullivan were humping naked on a table in our picture. That's what old age does for you."[25] (The sketch in question was likely the Act One closer "Was It Good for You, Too?" which, according to Wikipedia, "plays like the Marx Brothers at a sex research facility.")

When Cavett asks him if he thinks they might be on the verge of a new Victorian age, in reaction to present-day permissiveness, he snaps back, "Well that wouldn't be so bad!" (A visibly startled Cavett mumbles, "No, it wouldn't.") Again, we see that chasm opening. He had been taken to a production of *Hair* by Tommy Smothers, he tells Cavett, but walked out after the first act. "I'm not interested in seeing naked people on the stage," he explains, "because I can go back to my hotel room...." The audience erupts into laughter at this point, relieved to have been handed a bona fide laugh-line by the hero they were in no mood to see turn into a crusty reactionary before their hip, disbelieving eyes.

In these appearances, when he began to lament permissiveness on stage, indecorous talk in mixed company or the claims of the women's movement (his suggestion to Cavett that "as long as they're willing to take alimony, they have no right to ask for women's lib" may be the closest he ever got to an audibly negative reaction from an audience anywhere in recorded media) one can almost sense an invisible string tightening around his wrist, as "Erin" (for let us so name that bundle of generational certainties that she did more than anyone to ensure he lived up to) strains to pull him backstage and get him back on script.

His uncertainty whether to embrace or reject the more outré overtures he began receiving caused him to turn down Fellini's *Giulietta degli Spiriti* in 1965. A pity: it seems to me there was no better universe for an elder Marx Brother to end up, and I've long fancied that Peppino De Filippo is in fact Groucho in thin disguise. (I could easily see him in De Filippo's role in *Boccaccio '70* [1962], being chased through the city streets by a giant-sized Anita Ekberg.) It's hard to guess which if any of the especially rich assortment of roles assembled for *Giulietta* might have been intended for Groucho: there are few among the "real" characters that seem suitable, so it is possible that he would have appeared only briefly, in one of the vision sequences. (This may have even have been in some expressly-tailored capacity that, once declined, was then deleted entirely.) But the union of Groucho and Fellini is a fantasy I find irresistible. Did they ever meet? A curious passage in John Baxter's biography *Fellini* suggests they did, in New York before the shooting of *Giulietta*, and throws in a decidedly bizarre revelation on top:

> Strolling down Broadway, Marx took him into a sex shop to show him some porn movies. "He himself had seen an enormous quantity," says Fellini. "He said to me: 'You're Italian, yes or no? Then you can't have not gone to see porno films.' He was convinced that Italians spent their life going to see porno films and masturbating."[26]

It's a peculiar claim for a few reasons, not just because this porn-happy Groucho is not one we've encountered hitherto. However sexually adventurous the Marx Brothers may have been in their youth and early careers, there is no evidence that Groucho ever took interest in the clinical observation of others performing the sexual act, and, given what he himself characterized as a perhaps surprising strain of prudishness, strong reason to think he did not. (When Woody Allen asks him outright if he had ever seen a pornographic film in *Hello, I Must Be Going*, when there was neither the necessity nor the likelihood of tongues being tied in the interests of gentility, he replies instantly: "No, I'm not interested. I've seen naked girls.") More importantly, in Charlotte Chandler's book *I, Fellini* she quotes the director nominating Groucho, after his death, as one of the people he would most liked to have met but never did, adding that he had not even heard his real voice, only that of the actor hired to dub it into Italian.[27] Despite Baxter's use of direct quotation, therefore, this makes it difficult to imagine how this New York *tête-à-tête* could have happened at all.

But Fellini, I think, could have reinvented Groucho on screen in spectacular ways, not by simply giving him something radically opposed to type (as in *The Hold Out*) but rather by taking his essential persona and teasing out new depths and angles. He would have seen through to the hollow core of the character's bravado, and done so, what's more, without in any way diminishing the "classical" Groucho, merely adding to the experiences he is capable of offering. If that doesn't sound like your cup of tea, don't worry: it never happened. In fact, it never happened twice. After having his overtures rebuffed on *Giulietta*, Fellini took the interesting step of simply announcing Groucho's participation in *Fellini Satyricon* (1969), along with that of several other notables who likewise failed to respond to the summons, including Mae West, Jimmy Durante, Danny Kaye, Boris Karloff and The Beatles. Groucho was flattered by Il Maestro's attentions, and probably his impudence too, but pleaded old age, and unwillingness to travel.[28]

Between those two offers, however, he did take one chance. *Skidoo* (1968) was the first movie offer he accepted in ten years, and it would also prove the last. For a man who twice turned down Fellini, it is hard indeed to see what drew him to it, other than that it was a lot less work a lot nearer home, and almost certainly for a lot more money. The film was everything he had declared himself opposed to in his letter to Carl Reiner, and had he been in the audience instead of on the screen he'd have risen half way through, and exited in high dudgeon. But for some reason he chose to accept it, as if announcing that a decision had now, however uncertainly, been reached.

## *Skidoo* (1968)

"Every young person in the country should turn on mom and dad by taking them to this movie," a straight-faced Timothy Leary tells us in the film's trailer; "I think this movie's going to turn on the country." And how right he wasn't. When it wasn't actively turning off the country it was being blithely ignored by it, ending up one of the most ill-starred disasters of an age that specialized in such things. Simon Louvish suggests that Groucho must have accepted the role "in a moment of madness." The man himself claimed he got involved only at the express request of Jackie Gleason: "He's a great admirer of mine and so am I."[29]

The mention of Gleason reminds us that this most skittishly progressive of all Groucho's 1960s ventures plays almost as the flipside of an appearance which could be taken as the most wistfully elegiac of all those we have discussed in this chapter. His guest spot on the October 14, 1967 edition of *The Jackie Gleason Show* was, even more than his *Hollywood Palace* stints, an exercise in pure nostalgia. Incredibly, he enters—as he had not done even when reviving Spaulding with Margaret Dumont—in tailcoat and greasepaint mustache before launching with Gleason into a specially rewritten version of the "Mr. Gallagher and Mr. Shean" duet made famous by Groucho's uncle. There's even a laugh line about hippies, the joke being the sheer remoteness from context of that baffling modern phenomenon.

Fast-forward one year, however, and both men are in it up to their armpits. As we are informed by Harry Nilsson, the songwriter who sings the entirety of the film's end credits for our delight: "*Groucho Marx played God in the Otto Preminger film Skidoodley-doo-doo-doo.*" ("God" is an all-powerful crime lord who spends his life in a reinforced yacht with his only companion, the character termed "God's mistress" in the credits, played by the towering model Luna, who would go on to receive an effective showcase in *Satyricon*, the movie Groucho turned down. "I've often been a gangster but I've never played one,"[30] Groucho told the papers before production began.)

The film ends with "God" drifting from the camera in a boat with "Love" spray-painted all over the sails, wearing a kaftan and sharing a joint with Austin Pendleton. Gleason's character, by this time, has long-since dropped out too, having been turned onto peace and love halfway through the movie by unknowingly licking envelopes impregnated with LSD. (Mid-trip he sees visions of Groucho's disembodied head rotating on an enlarged screw, which, as anyone who ever went off their nut licking envelopes in those heady days will tell you, is testament to the painstaking medical accuracy with which the film reproduces the exact sensations of the experience.)

Attacking *Skidoo* is as easy as stealing money from a blind beggar's hat, and perhaps no braver. Harder, I suppose, to find something positive to say. Well, it is impossible for a film this misconceived to be uninteresting. Indeed, if you can grit your teeth through the almost unendurable opening two minutes, it becomes, for the first half at least, rivetingly weird, and in some ways it *is* bold and intriguing. This opening section has more dramatic momentum than might be expected, and the central narrative thread—retired gangster Gleason is smuggled into prison to assassinate another inmate—might fairly be described as gripping. (It's only when it gets to the big twist, and

**God on the line ... Groucho in *Skidoo* (1968).**

all and sundry begin to turn on and drop out, that the whole thing goes to hell in a handcart.) It is also not excessively long—that's the one display of self-indulgence they didn't think of.

And however many things are wrong with it, Groucho is not one of them. As the unseen mastermind, his very absence dominates the film's first half more powerfully than does the contribution of anyone who actually shows up. When he does finally appear it's a true star's cameo, and he *is* effective. This is not the indulged, twilight Groucho of the 1970s: it's a great performer giving an uncharacteristic performance with energy and aplomb. Otto recalled his star to Charlotte Chandler as "a complete professional. He came on time, he knew his lines and he was totally prepared. He was a star, but he didn't overact." (For his part, the star recalled Otto as "a good director. And he's a gambler. Not like Chico. I mean he's not afraid to take chances.")[31]

With a black toupee and dyed mustache—and no close-ups—Groucho evokes his earlier self more convincingly than most writers allow (at least from the fifth row back), and for a man nearing eighty years old, with a hell of a reputation to uphold, it is unquestionably a triumph of some sort. The only disappointment—apart from the way it reinforces how excellently used in movies Groucho might have been throughout this more or less lost decade of his professional life—is that Zeppo wasn't coerced into appearing as his personal assistant.

It is tempting to wonder what effect this exposure might have had on Groucho had the film been judged a success. As it was, the disaster propelled him into damage limitation, and the reclamation of his inner reactionary. "I don't think it ever played in a theater, did it?" Groucho asked the *New York Times* in 1970:

> I saw it one night with Preminger at a preview in San Francisco. I don't think anybody understood it. I didn't. He's a nice guy, but he's not a comedy director. I only did five days' work on the picture, you can't blame me. It had Gleason too, you know. I was lousy. When I say I was lousy.... I wasn't any worse than the rest of the cast. But, they gave me a lot of money and I only worked five days. I played God. Jesus, I hope God doesn't look like that. I think Preminger wanted to make a movie about the hippie movement. That's what I *think*. You know, they wanted me to testify in Chicago at the conspiracy trial. They wanted to bring me in as an expert on humor. I turned them down flat. I'm not too familiar with the case; I was

afraid I might be held in contempt of court. I kept my nose out of it. I told them, why don't you get Steve
Allen or Paul Newman, one of those guys always trumpeting about freedom of speech? ( … ) I spoke to
one of those fellows. Hoffman or Rubin, I don't remember. I asked him how he made a living. He said he
got $2,000 for a book about the case. How long ago was that? I asked him. Oh, about a year ago, he said. I
told them to get somebody else. Their request that I testify … it wasn't a compliment, I don't think.[32]

Two years later again he was even more frank regarding Otto to Rex Reed: "I think he's a big,
tall, fat man. But I don't think he should be directing pictures: he doesn't know a thing about
them."[33]

But there were other reasons for his scratchiness besides creative misjudgment. Melinda,
his chief source of personal pride and the focus of most of his professional aspirations, had
now grown and, as children are disconcertingly wont to do, become an adult. Back when he
was shooting *The Hold Out* in 1962 he had reflected on the production's themes by jokingly
envisaging a day when Melinda "might run off with some gas station attendant." And *Skidoo*
had begun with Jackie Gleason's middle-class existence being shattered when his Vassar-
bound daughter brings home a pretentious, long-haired hippy. (Sample dialog: "If you can't
dig nothing, you can't dig anything. You dig?") For Groucho, life was about to imitate art (if
*Skidoo* could be so labeled).

The prologue to it all had occurred in 1967, when he had grilled three likely suitors on
her behalf in an entertaining "Father's Day" edition of *The Dating Game*. With unerring paternal instinct, he turned down a rugby player and a skydiving motorcyclist before plumping
for "the assistant to the vice president of marketing for a major company." The lucky couple
won a chance to visit William Holden at a Kenyan safari reserve. The two runners-up each
took home a record player and a Bill Cosby LP. (It's probably just as well there wasn't a third
prize.) For Melinda, this was an obvious chance to make her bid for freedom. Having seen
all that Kenya and William Holden had to offer, she began globe-trotting in earnest.

In subsequent months, Groucho joked to Nunnally Johnson that she had been to Israel,
Africa, England, Greece and Paris and would likely turn up next in Vietnam ("in the northern
section"). What actually happened was even more worrying: she didn't turn up at all.

As time dragged on without a word, Groucho hired a private detective who discovered
that while in Israel she had fallen for one Jacques Gilloux, described by the press as "a $40-
a-week clerk in the St. Denis City Hall." Now ensconced together in Paris, the pair responded
by announcing their engagement. The wedding was hastily scheduled for her twenty-first
birthday, but Groucho, true to form and unconsciously recalling the screenplay of *The Hold
Out*, wondered publicly how far those forty dollars a week would stretch: "The main thing I
want to know is can he support her? I've been doing it for twenty-one years and that's enough."
Pressed by reporters for a characteristic bon-mot, the best he could rustle up was: "It seems
to me there is a great resemblance between a funeral and a wedding. There is no gaiety in
either affair." The marriage was first postponed, then discreetly called off. Melinda accused
Jacques of wanting her only for her father's money; her father, asked to comment on the
developments by French reporters replied, "It's none of your business."[34]

Still another engagement followed in 1968, when she took the leading role in a low-
budget movie, *No Deposit, No Return* (not to be confused with the 1976 Disney film of the
same name) and fell for the film's producer, Mack Gilbert. This time Groucho genuinely
approved, perhaps in ignorance of the nature of the film the pair were making, but certainly
aware that Gilbert had plenty of inherited money, and was a Gilbert and Sullivan aficionado

to boot. But to his profound embarrassment, less than two weeks after the wedding she dropped her husband and hightailed with the film's leading man, Sanh Berti—exactly the kind of character who could have wandered off the set of *Skidoo*. With the first marriage quietly written off, Melinda and Berti married the week *Skidoo* opened. (As for *No Deposit, No Return*, it wouldn't see the light until 1972, and God knows what Groucho made of it; most likely it passed him by entirely. Those who did encounter it mostly found it dingy and bleak, even as some scenes seemed to anticipate the high camp stylings of John Waters, though Melinda made a competent and certainly attractive lead. It was also, incidentally, a bona fide second generation Marx movie: Harpo's son Bill wrote the music.)

Baffled Groucho may have been by the frivolity that seemed to typify Melinda's generation in their attitudes to marriage and security, but his own domestic arrangements were on no sounder footing. The 44-year age gap between him and Eden had inevitably widened, and now, 79 to her 35, his behavior was fast descending into cliché. Increasingly jealous, he began baselessly accusing her of infidelity, first with her piano teacher, then her acting coach: the real issue, of course, being the threat they represented of her escape to professional freedom.[35] In 1969 she finally walked out. As was the custom, Eden charged him with extreme cruelty, but as soon as the divorce was finalized the two resumed a close friendship, frequently visiting each other and even travelling together. "I can't help it, I guess I'm a lousy husband," he told Dick Cavett in 1971. "I'm very fond of her, and she loves me, but we don't hit it off if we're married. Now that we're not married, we have a wonderful time together."

In his 1973 interview with *Gallery*, he reflected: "I had ten wonderful years with her, but by then the magic had worn off, and we got divorced. I've been single ever since, and propose to stay that way for the rest of my life. It would be folly, at my age, to start getting married again. I've paid a lot of money in three alimonies. It's not worth it."

A peculiar footnote to the story of *Skidoo* was the assertion by counterculture icon Paul Krassner that Groucho had taken LSD with him shortly before production.[36] The claims were made in a curious essay published in *High Times* magazine in 1981, and repeated in his memoir *Confessions of a Raving Unconfined Nut*. Krassner states that Groucho had come to him upon receipt of the film's script, claiming he was curious to experience the effects of the drug in the interests of authenticity and from a sense of responsibility towards the audience. According to Krassner, they made an appointment at the house of a well-known actress, and the session proved memorable and successful.

Readers must decide for themselves how far they are willing to suspend disbelief, though it's fair to guess that for many that will be until the point Krassner begins quoting Groucho mid-trip: "I never thought eating a nice juicy plum would be the biggest thrill of my life." "I may be Jewish, but I was seeing the most beautiful visions of Gothic cathedrals." "You know, everybody is waiting for miracles to happen. But the whole human body is a goddamn miracle." "That's funny, I'm not even sad." "Everybody has their own Laurel and Hardy. A miniature Laurel and Hardy, one on each shoulder."

The latter observation is curiously similar to an image evoked in Colin Wilson's essay *Consciousness and the Divided Brain* (later re-titled *The Laurel and Hardy Theory of Consciousness*), first published over a year after Groucho's death in *Second Look*, a New Age magazine with which Krassner may well have been familiar. Wilson and Krassner had many associates in common and had been published in some of the same magazines. Wilson re-introduced the bicameral Stan and Ollie in his book *Frankenstein's Castle* in 1980, and again in *The Quest for Wilhelm Reich* in January of 1981. Krassner cites Wilson's writing on Reich in his 2010 book *One Hand Jerking*.

It is relevant that Krassner, pioneer of "disinformation," is famous for his often elaborate published fabrications. ("Paul Krassner Lies Sometimes" was how *Oui* magazine announced its interview with him in August 1975. It also noted his claim to have dropped acid with the Manson family—no mention yet of Groucho who was, of course, still alive at that point.) On the other hand, it is also relevant that Krassner maintains his story today, along with the related claim that members of the "Hog Farm" hippie commune, serving as extras on *Skidoo*, "turned [Groucho] on with pot." Given the unlikeliness of the scenario, and his own reputation as a deft weaver of untruths, Krassner concedes the claims invite skepticism, but stands by them: "The story is true. Understandably some folks don't believe it, but that's not my problem."[37]

"I've never believed it, and neither has anyone I've talked to in his family or circle of friends," confirms Steve Stoliar, who as a young college graduate in Groucho's employ in the 1970s was well placed to judge how far Groucho's flirtation with his new fan base really extended:

> I wasn't there on the set of *Skidoo*, so I can't say it isn't possible; I'm just saying I've never believed it and neither has anyone else who was close to him. Groucho was extremely wary of losing control. He didn't drink to the point of inebriation. He had nothing but scorn for the recreational drug culture of the sixties and seventies, and there was such hysteria back then about dropping LSD and going out of your mind or jumping off a bridge, that he would be one of the last people I'd expect to say, "Sure, what the hell. Gimme a tab. I'll try it!" It's not just my lone observation; I've never found *anyone* in a position to have an informed opinion about Groucho's behavior who thought it happened.[38]

"I think it's nonsense to blame the parents when kids take LSD," Groucho had told an interviewer in 1969,[39] and his weird description of the so-called surrealistic quality of Marxian humour as "kind of an LSD effect"[40] similarly suggests a fairly remote level of familiarity with the point of reference.

Groucho's other major project at the end of the 1960s could not have been further removed from *Skidoo*'s desperate grasping at contemporary relevance. Like most of the other appearances covered in this chapter it looked backwards rather than forwards, but stands apart from them in two significant respects: first, it was an exercise in literal rather than figurative nostalgia, and second, he did not actually appear in it.

## *Minnie's Boys* (1970)

The idea to mount a dramatic life of the Marx Brothers had been kicking around for so long one might be forgiven for thinking it actually predated them. Plans for a movie biopic, announced as a certainty even by reliable Gummo around the time of *Love Happy* only to vanish soon after, re-emerged in 1956 at MGM, this time to be called *Minnie,* suggesting a switch in focus to their much mythologized mother. As before, the genuine quintet were said to be making appearances in linking scenes, but with actors playing the team in scripted scenes. ("None of us want to play it," Groucho told Erskine Johnson. "Harpo just bought a ranch near Palm Springs and he's through with show business. If I didn't have a TV show, I'd move to Palm Springs too. I don't want to work at all.")[41]

The following year we were told that Sol Siegel was to be the producer, the script was completed, Melinda had been added to the cast, and the title was now *Minnie's Boys*. (The double-act of Marty Allen and Mitch DeWood were said to have auditioned for the roles of Harpo and Gummo in 1958.[42]) This plan likewise faded away, but the title must have lodged somewhere. What actually appeared under that name in 1970, totally unconnected to the former project in any other way, was not a film biopic but a stage musical.[43]

The idea had been discussed with Groucho for a few years before it occurred independently to producer Arthur Whitelaw, who approached the senior Marx in 1968. Groucho liked his ideas, especially to limit the presentation of the Brothers to their childhood selves, thus avoiding the risk of overt impersonation, but he was quick to rule out any significant personal contribution, either on stage or behind the scenes. He was, however, officially taken on as a consultant to the production, a double-edged sword that gave the project legitimacy but also allowed Groucho to wield considerable power, such as when vetoing Whitelaw's suggestion for the lead role, Totie Fields, in favor of the more commercially viable Shelley Winters. ("You know," he then told Roger Ebert in the *New York Times*, "a lot of these big Broadway musicals these days, the stars sign short-term contracts. I don't know if Shelley Winters has or not. But I suggested that if she drops out after six months, they ought to get Pearl Bailey.")

Whitelaw had his songwriters in place (Larry Grossman and Hal Hackady) but responsibility for the book proved more difficult to assign. When Neil Simon turned the project down flat, Whitelaw suggested the fashionable humorist David Steinberg. Groucho was keen at first. Earl Wilson relayed the story under the splendid headline "Groucho Picks Hippie To Do Marx Play," quoting Steinberg: "Groucho said he thought I was an irreverent rascal but that my charm pulled it off. Which, he said, always worked for him, too." But when Steinberg's pages started coming in, Groucho seemed to have second thoughts (Hector Arce says he "hated" Steinberg's outline), and he pulled the plug on the idea. Perhaps in hope of a less iconoclastic take on cherished family lore, he cautiously suggested his son Arthur.

Out of all his children, Groucho's relationship with Arthur was ostensibly the healthiest, seemingly compromised by neither the excess of attention that had distanced Melinda, nor the lack of understanding that had caused so many breakdowns of communication with his oldest daughter Miriam. (At this point, and until just before Groucho's death in 1977, Miriam was, by her own account, "in and out of various clinics and hospitals being treated for alcoholism.") Nonetheless, there was at all times a curious scratchiness between Groucho and Arthur, infrequently boiling over into small feuds, the frequent irrationality of which gave them the characteristic of random eruptions around an ever fragile fault line.

Born in 1921 and named after his uncle Harpo ("He's the wealthiest one of the Marxes and hasn't any family so we thought the boy might get something out of it, but he hasn't given him a thing yet," Groucho told reporters in 1934), Arthur grew into a confident, independent and ambitious boy, and a highly ranked amateur tennis player while still in his teens. For a very proud Groucho this was ideal: a satisfying coupling of visible success with clear distance from his own sphere of activity. By the 1940s, however, Arthur had put down his rackets and was set on a writing career. He wandered between gag-writing, radio, stage and film scripts, both alone and in collaboration: Groucho tellingly advised him against working in films. By the 1950s he was moving into fiction and biography, and it is surely only in the context of what Groucho must have seen as an all-too successful encroachment into his own domain that we can make sense of the bizarre consequences of Arthur's decision to write a life of his father in 1954.

His recollections and observations, originally serialized in the *Saturday Evening Post* and eventually published as *Life With Groucho* (or simply *Groucho* in the UK) were for the most part entirely innocuous, and Groucho's approval had even extended to his okaying the inclusion of a series of jokey footnotes to the text, supposedly written by himself but in fact also Arthur's work. As publication loomed, however, Groucho's attitude inexplicably changed, and amidst threats of legal proceedings if the book went ahead as planned, he accused his son of writing a hatchet job and submitted a list of demanded cuts and alterations. It was a bizarre and transparent gesture, and one that Arthur could hardly be expected to accede to. He ignored him and the matter was dropped: Groucho had no real intention of suing his son, and his bluff had been called.

Nonetheless, the experience—revealing as it was of Groucho's insecurity and irrationality both—was a sobering and an educative one for his son. Normal relations were soon resumed but Arthur's display of independence could not be undone, and he ventured to go very much his own way from then on. Groucho noted the loss of control with resignation but, ever the last to argue with success, was mollified by the book's popular reception. Reviews were good, although many noted that the Groucho who appears on Arthur's pages was not always the one they were expecting. In *Saturday Review*, Bernard Kalb wrote that "Groucho is a lot funnier than the book," moving Arthur's wife, the former Irene Kahn (who had typed the manuscript and witnessed Groucho's behavior first hand), to pointedly reply:

> Does he mean the Groucho whom he sees on television doing his quiz show, or does he mean the off-stage, off-TV camera Groucho? Groucho in his living room can be, and often is, one of the sharpest wits I've ever encountered, but he isn't always that way. Mr. Kalb will have to take my word for it—there are times when the book is a lot funnier than Groucho.[44]

Arthur and his playwriting partner Robert Fisher enjoyed smash Broadway success with *The Impossible Years* in 1965, and it had just been adapted into a movie with David Niven, so in that respect securing their services for the Marx show was a sound move. But the freshness of approach Whitelaw was hoping to secure with the appointment of Simon or Steinberg was inevitably lost. The play they ended up with was an odd mix of general fidelity to the true story (or, as true as it is presented in *Groucho and Me* and *Harpo Speaks* at any rate) with a lot of tidying up to make an easier fit with the Marx Brothers with whom the audience would be more familiar. (For instance, the play's Gummo never joins the act; instead Zeppo is present from what was, in reality, far too young an age.) Other touches—such as having Minnie join the act dressed as a giant rabbit—were more elusive in their raison d'etre. "Arthur was too close to the material," Arce quotes Whitelaw observing, "and his thinking was very old-fashioned. He turned out an old-fashioned book."

After more than a month of previews and with the official opening delayed, Whitelaw called in Joseph Stein (adapter of *Fiddler on the Roof*) for some uncredited doctoring, and even asked S.J. Perelman to take a look in the hope of borrowing his expertise. (He declared it "a scalding descent into a tub of such merde as hasn't been seen outside a Catskill Summer camp show," but was otherwise at a loss to advise.) Whitelaw also replaced director Laurence Kronfeld with Stanley Prager because Kronfeld had proved incapable of handling Shelley Winters, still at this late stage giving erratic, undisciplined and ill-prepared performances, with her script in her hands. Whitelaw had considered her inadequate from the start, and would have much rather fired her, but in a crisis meeting she promised to learn her lines, take direction and give a good performance. "All of which she had not done," Whitelaw added. Totie Fields was still standing by and keen, but Groucho held firm.

An equally sticky problem was that Groucho's involvement, contrary to his own demand when first agreeing to associate himself with the production, was becoming increasingly hands-on. A constant presence at rehearsals, making suggestions that were often at odds with those of the director and, according to Whitelaw, "no good and not valid," he also had a habit of insistently shooting the breeze when they were supposed to be working. On many an afternoon, the cast, instead of trying to breathe life into the ailing play, would be found sat in a circle around Groucho, the latter holding court with anecdotes and reminiscences. Whitelaw eventually employed a secretary specifically to keep Groucho distracted and elsewhere; it worked to the extent that he proposed marriage to her.

To the press, Groucho displayed his usual defiant pessimism. "It doesn't make a damn bit of difference, anyway, what I say about *Minnie's Boys*," he told Roger Ebert:

It might be the most brilliant musical to hit Broadway in years. It might be a bomb. There's a big advance sale, but that doesn't mean a goddamn thing. The word gets around fast, with Newman on TV and three or four other knife wielders warming up…. The play won't have *any* Marx Brothers material. We're fooling them. It's about when we were youngsters. I'm the production consultant. That means they give me some money. I'm the guy who's supposed to holler if anything stinks. I'm keeping quiet. If anyone says I had anything to do with it, I can deny it. I might even say I never heard of it. It's got a big budget. Comes to about $100,000 a brother…. Of course, the play is absolutely based on the facts. Ha. It's so good not to be *in* the damned thing. I'll sit there on opening night and keep an eye on the guy playing Groucho. If I don't like him, I'll run down the aisle shouting, "I was *better* than that!" Well, maybe I wasn't….

A week before opening, the young cast, Shelley Winters and Groucho all assembled on *The Dick Cavett Show*. All were buoyant, including Winters, and there was much spontaneous laughter and sharing of party pieces (though Winters makes ominously heavy weather of what she says was her audition piece). Groucho seemed sincere in his estimation of the show as wonderful, and in his prediction of a hearty success. He attended the first night with his newly ex-wife Eden as guest, along-

Lyrics by **HAL HACKADY**  Music by **LARRY GROSSMAN**

ARTHUR WHITELAW
MAX J. BROWN  BYRON GOLDMAN
present

**SHELLEY WINTERS**

in

**MINNIE'S BOYS**

(BASED UPON THE LIVES OF THE MARX BROTHERS)

Book by
**ARTHUR MARX** and **ROBERT FISHER**
Music by
**LARRY GROSSMAN**  **HAL HACKADY**
Production Consultant
**GROUCHO MARX**
Settings Designed by  Costumes Designed by  Lighting Designed by  Choreography by
**PETER WEXLER**  **DONALD BROOKS**  **JULES FISHER**  **PATRICIA BIRCH**
Musical Direction and Vocal Arrangements by  Orchestrations by  Dance Arrangements and Incidental Music by
**JOHN BERKMAN**  **RALPH BURNS**  **MARVIN HAMLISCH**
Associate Producer

Directed by
**LAWRENCE KORNFELD**

**A Marx Brothers show without the Marx Brothers was a paradox that *Minnie's Boys* never quite outmanoeuvred (1970).**

side Gummo and Zeppo, and joined the cast on stage at the end for some impromptu banter and business. It wasn't enough to raise the spirits of reviewers. "Unless Groucho keeps turning up at every performance," wrote critic Raymond K. Bordner, "*Minnie's Boys* is going to be in trouble. Actually, it is anyway."

The commonest refrain was that of John Chapman in the *Daily News*: "What the show needs ... is a few real, live Marx Brothers." "We want to see the Marx Brothers, not the lower case Marx brothers," wrote Eric Takins:

> But we're not given that emotional lift until the very end. Too late. The transformation that puts a curly wig and smashed top hat on Harpo, a pointed fedora on Chico, and a broad, black mustache on Groucho could happen sooner, but the present story holds it back. The transformation could be used as a first act ending, then we would enjoy a full, final act of the zany antics we all remember so well. It would make a funnier, livelier production. But I think the producers still believe this is Minnie's story.

Few opinions could have mattered more than Zeppo's, but the one he volunteered, though diplomatic, was not encouraging: "Although the boys who played us were wonderful, it was hard for me to like it. I could hear Groucho doing those jokes and Harpo and Chico— it wasn't the actors' fault. It just wasn't the Marx Brothers for me."

Many, hoping for skilled impersonations of the comedians in their prime, were disappointed by the exclusive focus on their childhood, and Winters remained a liability. (Whitelaw maintained that she couldn't sing, "but then neither could Minnie," notes Simon Louvish.) The play closed at a massive loss after just over two months.

The players impersonating the brothers, at least, were generally praised, especially Lewis J. Stadlen as Groucho. (Stadlen was reluctant to become over-associated with the role, however, citing Groucho's own career as warning: "He has tried a few other things, but they never came off because people don't want Groucho to be anything other than Groucho. I understand that he has an offer to play Julius Hoffman in a film about the Chicago seven. I think he'd be very good for that part, but he probably won't take it.")

Nonetheless Stadlen was still in place for a tentative relaunch in 1972, this time with Kay Ballard in the lead. "It's a whole different show now," Stadlen told the press. "Kay is a stage performer, while Shelley is capable of doing something one time for the camera, although she's great at that. But Kay Ballard is a singer and a comedienne and ... well, it's better in every way." Lightning again failed to strike, and plans to resurrect it yet again in 1979 with Martha Raye proved to be just that.

Whitelaw remained philosophical, reflecting to Charlotte Chandler: "The real success of the show is it never stops being done somewhere by all kinds of groups." Chandler attended one such amateur production in the late 1970s with both Groucho and Whitelaw. Again at the end Groucho happily chatted with the audience and cast, of whom he opined, "They're much better than we were." "I just want to thank you," said a bearded audience member. "I don't blame you," replied Groucho. "Get a shave."

To a woman who asked if the show had made him relive all the old memories he answered, "Yeah. I wish I was dead."

# 7

# Lighted rooms

"I never retired, except from the late TV talk shows," a seemingly rejuvenated Groucho told Earl Wilson in 1972:

> I've got a new system. I get paid! Why should I do those shows? Those guys get all the money. I have a dog, a cat and a girlfriend—my secretary, who's in love with me. She's given up show business just to be close to me, especially at night.[1]

Which brings us, with the inevitability of sundown, to Erin Fleming.

A little-used Canadian actress, older than she claimed, Fleming arrived in Groucho's life in 1971. He was at that time in danger of being consumed by mountains of unopened fan-mail, and a mutual friend had suggested her as a likely secretary. She soon took charge of every aspect of his life and career, most importantly arranging for the one man shows that, whatever else they may have been, were spectacular affirmations of his durable drawing power.

Her micro-management extended to his dress sense, and ensured a definite goodbye to the sober suits, sport coats and quiet check shirts of his 1950s wardrobe. "Old age has caught up with the once brash and leering funnyman," opined columnist Mitch Woodbury in 1973. "Groucho is trying to cover it by dressing as a youngster. But it is no go. On the Carson program he came on wearing a beret and a white turtle neck shirt. Both seemed sadly out of place."[2] Like many another innovation habitually attributed to Erin, the beret and turtle neck in fact slightly pre-dated her, but under her guidance he would now match them with denim jackets and garish paisley shirts, like a child dressed up *à la mode* by pretentious parents. Erin's admonishment not to wear his trousers too high above his waist—no fashion *faux pas* more clearly revealing of a citizen of the 1930s and 40s—became a frequent refrain as he prepared for yet another night on the social circuit.

Her relationship with Groucho, though of course parasitic, was not so in any obvious, dime-novel way. Though she would be ordered to repay a vast sum of money to his estate after his death, it was not a simple case of rich man and designing woman; neither did she exploit the association as much as she could have done to further her own career. Instead, the commodity she seemed to want most from Groucho was glory by association, to be seen as Svengali and "sexy secretary" both. While her benignity and, ultimately, her sanity would often be called into question, the sincerity of her devotion to Groucho as a professional project was genuine and unwavering. Groucho's old bête noire Kenneth Tynan encountered the pair at Sardi's in 1972, and noted in his diary: "She is so unabashed that her ambition seems almost innocent." Describing her as Groucho's "sexy but undoubtedly daunting young secretary-manager-girlfriend," he writes that she "makes no secret of her hope of making a fortune out of his memoirs."[3]

The belief that she was good for him, turned his life around, and gave him something to live for in his final years is not without substance—at least it wasn't at first. Talking to Dick Cavett in 1971, discussing Groucho's fan mail and their daily routine, she seems disarmingly sweet and likeable, and her rapport with Groucho on the same show is charming. Interviewed in 1979 for Barry Norman's *Hollywood Greats* profile, at a time when she was embroiled in a vindictive legal battle with Groucho's son and beginning to make public display of plainly disturbed behavior, there is a touch of psychosis in her revised version of everyday life with Groucho. Recasting him as a domestic tyrant, she describes a household trained to quake in fear at his moods—a clear description not of him but of herself. Eyewitnesses would later recall her screaming at Groucho, manhandling and even slapping him, episodes that would often leave him shivering and in tears. This and much similar testimony emerged in court, and is detailed at first-hand in Steve Stoliar's book *Raised Eyebrows*. It is hard to read and difficult to think about.

And yet, might it not still be a little too convenient for us to lay blame for all the tragedies of Groucho's final years at the door of one mentally disturbed woman? Should we, his public, who demanded this foolish pretense of agelessness and invincibility, not collectively shoulder at least some of the responsibility? Stoliar likens Erin to the archetypal Medusan wives of showbiz. I prefer to see her as the almost inevitable figurehead of that entire cultural moment, and thus not so much Groucho's Mary Livingstone as his Ralph Schoenman. As with Erin and Groucho, Schoenman had exploited the youth appeal of Bertrand Russell to inveigle himself into a position of influence with the great logician, permanently compromising his intellectual standing. Russell, like Groucho, became little more than a bewildered, wraith-like adjunct to his own fame and coin value. But in both cases it was the public's willing acceptance of the charade, as much as any behind the scenes manipulation or coercion, that prolonged the indignity. Erin was the controlling influence, but it is not too flighty to theorize that if she hadn't come along, somebody else would have done. The zeitgeist laid the groundwork: bad luck merely made the final choice of candidate.

As this book was being written, plans were announced to use *Raised Eyebrows* as the basis of a cinematic film. But what I did not realize until later was that this will not be the first attempt to translate the Groucho and Erin story into movie magic. *Marriage Is Alive and Well* is

Groucho and Erin at Groucho's 85th birthday party in 1975. Looking shocked is Groucho's glamorous cook Robin Heaney. Loitering in the half-light is Peter Sellers (courtesy Frank Diernhammer).

a 1980 TV movie in episodic format, in which a wedding photographer, going through a marriage crisis and given to talking to the camera about it, recalls for us three encounters from his professional life that support the thesis of the film's title. The last of these is truly extraordinary. Stop me if you've heard this before, but it seems the tennis-playing son of one "Manny Wax," an ageing comedian with a mustache and a blue turtle-neck sweater, is trying to legally prevent his association with his pretty young secretary, who he claims is receiving a fortune from him in gifts and financial assistance…

It would be contentious enough under any circumstances, but when you add to the brew the fact that the legal battle between Arthur and Erin was very much ongoing at the time it was produced and shown, it becomes almost impossible to comprehend how they ever got away with it. For the really incredible thing about *Marriage Is Alive and Well* is not just how transparently the main players are based on Groucho, Arthur and Erin but that, in its effort to dilute the complexities of the real story to the manageable dimensions of soap opera, it removes all of the elements supportive of Arthur's case and plays him unequivocally as the villain of the piece. Far from accurately reflecting the complex relationship of Groucho and Erin, Manny and "Lou Anne" simply love each other, and want to marry, as our hero (unattractively named Brian Fish) discovers when he turns up at Wax's house to take a photo for the jacket of his book "An Unauthorized Autobiography":

> **Wax:** We want to get married. We got the license. All we've been waiting for is the right time. Why not now, when we have a wedding photographer who can also be our best man?
> **Fish:** I don't even know you.
> **Wax:** Nobody who knows me would be my best man. They all think my marrying this gorgeous young peach is a sick, dirty thing. What do you think?
> **Fish:** I think it's your business.
> **Wax:** Right! And I think it's a sick, dirty thing. But I love sick, dirty things so let's get on with it! Von Stroheim!
> **Butler:** Yes, sir?
> **Wax:** Call me a preacher.
> **Butler:** You're a preacher, sir.
> **Wax:** Isn't he well trained? No, no, I mean get me a preacher. We want to get married.
> **Butler:** Any particular kind of preacher, sir?
> **Wax:** Better make it a short preacher. I'll be sitting down.

As this sparkling banter shows, there is no question of "Manny Wax" being vulnerable or unable to make his decisions: he's wily and sharp, and, a far cry from the often oblivious Groucho, he attends court in person and represents himself against his son. The son's objection to the secretary is not that she is an unstable and volatile influence in his father's life, but simply that she is a gold-digger. As a sweet old lady watching in the courtroom sums it up for us: "Isn't it awful? His son's trying to prove he's crazy so he won't marry that pretty girl. His son's just after his money. I think Manny's crazy if he gives him any."

Yet somehow this incredible travesty managed to avoid any attention from Arthur or the Groucho estate, even though the latter was incredibly jumpy and litigious at this time. (*Playboy*, which had always enjoyed a good relationship with Groucho in life, was walloped with a suit, settled in the estate's favor in 1978, when its sister magazine *Oui* used Groucho's image without permission "in scenes with nude and semi-nude women," in a pictorial called "A Night in the Stateroom."[4] Compare that minor indiscretion with this!) In the end, all parties come to reason and Manny and Lou Anne tie the knot; Mr. Fish then informs us that they remain knotted to this day. Would that the real story was so neat, so explicable, so reassuringly turgid, and ended so happily.

Back on earth, the Arthur–Erin circus rolled on more grimly than ever after Groucho's death. Of all the terrible, credible claims made against Erin, that she was morally obliged to pay back some $40,000 from gifts and business interests seems to me by far the least reasonable, and her lawyer David Sabih surely made a telling point when he wondered if the same attitudes would have prevailed if she were male. The court found against her in 1983, though appeals dragged on until 1988. By this time she was plainly and seriously mentally ill. For many years she dropped out of sight entirely, suddenly popping up to send rambling letters to those she still considered confidantes, or subjecting them to confused, paranoid telephone calls. She apparently lived on the streets for some of this period. Then, on April 15, 2003, she put a revolver in her mouth, and pulled the trigger.[5]

Groucho's last published comment on Fleming was in the wistful interview with Barry Dillon, conducted after she had been legally removed from his employ and published in June 1977, less than two months before his death. "She was not all that bad," he told him.[6]

If I have seemed to dwell disproportionately on the subject of Fleming, it is precisely because, unlike his wives, she had a profound effect not merely on his personal life but also his professional one, and because it was the precise nature of her influence that explains the professional choices he now made. The most tangible manifestation was the LP record *An Evening with Groucho*, which served as souvenir to one of the most surprising and important developments of his entire career.

## An Evening with Groucho (1972)

"I'm very fond of Dick Cavett, but it's foolish for me to do his show for $250," Groucho told reporters in 1972, stressing once again that he no longer needed the talk show appearances that had been his bread and butter for the previous few years. "I'm going to start getting paid again. In the next few months, I'm going to do one night at the University of Iowa for $6,000, an evening at Carnegie Hall for $10,000, and a week on Long Island for $50,000. Now that's more like it."[7] Groucho would in fact give four performances of his one man show: a test-run in Iowa, then the famous Carnegie Hall show, then San Francisco, then finally Los Angeles. Asked by columnist Vernon Scott what the show consisted of, he shot back:

> I'm not going to tell you what I do in my act. Pay $10 and buy a ticket. If you don't like the show I'll give you back a dollar. Seeing the crowds out there is tremendously gratifying to me. I tell the same lousy old jokes. If they didn't used to be lousy, they are now. But they come and see me. Why not? Buster Keaton, Laurel and Hardy, Harold Lloyd, W.C. Fields and all the rest are dead. Who the hell is left today who can amuse an audience?

Many must have been dubious at the very idea of Groucho appearing all by himself at New York's Carnegie Hall—still more that the show was to be sound-recorded and released as an LP by A&M Records. Unlikely they were still skeptical when the tickets sold out, and a crowd of 3,500 had to be turned away from the doors.

The answer to Vernon Scott's question proved, in fact, to be: not all that much. He simply retold the same old anecdotes and sang the same old songs as he had used in his TV interviews, only now with an unmistakable reduction in comic and physical power. None of which mattered to his audience: the show was more than a hit; it was a culmination and an affirmation. Few political meetings, rock concerts or religious revivals ever evoked such uncritical rapture. The audience cared nothing of the gulf between the frail man reading from cue cards on stage and the one they had really come to see, the ageless Captain Spaulding. This was a date with destiny, for both parties. What must he have thought, that night, as he sat in his dressing room, and surveyed not only his present circumstances but the history that had led him to them?

Launched with a star-studded party attended by the likes of Elliot Gould, Tommy Smothers, Victoria Principal and Edward G. Robinson, the LP proved hugely successful with fans old and young alike. (At the press conference before the LA show, which Groucho claimed he had called "because it was raining and I couldn't think of anything else to do," he cryptically advised fans to buy the forthcoming LP but not to play it.)

It had been a shrewd move to make the show available in sound only. For the audience watching him live, the sheer thrill of being in the same room as a living legend partially masked the reality of his condition, but a film recording would have had no such buffer. On disc, fans were free to imagine their hero, with only the faint, tremulous voice standing between them and the commanding stage presence of their fondest demand. The fragile body, the slow, pedantic movements, the rheumy eyes straining to read the cue cards, the moments of bewilderment ... all of this they were spared.

Though generally promoted as a recording of the Carnegie Hall performance, the LP version was in fact culled from tapes of more than one show. The jumps between the different performances on the disc are fairly obvious: changes in sound quality are quite distinct, with varying degrees of echo and ambient noise. According to the album's credits the disc uses the New York, San Francisco and Iowa shows, but a separate recording has lately emerged of the entirety of the San Francisco concert, revealing a puzzle that begs two questions. First, while it was always stated that the latter was a notably successful show compared to the others, nothing prepares the listener for the experience of actually hearing it. Groucho sounds *vastly* more energetic and articulate; his performance level seems entirely distinct from that of the LP. It is as if years rather than weeks separate the two, and it's so different that it suggests this was not, in fact, used as

**On the road again: Groucho announces his one-man shows in 1972.**

insert material on the LP, and that only the Iowa and New York shows were featured. (The record does sound to me as though two recordings are being alternated, rather than three.)

The second question raised is therefore why the much superior SF show wasn't used as the LP's default performance. Possibly the Carnegie Hall show was felt to be the main "showpiece" of the four and so had to be the principal source—and compared to it, the SF show just presented too great a contrast to be used even in part without drawing attention to the substitutions. If so, a better performance was knowingly rejected (and remains largely unknown): a decision that feels oddly of a piece, somehow, with the Alice in Wonderland world through which Groucho was now helter-skeltering.[8]

But even the San Francisco recording cannot really be considered vintage Groucho, without considerable generosity on the part of the listener. A far better self-valediction is his 1969 appearance on *The Dick Cavett Show*, smaller fee or not. Groucho had appeared on Cavett's show many times, interacting with other stars as diverse as the cast of *Minnie's Boys*, Truman Capote (to whom he proposed marriage), Debbie Reynolds (whom he claimed to have personally inspected to check for the presence of breast enhancements) and naturalist Jim Fowler (whose two-toed sloth he described as "the lousiest-looking dog I've ever seen.")

For the show on September 5, 1969, however, Groucho was the sole guest, and with an hour at his disposal he proved expansive and delightful, doing exactly what he does in the later live concerts—the anecdotes, songs and asides—but just before, as opposed to just after, his powers as a conversationalist began to desert him. With only the occasional interjections of his host to keep him on course, it was, essentially, the one-man show that everybody wanted the 1970s concerts to be. The latter were a triumph in many ways, but perhaps better left to the memories of those who were there, and the imaginations of those who were not.

The last of them, in Los Angeles, had to be rescheduled when Groucho suffered the latest in a series of strokes, though it was at first reported to the press only as extreme fatigue, coupled with emotional distress caused by the Munich massacre (in which eleven Israeli Olympic athletes had been kidnapped and murdered by the terrorist gang "Black September"). Unsurprisingly, it proved the weakest of the four. This time nothing could disguise the truth. The film clips that were intended as punctuation seemed more than ever to be the highlight of the show, and Erin's efforts to inject energy by bantering on stage with the star carried a strong whiff of the grotesque. Groucho had to be helped with his lines on several occasions and his stories meandered aimlessly: it is understandable that none of it was used on the LP. Sadly, this show was filmed, by a TV crew. The quality only barely manages broadcast standard and the show itself, according to Stefan Kanfer, is "heartbreaking." (It was not transmitted until 1990.)

By now, the initial euphoria had given way to the realization that Groucho was simply no longer up to the rigors of live performance, and columnists began suggesting that, point now very much proved, it was time for Groucho to rest on his laurels. Most candid of all was Zeppo, who told Richard Anobile in *The Marx Brothers Scrapbook* that it was "just terrible that he is still working."

> I went to see his one man show. He couldn't remember a goddamn thing. The piano player had to keep cueing him. After all, he had to do something for this man who couldn't remember what the hell he was going to do next. And he was reading the stuff and he couldn't do it well! Jesus, I think he's spoiling a great image. He's just tearing down something it took years to build. Why does he have to do it?

But to the world at large, and especially in the warm air of its college campuses, Groucho was now the last word in elderly cool. ("Why should there be this incredible revival of interest in our movies?" he pondered to a reporter in 1972. "Maybe it's because the kids today think we were attacking the establishment. We were just trying to be funny."[9]) His 85th birthday in 1975 was nationally recognized, and the requests for interviews and profiles kept coming. Unlike in the days of *You Bet Your Life*, when he was partially obliged to reinvent himself as a more avuncular character, his new audience liked him as waspish as possible. He was happy to oblige. (Elaine Tyler May, daughter of his TV writer Ed Tyler, recalled: "I saw Groucho for the last time at a Writers' Guild dinner in the 1970s. He was pretty cynical at that point. I told him I was married and introduced my husband. He looked at me and he said, 'Why would you want to do something like that?'"[10])

One of the odder indicators of his new status was William Friedkin's invitation to make a joke cameo in the rushes for *The Exorcist* to startle Warner Brothers executives viewing the dailies—an offer sadly not taken up.

Scenes from Groucho's 85th birthday party. At the piano is Harpo's son Bill (courtesy Frank Diernhammer).

Another no-show was for British maverick producer Antony Balch, who wanted him for his aborted 1972 version of *The Naked Lunch*. It's unlikely this ever got as far as a formal offer, but, just as Fellini had done with *Satyricon* in 1969, Balch announced his involvement straight away, and included his name in an optimistic promotional poster.[11] All of this is testament to the new, hip image he had acquired. Had he been so inclined, Groucho could again have plunged wholeheartedly into the counterculture at this point: his false start in *Skidoo* was now long forgotten, and his new audience would have loved it.

Nonetheless, he did not plunge.

## *The Marx Brothers Scrapbook* (1973)

The one big chance he did take rebounded spectacularly in 1973. This was his decision to relax entirely his old sense of propriety while conversing with author Richard J. Anobile for his book, *The Marx Brothers Scrapbook.* In the course of the interviews, which appeared verbatim, Groucho talks about how he "wanted to fuck" Thelma Todd and Marilyn Monroe, recalls Chaplin "living in a huge home and fucking all the leading ladies," and describes another acquaintance as "an old cunt." At a horrified Erin's command, Groucho launched a ten million dollar claim against the book, saying that he had been used under false pretenses. Suit was filed and a temporary restraining order placed on the book, halting its further distribution, but as Darien House president Jack Rennert gleefully noted at the hearing, it was already in "all the bookstores in the country."

*The New York Times* detailed the substance of the complaint, essentially Groucho's assumption that Anobile "would substitute words every time he used the Anglo-Saxon verb and participle for intercourse." According to the same article, he regretted describing his first wife, Ruth, as "a hell of a drunk" and "summing up President Eisenhower in one Yiddish word." Incautious references to Nixon ("a cocksucker"), Harry Weber ("a dirty cocksucker"), Truman Capote ("a fag"), Noel Coward ("a notorious fag"), and Alexander Woollcott ("feminine but not a fag") were also cited. We can surely sense Erin's stage-management in Groucho's assertion that, as a result of the book's appearance, "I became ill and had a serious increase in my blood pressure." "I've read of your goings and comings (so to speak)," joked Leo Rosten in a letter to Groucho when the scandal first broke, "and would like to have you talk into a tape recorder for *me*."[12]

Anobile recalls today:

> Until it was released, no one in the family was involved with the book. Arthur never once asked to see it nor did any of the other Marx family members. Only when the first copies came off the press did any of the family get involved to stop the book's publication. I can only assume—I'm giving them the benefit of the doubt—that they really did think it was "scandalous and defamatory" and were trying to protect what they perceived as an asset. Fortunately they failed at halting publication.[13]

The only real charge against the book was that Groucho had assumed his comments would be edited for discretion, but the conspiracy theory grew in the telling. Soon it was believed that he had not merely assumed there would be edits but had been *assured* of it, with the reality deliberately withheld from him until it was too late. It was even suggested that a phony edition was actually prepared and presented to him for his endorsement. None of this had any basis in fact.

For Fleming, however, even these variations were insufficiently Woodward-and-Bernstein, and she became obsessed with proving the transcripts inaccurate, apparently in the belief that a demonstration of error anywhere would somehow cast doubt on the whole. In *Raised Eyebrows*, Stoliar recalls the weary ensuing days as "an exercise in absurdity," as he and two colleagues were instructed to pore over the transcripts, searching for discrepancies. "Now we've got 'em!" Fleming would exclaim, as each irrelevant, trivial anomaly was unearthed.

Transcription errors are to some degree unavoidable with oral testimony (*Harpo Speaks* is no more innocent of them: note Rowland Barber's rendering of Sidney Legendre as "Lejon") and Erin's detective work only reinforced the fact that the truly contentious material was said by Groucho exactly as it was presented in the book. (Ironically, it is in the subsequent, authorized collaborations with Hector Arce, *The Groucho Phile* and *The Secret Word Is Groucho*, that Groucho's text is actually ghosted.)

"There is nothing in the book that is not on tape," Anobile still stresses:

> My editors saw to that. I spent a little over three months speaking with Groucho—usually three to four days a week over that period. We talked a lot—sometimes not on tape—but only what is on tape made it into the book. He was certainly on his toes during that period; a bit slow as one would expect from someone his age. He knew what he was saying. He knew he was being recorded and he wanted to set the record straight. Groucho reviewed the blue galleys—they were the galleys printed in blue for final editorial review; I'm not sure if they have these anymore—and it was the last time in the print process when changes could be made. He did make changes. He initialled each page; crossed out a few things he didn't want, as did I. It went through a final proofread at that time (though there are still some typos in the final)–and after Groucho's and my revisions were incorporated, it went to press.

The truth, of course, is not that Groucho was duped, but that he capitulated to what he thought was the spirit of the age, then changed his mind and tried to rewind time. He's talking dirty to a young guy because he thinks that's what young guys want to hear now. Only the horrified reaction of others convinced him he'd made a major mistake. Nonetheless, the popular notion that the *Scrapbook* was a notorious and much-maligned endeavor is a result purely of the attempts to suppress it. The public at large rather took to it, with all but the easily shocked fascinated to experience so candid a window into the subject. Anobile remembers:

> The floodgates broke after Vincent Canby's good review in *New York Magazine*. The book came out in several editions and even a dolt could see that there was no diminishment of the value of team's work that could be ascribed to the book's publication. In reality the lawsuit brought attention to the book that I am not sure it would have gotten otherwise. For that I guess I should thank the family.... Up until the day the family saw the book, Groucho and I were in contact. Plans were being made for joint interviews about the book. That, of course, all fell by the wayside when I called one day and Erin Fleming picked up the phone to say that the family would not allow me to speak with him anymore. That was the end. I never had another conversation with Groucho, and the case never got to court. Once he passed on, his family ended the lawsuit as they would not be able to divvy up the estate with the outstanding lawsuit that could have evolved into a countersuit had they lost their case—which I believe they would have done, as there was no merit to it.

For the buffs, it quickly became one of the key texts, and remains indispensable for its trove of rare photographs, and interviews with vital first-person witnesses that, had they not been recorded, we would be much the poorer for the lack of. That it contains errors of fact is inarguable, as Anobile readily concedes:

> There *are* errors in the book. It was a book of conversations, and it was always meant to be an overview of the team from Groucho's personal perspective. I had researchers in the States and in the UK feeding me

material that formed the basis for my questions with our conversations. The book was not supposed to be in question and answer format, but as the material came rolling in it cried out for it. I had editors in New York who were constantly checking the material as it was being transcribed. If they came across factual issues that seemed at odds with what others had said or what had been previously published, they flagged it for me to go back to. And I had a series of index cards broken into decades, covering their career, from the early days to the fifties and sixties. They allowed for two things; they kept me organized and reminded me of areas that should be covered, if possible, and because of their chronology they helped Groucho to focus. I was fortunate that I had so much time with him and could use the supplementary interviews I was compiling to jog his memory and allow him the time to think, and finally to respond. As a young and not very experienced interviewer I had to learn to give him the time he needed.

Today, Richard Anobile is far removed from what he views almost as the events of a separate lifetime. ("I am beginning to understand how Groucho felt when I was prodding him to recall some moments and he'd look at me and suggest that it was all a long time ago!") But his recordings of Groucho's conversation—which Rennert threatened to introduce as evidence at the hearing—thankfully survive, and represent an additionally priceless resource, as yet untapped. Anobile again:

I would love to take the tapes, edit me out and leave it to Groucho to narrate their life and times. I only used a cassette recorder for the interviews but the tapes have already been sweetened for the CD collection that is in the Academy Library and I know that with new technology they can be sweetened even more.

He concludes:

I don't have any reservations about the book that we published: it reflected Groucho's memories and his opinions. It reflected an 83 year old man who was instrumental in creating what we understand to be modern American humor, and these reflections are of the whole man, showing strengths and supposed failings—and humanity. I appreciated the support of serious reviewers and was bothered at times when the book was negatively reviewed. But the nasty comments of some other film-book authors never really mattered as I was never a part of their little group. I am the first to say this–I stumbled into the *Scrapbook*. And did my best to make it as good a book as possible. I haven't read it in a number of years but about ten years ago I did give it a read and I still liked it—though I did cringe at some of my naiveté. Given that I was not a trained or seasoned interviewer I did the best I could—and I think that best was a damn good job, if I do say so myself.

Steve Stoliar agrees with Anobile that Groucho was singularly unbothered by the sensational potential of the book, and that the shock and horror was instead registered by influential parties around him. This view is also endorsed by the book's publisher, Jack Rennert, who likewise recalled this turbulent episode for me:

We met with Groucho at his home in Beverly Hills, and he was helpful and enthusiastic about the project. It was after the book was published that I was sued by him, but, in fact, this was instigated by his son. The charges were dismissed, as we had a contract. But although it was expensive, this suit proved most entertain-

**Richard Anobile took this delightful portrait of a contented Groucho during the writing of *The Marx Brothers Scrapbook* (courtesy Richard J. Anobile).**

ing, as the pre-trial discovery was held at Groucho's suite at the Sherry Netherland Hotel, where he regaled us with his piano and wonderful stories. It was worth it.[14]

## Joys (1976)

Since the one-man shows, audiences had seen little of Groucho. His declining health, and his obvious bewilderment at the LA show, had convinced all but the reality-blind Erin that the time had come to begin a decorous retreat from public life.

In 1974 he accepted a special Academy Award, dedicating it on stage to his absent siblings, his mother and to Fleming; the following year he teamed up with a seemingly inebriated Lucille Ball to give someone or other an Emmy. Other screen appearances were limited almost entirely to the occasional talk show, in which he would usually appear waspish and distant. (Though 1975 did also see him in his element, appearing as a judge at the *Playboy Bunny of the Year Contest*.) But in 1976 audiences were given one last chance to see at least an approximation of Groucho in performance mode, in a star-crammed Bob Hope special.

*Joys* is (supposedly) a riff on the previous year's mega-hit *Jaws*, but the only real association comes in a couple of reasonably bright gags in Hope's opening monologue. ("*Jaws* was nominated, and if it wins it'll be exciting. I can't wait to see who hands him the Oscar.") The premise is that various famous comedians have been invited to Bob Hope's house, where they are then mysteriously killed one by one. Several sources, confusing it with a popular sketch on the TV series *Saturday Night Live*, claim the deaths are the work of a walking "land shark." In fact the link to *Jaws* is much more tenuous: the killings are being carried out by an ordinary man, albeit described meaninglessly in Vincent Price's introduction as "a sinister human shark." One by one, the guests all end up floating dead in Hope's pool, until in a final reveal the killer is shown to be Johnny Carson.

Scores of celebrities pass through the special, some doing a bit, some doing a lot, some doing almost nothing. Harry Ritz is among them—the only time a Ritz and a Marx shared billing in the same production. The contrast is startling: over a decade and a half Groucho's junior, Ritz makes an energetic and top-form contribution to the show. Groucho, on the other hand, seems as fragile as Limoges porcelain. In deference to his condition he appears (with George Burns and Billy Barty) in a self-contained insert, and does not mingle with the other comedians in the main section, which was shot separately. He wears a baseball cap in place of the expected beret, and appears baffled but amused by the proceedings. He remains seated throughout, and Burns very much leads and directs the brief exchange of banter between them. "George, tell me something," Groucho says at one point. "Am I having a good time?"

Steve Stoliar (who was present at the filming, and proves it with a terrifying anecdote about Hope haranguing his hairdresser) recalled Groucho's scene in his book *Raised Eyebrows*:

> Personally, I thought Groucho did a pretty good job…. After all, this called for genuine *acting*, complete with remembering lines and reacting to what was being said. It was a far cry from relating a humorous anecdote over lunch or singing "Show Me a Rose" in the relaxed comfort of his living room. Later I sent (producer) Hal (Kanter) a note thanking him for allowing us to come and watch, and telling him that I thought Groucho had come off surprisingly well, all things considered. Hal sent me a note in response, saying that if I thought Groucho had come off well, I must never have seen him at his best. He confessed

that he'd shed many a tear in the editing room fighting tooth and nail to keep even those precious moments in the final edit.

If Stoliar was, as he concludes, viewing the scene too generously, then certainly I would argue that Kanter was allowing the effort needed to make it play to affect his judgment just as surely in the opposite direction. It is what it is, of course. It's pretty clear the scene has been painstakingly compiled using variant takes, and very tightly edited in an effort to make Groucho seem consistently on the ball; even so, there remain moments where he seems to drift off, only to instantly revive in the editing. Nonetheless, he is twinkly and loveable, and his face lights up as he asks Burns, "Remember the old days, when we used to chase the girls?" And he scores a big laugh when the diminutive Barty suddenly enters doing an eccentric impersonation of the movie Groucho, whereupon the real thing perfectly deadpans: "That's me as a young boy."

Never say die: A year before *Joys*, Groucho greets Bob Hope at his 85th birthday party (photograph courtesy Frank Diernhammer).

## *Beds* (1976)

"You know, I don't believe in religion, or the hereafter," Groucho told the *New York Times* in 1970. "Not at all. I discussed the subject with Chico and Harpo a couple of years before they died. They said they'd get in touch with me if there were a hereafter. But you know what? I never heard a word. Not a goddamn word."[15]

And so on August 19, 1977, as it must to all men, death came to Julius Henry "Groucho" Marx.

The man who had attributed his ailing condition to "too many birthdays"[16] was, numerically speaking, eighty-six years old. But in terms of lifetime lived, he was much older than that. He had spanned two centuries—a Victorian who had seen men walk on the moon. He survived vaudeville, Broadway, silent movies, talking movies, singing movies, television, two world wars and Vietnam. He *remembered* the Spanish-American war, *performed* at a benefit for the victims of the San Francisco earthquake … and still, somehow, released a hit LP in the 1970s that sat in thousands of record racks between Led Zeppelin and Nektar. This was the end of much more than merely an era.

*Beds*, the last appearance Groucho made before a film camera, was shot in 1976, but the finished product, which is haunting and beautiful, and sweet, and poignant, gently funny, and redolently nostalgic, feels like a conscious preparation for that final moment, requesting our acceptance of it, our permission. Groucho will only die if we let him.

In actuality, it is a three and a half minute promo for the paperback reissue of his and Sheekman's 1930 book of the same name. Groucho is, appropriately enough, in bed. He's wearing pajamas, his beret, and a big bow-tie. He looks like the ghost of a kindly clown.

George Fenneman is with him, sat on the bed, interviewing him about the book. Groucho frequently smiles in a beguilingly natural way, and we realize just how rarely we've had a chance to see that in his long career. The mention of his headboard, made from the doors of a nineteenth-century circus wagon, prompts a rambling memory of his grandparents. There are some pretty good scripted jokes, and, I think, an ad lib or two. Fenneman's deep affection for the man is touchingly obvious, and his constant, non-genuine laughter is no less infectious for being so plainly voluntary. Groucho's voice rarely rises above a whisper.

> "Why did you write a book on beds?"
> "Because I had a lead pencil and I didn't know what to do with it."
> "I'm not sure that our viewers are aware that you are a man of letters."
> "Yes, letters and tomatoes."
> "What do you think your readers will get from the book?"
> "Probably a good night's sleep."

"Perhaps being old is having lighted rooms inside your head, and people in them, acting," wrote Philip Larkin. "People you know, yet can't quite name; each looms like a deep loss restored."

Here Groucho seems, finally, happy in his lighted room. Every few seconds he returns to us, makes an observation in his tiny, soft voice, then withdraws to his room again. Eventually, he will stay there. We must remember him here, like this: drifting between memories, dredging old jokes from deep storage, a good friend by his side.

The indelible impression that *Beds* leaves is of a great comedian and a great man, old now, and tired, contentedly preparing to sleep.

# Afterword[1]

If an old man is the sum of his memories, a dead man is the sum of other's.

Our duty, then, is to acquire as many memories as possible, and to keep them all alive in their progenitor's stead, to let as few as possible be unheard, or to drift away. With a man like Groucho, the temptation to assume that the memory pool *must* now be dry may seem overwhelming, but we should keep our ears open, all the same.

And we should remember, as I warned at the beginning of this book, to always bear in mind the distinction between "Groucho" (a figure of fantasy), Groucho (a performer, intent on perpetuating "Groucho" as a living presence) and Julius (the real man, hiding in the shadows cast by the other two).

Julius is glimpsed only occasionally in the public record, but it is Julius that we should be keenest to get to know more of, especially if there lurk among us lofty biographers, aiming to pass judgment. Alas, like Captain Spaulding, one of the many costumes behind which he hides, no sooner have we met him than he must be going, pushing Groucho to the forefront in his place. When you hear a Groucho story you've not heard before, it's like discovering an artifact on an archaeological dig. When it's a great story it's like finding buried treasure. When it's a great *Julius* story, it's like finding King Tut.

At the beginning of this book I said that Groucho was basically a good man, and that he had a natural passion for justice. Here is a story I was told some considerable time *after* writing those words.

In the early 1950s, the child actress Lesley-Marie Colburn lived in the same street as Groucho in Beverly Hills. By this time divorced from Kay, and just before his marriage to Eden, he shared the house with the young Melinda: this is the period of his life captured in the well-known *Person to Person* interview with Ed Murrow. Lesley-Marie was friendly with Melinda (they would later appear together in the movie *Bye Bye Birdie* in 1963) and would often be greeted by Groucho with the friendly growl, "Hey, kiddo!"

Lesley-Marie's mother employed a young woman called Florence as live-in domestic help, and (uncommonly for the time) did not oblige her to wear a uniform. One evening, Florence left the house briefly to walk to the mailbox, when two police officers pulled up and asked her what she was doing. The Beverly Hills Police Department at this time not only had a stated policy of stopping and questioning blacks without cause (on the assumption that they would not be residents of the area and, in their eyes therefore, potential criminals) but even imposed an unofficial curfew in the evenings. "We're sorry," they told her on seeing that she was carrying an envelope of money, "but you'll have to get in the car. We don't know you."

They frogmarched her to their vehicle and demanded she tell them where she lived, but given her casual manner of dress (she was also visibly pregnant), they refused to believe her answer. On arriving at the address, Leslie-Marie quickly confirmed that Florence lived with her. But the police told her that they could not rely on the word of a minor, and that they would still have to take her to the station. Panicked, the child ran into the street and jumped into the back of the car, shouting, "She's my friend and she doesn't want to go alone!"

A parked patrol car was a relatively unusual sight outside a Beverly Hills residence, and at that point the owner of the opposite house appeared, disturbed by the commotion.

"What's going on here?" demanded the beloved TV star. As he did so, he saw the occupant of the vehicle, and asked, "Where are you going, Florence?" Sobbing, she replied that she didn't know. "Then I'm going too!" he exclaimed as he pulled open the car door and got in.

"Mr. Marx," the officer warned him, "this has nothing to do with you."

"Yes it does," he told them, "this woman works for me too, on weekends."

"She was ignoring the curfew," the police continued, "It's our policy to take her to the station and make a record of it."

"Then book me too—I'm ignoring your curfew!"

"You're a householder, Mr. Marx. And you're not colored."

"Well I'm Jewish! What's the damned difference? If she's not safe to be in the street, neither am I!"

The stalemate was ended only with the exchanging of money—Groucho's, in cash—after which the police agreed, this time, to let the miscreant off with a warning.

After they had driven away, he invited both neighbors into his house. He mixed cocktails for himself and Florence and poured Leslie-Marie a Hawaiian Punch, and the three drank together. "Don't you ever worry about this," he said, turning to Florence. "It will never happen again."

Fragments of unfamiliar, perhaps surprising testimony such as these are the lightning flashes by which we briefly glimpse a man we'd like to know better than we do. Clearly, this was not any kind of public performance. It was not "Groucho Marx." There were no reporters there. There were no cameras. He had nothing to gain from his actions, and he could well have made trouble for himself. And he never publicly told the story himself. As far as he would have presumed, there wasn't anybody present that his gesture would have even particularly impressed. (But, luckily, there was: a child who never forgot what she saw.)

This is the genuine article. This is Julius Henry Marx, at his home in Beverly Hills, one late afternoon in 1954, lit briefly by the lightning flash of memory.

A good man?

You bet your life.

# Appendix I

# Evenings with Groucho

*by Matthew Coniam*

And so, as I settle into my seat in April of 2016, in eager anticipation of Frank Ferrante's live show *An Evening with Groucho*, it would seem that Groucho *has* endured, after all.

As the fortieth anniversary of his death approaches, he remains among the select few golden age Hollywood personalities to retain a cultural afterlife, divorced from their work. Just as everyone knows who Chaplin was, even if they have not seen a single one of his films, Groucho's name has held its ground, and remains accessible to non-specialists, somewhat in the manner of Garbo, or Bogart, or Valentino. The face, too, is still alive, even if not identified. "Which Marx Brother played the piano?" may be for most a distinctly fiendish trivia question, but thousands of kids will be laughing as they put on their "Groucho glasses" today, same as yesterday, and tomorrow.

More importantly, he remains a *viable* comedic presence. The various obstacles a Marx Brothers movie might present to a modern audience—the obscure references, the old-fashioned music, the sappy subplots, that oh-so-daunting monochrome—do not apply to the specific matter of Groucho's style of comedy, which remains refreshingly modern in its iconoclasm, sarcasm, savagery and fearlessness. Groucho in attack mode, even though fenced within the limits of a Hays-era phrasebook, would work every bit as well to a modern audience, and in a modern context, as he did to and in his own.

It is the confrontational element, the sense that he not merely entertains but engages with and challenges his audience and surroundings, which gives him that continued potential as a live comic presence denied more sedate and self-contained acts. The idea of Laurel and Hardy lookalikes touring a live show based on their routines, though perhaps a charming one, is distinctly unlikely. Groucho, on the other hand, is revived frequently, and in the presence of Frank Ferrante, has been entirely resurrected as a live comedy act, one that is not only still breathing but still developing.

It has been my great pleasure to get to know several professional Grouchos: Ferrante, George Bettinger, Noah Diamond, Michael Roberts. All are delightful fellows, and all take very seriously their responsibilities as custodians of the legacy. But what sets them apart from mere impersonators is that they are all comedians in their own right. They have to be: Groucho is not a role that can be conveyed through slavish imitation, by immaculately learned lines and mastered delivery. The modern Groucho must be a living commodity, alert to all around him, he must have the freedom and the ability to break off, change direction, comment and ad lib.

The audience wants to know that if, say, an actor fluffs a line, Groucho is not going to stand there silently while they try again, but will rather leap in and milk the moment for its full comic potential. Roberts, for example, found that audiences for the BBC radio remakes of *Flywheel, Shyster and Flywheel* responded as much to his spontaneous interjections as to the carefully crafted authentic material being delivered. Audiences demand this of Groucho: it's part of the role, and in such moments a museum piece becomes a live act. And it's the reason why Ferrante has been able to develop a live show that can tour America and the world, and to which people return time and again. Only Groucho could enable that.

Watching *An Evening with Groucho* as part of a Marx Brothers weekend I had organized in England was a unique experience. (Precious few vintage comedy festival programmers have the liberty to include the subject himself on the bill!) It is, in effect, three separate shows. The basic structure is that of Groucho reminiscing about his career: as such it serves as a potted history of the man and his art that is invaluable to audiences unfamiliar with the details. Then, studded within that are the highlights of that career: the songs and routines, the African lecture, *Lydia*, and all the other expected bits of classic Grouchiana. But it is the third layer that makes it exciting. This is the all-new Groucho, brought supernaturally back to entirely unpredictable vitality before our eyes. This "living" Groucho is an *observer*, same as the audience. He watches the performance, comments on it, plays with it and frequently stops it completely to follow some entirely new tangent, or to jump from the stage and converse with the audience. And this is where Ferrante's decades of living this role really assert themselves.

From the first, no doubt, he was an able mimic of the man - he must have been, to have caught the eye of Arthur Marx, who cast him in the play *Groucho, a Life in Revue* (a more tightly scripted and comprehensive piece, of which the current show is a direct if increasingly independent heir). Now, however, we sense we are watching not a performance so much as the free exercise of an alternative personality, living within the outer man. I had privately noted the ease with which Groucho seems to come and go in Frank's off-stage conversation: if the moment calls for Groucho he duly appears, only to then disappear until summoned again by some impossible-to-resist situation or feedline. But the effect is not simply that of a versatile actor switching between characters: it's more instinctive, more primal, and the effect is magnified a hundredfold in performance.

**Frank Ferrante at the end of another evening with Groucho (copyright Andy Hollingworth Archive).**

A "tribute act" is by definition a kind of mutual wish-fulfillment, a fantasy that demands the audience's prior knowledge of what is being evoked. But you no more need be a Groucho fan to enjoy this show than you do to enjoy your first Marx Brothers film, because it feels entirely spontaneous. If a chance development prompts a comic inspiration Ferrante will seize it and work it for as long as it holds, sometimes for many minutes; sometimes he will leave it and then, when least expected, pick it up again many minutes later. As such Groucho is restored as a vital presence, and all that matters to the audience is that it's funny. You don't technically need even to know who he is.

One technique I found particularly impressive was his tendency to begin a familiar routine, play it as expected for a while, but then take it off on a tangent, so that it becomes entirely new, original comedy. The *Animal Crackers* piano routine, with his brilliantly talented accompanist Mark Rabe standing in for Chico and unable to "think of the finish," may have been the most notable example of this: we were already laughing at the original set-up, but the laughter was complacent because we were confident that we knew exactly where we were being taken. Then suddenly Frank and Mark take an abrupt left turn and a brand new sketch begins, but one rooted not only in pre-established character but also in a pre-established premise.

After all, Ferrante clearly knows he's playing to two audiences at once: newcomers who may be completely unfamiliar with, say, the African lecture, and enthusiasts who know its every word and emphasis as well as Frank himself does. How can he possibly accommodate the demands of both simultaneously? The answer is: by being dexterous, by being alert, and by reading the audience's collective mood on a second-by-second basis. On this occasion he was doubly challenged: not only were there large numbers of Marx obsessives in attendance, they were obsessives who had just come away from a festival in which they had watched a bunch of Groucho interviews and *Animal Crackers*! So he would start a routine, read the depth and length of the laughs it received, and then frequently break off, interject, and freshen it with spontaneous material and a self-deprecating acknowledgment of the particular circumstances of the occasion. ("You've heard this already today?")

In truth, Frank does things that Groucho himself would not have done: the athletic abandon, and the absurdist spontaneity, are an *amplification* of what makes Groucho's comedy great, not an accurate representation of any actual performance we have of him. It's a fantasy of Groucho in that it is visually the mature Groucho of the Marx movies transported to the stage, but performing with the youthful irreverence and physical energy that we imagine from that great vanished chunk of his career before the cameras showed up. The *actual* Groucho that Frank embodies—the Groucho that was this age and at this point in his career—could never have dominated the stage the way Frank does: he would have had neither the energy nor the performing hunger. This is the Groucho of our dearest dreams, the Groucho's Groucho—the spirit of Groucho condensed, distilled, and then exploding from the bottle.

There is no small significance to this: these performances literally keep Groucho alive. Spike Milligan famously took a role in the BBC version of *Flywheel, Shyster and Flywheel* so as to fulfill a lifelong dream of working with the Marx Brothers. Likewise, I can now proudly boast that Groucho has made an onstage joke about me. When he recalled the Brothers' disastrous performance in Britain in the 1920s, he stopped to check the details: "That's right isn't it, Matthew? You were there."

# Appendix II

# Anatomy of a Mustache
## by Noah Diamond

> Comedians had long resorted to mustaches as comedy props. But Groucho's mustache, painted on his upper lip, had a Rembrandt quality that lifted it into another realm. It gave him the status of a Royal Academy canvas, fitted him for membership in the elite of the Metropolitan Museum.
> —Ed Sullivan's "Hollywood" column, June 11, 1939

Was it war paint, for battle against reason and conformity? Was it armor, to protect a melancholy heart? Whatever the reason, when Julius Henry Marx made the fateful decision to draw a mustache on his face, he chose an impossible rectangular affair, a slab with rounded corners, overlapping the upper lip—and eyebrows to match. It was a mustache that could never exist in nature, smeared across the face without regard for realism. It was cheeky. It was satirical. It was like Groucho's character, a blatant fraud, daring you to object. But *why* Julius created this particular work of art over and over again for decades, we can only theorize:

(1) It was distinctive and memorable. People often had trouble telling the Marxes apart, and this was a way to stand out.

(2) The stage glasses and the greasepaint de-emphasized the lazy eye. In pictures of a clean-shaven and unbespectacled Julius, the exotropia is unmissable; in *Groucho* pictures, it's only there if you look for it.

(3) "The enormous greasepaint mustache and the enormous painted eyebrows ... allowed him to communicate ironically with a big theater audience—to comment on the jokes even as he made them."—Adam Gopnik[1]

(4) It made him a favorite subject for portraiture. (One frequent Groucho renderer, John Decker, insisted that the term *caricature* could not apply to drawings of the Marx Brothers: "They're such living caricatures themselves that all I had to do was draw them from life."[2])

For about a decade in vaudeville, Julius had played an elderly schoolteacher, variously Dutch or Yiddish. Photographs of Julius in character show that the wire-rims were already in use, and sometimes the tailcoat. The hair was thinned and grayed and sometimes hidden under a bald cap. He looked much the way he would actually look when he got to be an old man, but one thing was missing: the mustache! It wasn't part of the picture at all, throughout most of the vaudevillian odyssey. There was not necessarily a single day on which Julius decided to wear a mustache, and wore one forevermore. It's possible that the old character *did* develop one, or use one occasionally, at some point in the long evolution from *Fun in Hi Skule* to *Mr. Green's Reception* to *Home Again* to *N'Everything*. But the first time we *know*

Groucho wore a mustache was when he took on a new character in *On the Mezzanine*, the character we would come to know on film.

*On the Mezzanine* was a major break from the act that had been developing since 1911, with *Variety* noting the Marxes' intention to "do away with their former characters."[3] Until now, the major influence on the act was Uncle Al Shean, who provided the model for Groucho's early stage persona, and wrote and staged *Home Again*, their greatest vaudeville success. (He also directed their worst failure, *The Street Cinderella*.[4]) Now, at the dawn of the 1920s, the team sought a new collaborator, a more modern artist, to help conceive a more modern Marx Brothers. Herman Timberg was a comedic powerhouse, always one step ahead of the Brothers in vaudeville. He rose to fame as the star of Gus Edwards' school act, from which the Marxes' *Fun in Hi Skule* had liberally borrowed.[5] Now, engaged to create a new tabloid for them, Timberg had a hand in the creation of the Groucho character.

For the first time, Julius would not be playing an immigrant; he would be what he was, a first-generation American Jewish New Yorker with a big mouth. The jokes Timberg wrote for him replaced Uncle Al's singsong Dutch with syncopated New York patter that perfectly fit Julius's once-in-a-generation voice and timing. This new character was called Mr. Hammer, a name which would recur in the film version of *The Cocoanuts*, and this Mr. Hammer had a new look. It was written right into Timberg's script, when Mr. Hammer is on the telephone and is asked to describe himself: "Did you ever see Lincoln without a beard? Well, I look like Washington with a mustache."[6]

**Fig 1. The Greasepaint Classic.**

If we believe the traditional origin story of the Greasepaint Classic (Fig. 1), then it did not appear in early performances of *On the Mezzanine*. But of course, the story exists in several forms, each at odds with verifiable fact in one way or another. The man himself, in *Groucho and Me*, explains that "I had always worn a hairy mustache which was stuck on with glue," and that applying and removing it had become painful. One night, having "dawdled over" a "sixty-five cent dinner," the Brothers were late getting to the Fifth Avenue Theater, and Julius hastily smeared on some greasepaint and that was that.

Or not quite. Groucho has the theater manager confronting him after the show, and demanding that he revert to "the same mustache you wore at the Palace!" Groucho tells the manager off and orders him to leave the room, noting, "I was unusually brave that unforgettable night. The reason? My three brothers were standing right behind me, casually swinging their blackjacks as a harbinger of mayhem." There they are, four of the Three Musketeers, ready to do physical battle in defense of a mustache. Groucho doesn't place the story in time, though his claim that "I had *always* worn a hairy mustache" misleadingly suggests that it had been part of his stage persona all along.

That impression is reinforced in the second major telling of the story, by Arthur Marx in *Son of Groucho*. Arthur places the story at Keith's Flushing in Queens, and tells us specifically that Groucho "usually wore" a "hirsute mustache … in his characterization of a school teacher," that the show was *Home Again*, that the greasepaint substitution took place within a week after Arthur's birth, and that Groucho was late to the theater because he'd been at the hospital doting on his newborn son.

The earliest known photograph of Groucho with a mustache was taken in the autumn of 1921.[7] It shows Groucho outside a theater, in his undershirt and suspenders, holding the infant Arthur. (Chico's daughter Maxine, then almost four, stands nearby.) Groucho is seen in profile, sporting a clear Greasepaint Classic, though seemingly nothing on the eyebrows. Then we have a pair of publicity shots taken on December 16 of the same year, in connection with *On the Mezzanine*.[8] These are apparently the first images of the total classic Groucho look. In one, he's sprawled on the floor in a mock-provocative pose, eyeballs rolling, while his brothers cavort above him. Harpo's coat and hat look a little too crisp, and Chico doesn't have exactly the familiar clothes yet, but it's unmistakable: posterity's first glimpse of the Marx Brothers as we know them.

But *On the Mezzanine* had been a going concern for almost a year by the time these pictures were taken; it premiered in February of 1921. Arthur was born on July 21, and the Brothers indeed played several engagements in and around New York City that summer. (Every version of the story places it in a different theater, but always in New York. Kyle Crichton's *The Marx Brothers* puts it at Proctor's Twenty-Eighth Street.) It's entirely possible that Groucho began using a glued-on mustache in February, and switched to the greasepaint in the summer. But as far as I've been able to determine, there is no photographic evidence of the earlier mustache.

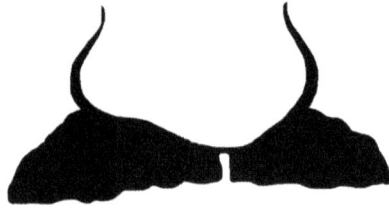

**Fig 2. The Twenties Experiment.**

The greasepaint stripe remained mostly constant for the next twenty-five years, with only a couple of incidental or theoretical exceptions. When the boys toured England in 1922, they started with *On the Mezzanine* (retitled *On the Balcony*), but then reverted to *Home Again*; did Groucho revert to his old makeup? Then we have a few portraits of Groucho out of costume in 1925, sporting a real mustache, which he's grown himself (Fig. 2). It looks a lot like the later *You Bet Your Life* mustache. A similar one (with seemingly unenhanced eyebrows) appears in some early publicity shots for *I'll Say She Is*, taken in the spring of 1923, though it's hard to tell if that one is real.[9] But except for these brief anomalies, the Groucho mustache was unvaried from *On the Mezzanine* through *A Night in Casablanca*.

In 1924, during the epochal Broadway run of *I'll Say She Is*, Percy Hammond noticed a physical resemblance between "Julius H. Marx, the least beautiful of the Marx Brothers" and

George S. Kaufman (who, of course, would soon write for the boys). Kaufman sent Hammond a letter of protest, noting that "Mr. Marx is just a wee bit terrible looking." Moreover, "Mr. Marx wears a black mustache, and you can appoint one person and I will appoint one and together they will pick a third impartial one, and they can search high and low on me without finding a mustache of any color." Groucho wrote in next, helpfully confusing the question of whether Kaufman had a mustache, "although some authors find it advisable to wear something on the opening night." Another columnist chimed in with the argument that Groucho *didn't* look like Kaufman, but resembled the director Frank Tuttle: "Julius denies that he is copying Frank, but no one is going to believe that such a startling similarity could be an accident." But Tuttle's mustache was *real*, and it was rational; and had Kaufman grown a mustache, he would have looked more like Frank Tuttle than Captain Spalding.[10]

By the time *The Cocoanuts* was filmed in 1929, the mustache was a trademark of a famous stage persona. But now that persona was about to debut in a new medium, and there were officious conversations about whether the mustache would be "accepted" on film. Sources differ as to whether Walter Wanger or Monta Bell was the executive who insisted that cinema audiences wouldn't "believe" the painted mustache. Groucho's response, in his autobiography: "The audience doesn't believe us anyhow!"

The mustache is a bluff, and this bluff is part of the premise of any Marx Brothers comedy. One of the principal characters has a mustache and eyebrows, very obviously painted onto his face, and nobody is ever going to mention it. In *Animal Crackers*, Roscoe W. Chandler gets to imply that Chico isn't really Italian, but nobody *ever* says of Groucho, "Is this guy kidding—that's not even a real mustache!" The people who cross paths with the Brothers are too constrained by social courtesy, or too preoccupied with their own agendas, to recognize that Groucho is a fraud in the most blatant way possible. Once they've accepted the mustache, they can accept anything. (In the real world, however, the peculiar qualities of the mustache did not go unnoticed. A 1929 Broadway column asserts that "Gotham's most famous mustache belongs to Police Commissioner [Grover] Whalen," but an honorable mention goes to "Groucho Marx, whose mustache is painted on.")

The mustache assumed its rightful place in the *Cocoanuts* film, but it remained a point of consternation. Director Robert Florey wanted to go to Florida to shoot backgrounds and establishing shots. Monta Bell famously asked him, "Why are you so concerned with having real backgrounds when one of the leading characters wears an obviously false mustache?" Florey later explained that Groucho's mustache "was very glossy and at certain angles the light reflected onto it and created a hot spot ... but I did prevail upon him to powder it a bit. If you look at the film closely, you'll notice that the mustache shines in a couple of reels more than in others."[11] There are photographs of the Brothers on stage in which the mustache is shiny indeed, or smeared, or dripping right off. (There is one unspeakable photo from a performance of *Animal Crackers* in which the mustache is crookedly bisected by what seems to be a stream of liquid coming from Groucho's left nostril.[12]) On *Cocoanuts*, Bell threw up his hands. "As far as I am concerned, I am giving up," he told Florey, "and I don't care if the SOB wears a monkey suit in the picture or what he does."[13] No blackjacks were necessary.

During the Hollywood Paramount years, the mustache was occasionally referred to on film. It's discussed twice in *Monkey Business*. First, when the dense captain describes the stowaways: "One of them goes around with a black mustache!" This leads to Groucho's profound question, "Don't you think a mustache ever gets lonely?" Chico suggests that his grandfather's beard should meet Groucho's mustache. "I'll talk it over with my mustache," comes the genial response. Later, when claiming to be Maurice Chevalier, Groucho explains the facial discrepancy with, "The barber shop wasn't open this morning," as though that mustache could possibly be the result of one missed shave.

Fig 3. The Teasdale Variations.

Two years later, in *Duck Soup*, we are afforded an even more compelling meditation on the nature of the mustache. Sneaking around Mrs. Teasdale's mansion, spies Harpo and Chico both get the idea of disguising themselves as Groucho (Fig. 3). So they grab some extra wire-rimmed glasses and greasepaint that just happen to be lying around! As Matthew Coniam suggests in *The Annotated Marx Brothers*, this is the closest we ever come to an acknowledgment of mustache fraud. The mustache *is* fake, even within the reality of *Duck Soup*, because now Harpo and Chico have mustaches just like it, which we've *seen* them paint on. And when Margaret Dumont confronts them, she's convinced that they are Groucho, which means that in this world you can paint on a powerfully convincing mustache—or at least *they* can.

At MGM, Irving Thalberg's calculated taming of the Marx Brothers' characters did not include a rethinking of Groucho's mustache. They made *Room Service* for RKO, assuming characters that were even less fanciful than in Thalberg's vision, and less connected to their traditional roles. If there's any Marx Brothers movie in which it would have made sense for Groucho to wear a more realistic mustache, it's *Room Service*. The idea was apparently toyed with,[14] but in the finished film the greasepaint endures. Three more MGM vehicles followed, but after *The Big Store*, Groucho was determined to move on from the mustache as well as the Marx Brothers. In 1942, Irving Berlin asked him to headline *The Music Box Revue* on Broadway, "but that would mean the black mustache again," Groucho wrote to Arthur Sheekman, "and I'm ducking it as long as it is economically feasible."[15]

Fig 4. The Devereaux.

During radio and U.S.O. appearances throughout the 1940s, he did don the greasepaint sometimes, if only for reassurance that he was famous. He supposedly rushed to apply his greasepaint in order to be recognized by adoring crowds on the Hollywood Victory Caravan.[16] As it turned out, the mustache was not so easily forsaken. With the exception of his appearance in *Twentieth Century* in Skowhegan in 1934, Groucho had not performed before a large audience without a mustache since vaudeville. The Greasepaint Classic was a foregone conclusion when he agreed to reunite with Harpo and Chico for *A Night in Casablanca* in 1946. One year later, in a *New York Times* profile by Brooks Atkinson,[17] Groucho was adamant: "Just get that greasepaint mustache out of your mind, will you? The mustache is out for good." Yet within months of that pronouncement, it had a nostalgic cameo in *Copacabana*.

In his proper role in that film, Lionel Q. Devereaux, Groucho looks essentially the way he will as "the kindly old quizmaster"[18] on *You Bet Your Life*. The Devereaux mustache (Fig. 4) happens to be fake, but it's realistic, a mature, earthbound version of the crazy mask of yore. A sign that he had really finished with the greasepaint came in 1949, when his reluctant participation in the quasi–Marx Brothers film *Love Happy* did *not* include a reversion to the classic look.

**Fig 5. The Kindly Old Quizmaster.**

In the 1920s, Groucho had fought for the greasepaint, but by the 1940s it was a quaint relic of vaudeville. Even Chaplin's Little Tramp was history. Chaplin solved the problem by playing new and different characters. Groucho solved it by mostly refusing to play a character at all. He became a personality. He wasn't an actor or a comedian in the usual senses of these words; he was simply himself. He was a Groucho Marx. He didn't talk to the contestants on *You Bet Your Life* the way he talked to the students in *Horse Feathers*. He couldn't have. Nevertheless, the show's producers did ask him to paint on the old mustache. "The hell I will," he said. "That character's dead. I'll never go into that again."[19] How the tables had turned: Now management *wanted* the mustache, and Groucho had to argue *against* it. Their compromise, of course, was a *real* mustache, grown and maintained forevermore (Fig. 5).

*You Bet Your Life* was a reconciliation of the dual identities of Julius Henry Marx. He had transcended the Marx Brothers and made himself real. By simply growing a mustache instead of painting one on, Groucho was also submitting to the full measure of his celebrity status. In the greasepaint era, he could move through the world with an anonymity not usually available to superstars. But now he woke up every morning already wearing the mask. In one episode, a contestant asked why he had that mustache on his face. "I have no other place to put it," said Groucho.

**Fig 6. The Living Legend.**

Over the years, the real mustache got whiter (Fig. 6), but he always had it, because the world had convinced him that Groucho Marx had to have a mustache, because he had convinced the world. When he proudly appeared as Ko-Ko in a TV version of *The Mikado* in 1960, he was given the faux-Japanese costume common to all productions of *The Mikado*—but *this* Ko-Ko also had glasses (chosen for the character and distinct from Groucho's usual frames) and a mustache. The mustache was Groucho's real one, augmented to a style we might call Fu Grouchu (Fig. 7).

**Fig 7. The Fu Grouchu.**

The classic greasepaint rectangle was retired but not deceased, and it occasionally returned to the spotlight. In 1955, Groucho performed "Dr. Hackenbush" on television's *Swift Show Wagon*, and he painted the old mustache right over the new one. He did this again in 1967 for *The Jackie Gleason Show*, entering to the strains of "Hooray for Captain Spalding." There was great joy in the interplay between Groucho and Gleason, and several hilarious, apparently impromptu moments. They performed a delightful variation on the Gallagher and Shean song. It's appropriate that this late return to the greasepaint would include an evocation of Uncle Al, effectively bookending Groucho's career. "I'm getting pretty sick of this walk," he announces to the audience, looking like he's having the time of his life.

It would be lovely if this nostalgic *Gleason* turn was the final appearance of the old Groucho character and his legendary mustache. Alas, the indignity of *Skidoo* lay just ahead. Groucho's presence in Otto Preminger's cinematic acid trip was surprising enough; what's even more surprising is the return of the old look, or a misguided approximation. For some reason, when seventy-eight-year-old Julius sat down at his makeup table on the set of *Skidoo* and confronted the tube of black greasepaint, he didn't revert fully to the parallelogram. The *Skidoo* mustache is a trapezoid, conforming to the now-deeper lines of the face (Fig. 8). And the eyebrows, though darkened, aren't the thick smears of yesteryear.

**Fig 8. The Lysergic Trapezoid.**

Groucho Marx died in 1977, but his mustache lives on. For posterity, an inadvertent benefit of Groucho's 1921 makeup choice was that his look could easily be approximated on other faces. We know the legends about Zeppo understudying Groucho on stage, or Irving Brecher standing in for him at a photo shoot. Numerous performers who don't particularly look like Julius Henry Marx out of makeup—including George Bettinger, Frank Ferrante, David Garrison, Gabe Kaplan, Michael Roberts, Lewis J. Stadlen, and even Noah Diamond—have convincingly embodied the Groucho character. Add to us the three or four generations of Marx Brothers fans who borrowed their mothers' eyebrow pencils to emulate their hero, or bought a tube of black cream makeup and a big plastic cigar every Halloween.

All you have to do, to understand the power of the Greasepaint Classic, is paint it across your own face. Its effects are magical and immediate. Woody Allen, who wears the iconic mustache and eyebrows (and credibly imitates Groucho) for a few minutes in his 1996 film *Everyone Says I Love You*, was asked about the experience by a reporter. "I liked it," Allen said. "I wish I could have done it more. I could see the appeal it had for people who played him on stage. It's great. You do what all actors do, and that is start playing your costume."[20] The Groucho character had so many moving parts—the mind, the walk, the talk. I'm not sure it would have added up to an eternal comic archetype without that careless, brazen, revolutionary black stripe. Sometimes genius is right under your nose.

**Noah Diamond** *adapted the book and lyrics for the lost Marx Brothers musical* I'll Say She Is, *and played Groucho in the show's first-ever revival. He is also the author of the book* Gimme a Thrill: The Story of I'll Say She Is, *as well as two earlier books,* Love Marches On *and* 400 Years in Manhattan. *The reader may learn more about the* I'll Say She Is *revival at illsaysheis.com.*

# Appendix III

# I Saw It with My Own Ears

## *by Gary Westin*

**Groucho** (to the mother of 19 children): Why do you have so many children?
**Mrs. Story**: I love my husband!
**Groucho**: I love my cigar, too, but I take it out of my mouth once in a while.

If you know anything about Groucho (presumably you do, if you've just finished reading this book) you've likely heard this brilliantly funny line from *You Bet Your Life* quoted before many times. It's perhaps the single best known Groucho joke outside of the Marx Brothers' films, and a pitch-perfect one-liner: short, unexpected, witty. While it deftly avoids overt lewdness, the sexual implication is undeniable, the line very clearly more than a little too blue for audiences of the time.

It certainly does sound like a line Groucho would say, a whole lot more than many of the widely accepted but false quotes attributed to him over the years do. (Attributing random quotes to Groucho has become something of an internet cottage industry.)

There's just one problem. He probably didn't say it. Not even just *probably* not, but I'd say almost if not quite entirely *definitely* not. But that won't stop people from swearing on their respective Aunt Minnies' graves that they remember having seen it personally.

I run several YouTube channels featuring vintage entertainment. It's pity enough to see the degree to which so many truly brilliant, highly influential performers have been forgotten by large sections of the public, including Groucho. But it's something more again when all that people *think* that they remember about these performers are things that aren't true.

I can personally attest that if you post a video featuring Jack Benny, sooner or later someone will leave a comment citing the "your money or your life" gag as the longest laugh in the history of the Benny show (it wasn't). If you post a video featuring Burns and Allen, sooner or later someone will leave a comment "quoting" Gracie answering George's "Say goodnight, Gracie" with "Goodnight, Gracie" (it never happened). And if you post a video featuring Groucho, sooner or later someone will leave a comment claiming to have personally seen the cigar line in a video recording of the show (no one ever has).

It's easy enough to shoot down the "Goodnight, Gracie" line, and even easier to shoot down the claim that "your money or your life" was the longest laugh Jack Benny ever got, because we still have the vital evidence: the actual shows. The problem with disproving Groucho's cigar line, however, is a generalized logical problem, that you can't ever prove a negative in the absence of a key piece of evidence: in this case, an unedited, pre-broadcast recording of the show in which the moment would have taken place.

*You Bet Your Life* was produced in a highly unusual way: in order to maximize the laugh quotient for what was largely a spontaneous and ad libbed program, an hour's worth of material was recorded every week and meticulously edited down to the best 25 minutes for broadcast. This freed Groucho up from worrying about lines falling flat or saying something inadvertently naughty (his mouth tended to operate ahead of his brain). So because it was pre-recorded and edited, if the cigar line had ever happened there is absolutely no question that it would have been cut out of the broadcast version, solely on the basis of how far beyond acceptable broadcast standards of the time it would have gone.

This would be as certain as certain gets, even if the episode in question was unavailable. But it turns out that the broadcast version of the episode that this line is claimed to have taken place in is, in fact, available. And, no surprise, the line isn't there.[1]

"Of course it wasn't in the broadcast version," you say. "I saw it as an *outtake!*" No, you didn't, I say, unless you have your own reel of hitherto unknown outtakes in your attic, presumably lying beside a slowly decaying copy of *Humor Risk.* Let's face it: if this line had occurred after the debut of the series on television—a line so great it became a classic and an indelible public memory despite the fact that no one has seen it—then it surely would have been preserved by the show's editors as part of those precious outtake reels they compiled for the staff holiday parties. All manner of other naughty Groucho lines snipped from broadcast were saved in those reels—but no cigar.

As for the Mrs. Story episode, well, that was on *radio only,* aired on January 11, 1950, before the TV series even debuted. So we can dismiss completely anyone's claim to have personally seen the Mrs. Story episode, because it was never filmed, or heard an outtake from this show, because the unedited version has never surfaced, *or* seen the line in the outtake reels from the TV years, because it simply isn't in there.[2] Unless you were physically in the studio the very day the show was recorded, or are sitting on a previously unknown copy of a never-broadcast recording containing the line, it's literally impossible for you to have heard it.

A new collection of hour-long pre-broadcast *You Bet Your Life* episodes surfaced on the Internet Archive recently, a truly major addition to the publicly available material from the series. It's aggravating, though, to find that this collection includes the unedited recording from the week *before* the Mrs. Story show and the one from the week *after,* but not the one we need in order to settle this question once and for all.

In the absence of this pre-broadcast recording, and with incontrovertible evidence that the line never made it to air, there's very little left to support the notion that Groucho said it beyond the fact that it *sounds* like a genuine Groucho line. Nothing but the confused testimony of Groucho and Robert Dwan decades later, after they had both long denied it ever happened.

This poses quite a thorny logical problem for the believers: if the line had never been broadcast, and if everyone associated with the show who was on record about it denied that it ever happened until decades after the fact, how could this line ever possibly have reached the public consciousness in the first place?

The earliest reference I can find to it is in an *Esquire* magazine profile of Groucho from 1972, in which he said, "I get credit all the time for things I never said. You know that line in *You Bet Your Life?* The guy says he has seventeen kids and I say: 'I smoke a cigar, but I take it out of my mouth occasionally'? I never said that."

Note that this was more than 20 years after the fact, in reference to the quote being offered by *Reader's Digest.*

Now, just think about that for a moment: Who on earth could *Reader's Digest* have gotten this line from if not Groucho himself? Was the person who offered this quote in the audience that day in 1949? Or was this just a very clever line misremembered or (even worse) dreamed up by a *Reader's Digest* staffer desperate to fill column inches?

Here we have Groucho, still in good mental shape, unequivocally disowning the quote the first time I can find any public reference to it. What reason do we have to doubt his word on the matter? Producer John Guedel was also on record denying that the line ever happened, as was George Fenneman, and director Robert Dwan.

For decades the only person associated with *You Bet Your Life* who believed the truth of the Story story, according to Dwan, was co-director Bernie Smith. Unfortunately, we have no way of understanding why Smith believed the line was authentic, or when he started to believe it, because we have only the maddeningly incomplete second hand testimony offered in Robert Dwan's book *As Long as They're Laughing!*

As if only to muddy the waters further, Dwan reversed course after years of his vehemently denying it, claiming he had been convinced at long last by Bernie Smith that the line did in fact happen. Infuriatingly, Dwan declines to offer the barest scintilla of a reason for having been convinced out of his long-held firm conviction to the contrary. He merely says that Bernie Smith convinced him otherwise and leaves it at that, a totally worthless statement without at least *some* kind of logical or evidence-based argument behind it. "Cause Bernie said so" doesn't really cut it.

If Smith had played back an actual recording of the incident for Dwan, that would of course be a different matter, but I have to presume that if Dwan had access to a recording he would most certainly have said so, and put the issue to rest once and for all. Since he declined to offer any support for his reversal, I tend to believe that Dwan was convinced solely on the basis of Smith having had a very strong contrary memory. Casting no aspersions on Bernie Smith in particular, I simply don't consider human memory in general to be reliable enough to ever change my mind about something I consider illogical simply because someone else remembers it differently.

The only other direct confirmation, of a sort, is in the 1976 history of the show *The Secret Word Is Groucho.* Here Groucho himself apparently changes his mind and decides to take full and unabashed credit for the line, but there are major problems with taking this at face value.

For one thing, it's important to understand that *The Secret Word Is Groucho* was really written by Hector Arce, with minimal participation from a then ailing, aged Groucho. Groucho was about a year away from death when *The Secret Word Is Groucho* was written. As already noted, just a few years earlier he had firmly denied saying the line. I think it stands to reason that Arce attributed this confirmation to Groucho for the sake of including an irresistible anecdote in the book, perhaps unaware of Groucho's earlier denial, or possibly that Groucho's mental faculties were diminished enough by this late stage in his life that he actually came to believe he did say it after all. (Shades of the "Christmas card painting" episode—see the introduction of this book for this and other examples of Groucho's latterday unreliability.) He was by all accounts significantly impaired by the end of his life, and it must be conceded, was always quite an egotist, as so many great performers are. As such, I can't see any rational reason why, just a few years prior, in more lucid but equally egotistical days, he would have *denied* it ever came out of his mouth (the joke, not the cigar).

There's an interesting parallel with George Burns's statements over the years about the "Goodnight Gracie" line. George repeatedly denied that they'd ever used it, his explanation a typically modest one: "Because we never thought of it." Only when he reached his mid–90s, when his razor sharp mind began to slip just a little, can you find a couple of examples of George reversing himself and suddenly, casually claiming credit for the line he'd spent 30 years denying he ever used. Unlike Groucho's cigar line, we can definitively disprove the "Goodnight Gracie" line having been said by simply looking at all the closings of the TV shows. Like Groucho, George reversed himself only in extremely advanced old age, and George was definitively wrong; in Groucho's case, we can't be quite so definitive, but the parallel is otherwise striking.

I don't mean to rain on anyone's parade. I'd honestly prefer to believe that Groucho said the line, and I readily concede the *possibility*, however unlikely. I certainly believe Groucho capable of this level of spontaneous wit, and despite his almost Victorian aversion to blue material in mixed company, I don't think the line goes too far beyond the realm of other obviously sexual jokes preserved in the *You Bet Your Life* outtake reels to be out of character for Groucho. There are far nuttier widespread Marxian legends.

But let's face it: there's just no credible direct evidence to support that the line happened, only weak and contradictory testimonials offered decades after the fact, and a lot of folks who run around claiming they've seen it when they couldn't possibly have. It can't be debunked definitely unless an unedited recording surfaces, so go ahead and believe it if you want to. Just *don't* believe you've seen (or even heard) the moment personally, because you quite simply haven't.

If that unedited recording ever surfaces, I'll gladly eat a bug as punishment for my transgression if I'm proven wrong. But until that happens, I firmly contend that the prevailing belief in this incident relies on three things: the limitless fallibility of human memory, a general ignorance of the relevant facts, and wishful thinking.

As Sigmund Freud so famously said to his daughter Ana, "Sometimes a cigar is just an apocryphal story." But that's probably apocryphal, too.

*Gary Westin is a lifelong collector and student of vintage entertainment. Among the many digital archiving projects he has worked on are a set of high quality mp3s of the entire Jack Benny radio series and a restoration of the Burns and Allen television series on DVD. In recent years, he's been running several popular YouTube channels featuring the most complete collections available online of programs such as* You Bet Your Life, Your Show of Shows, Hollywood Palace *and* What's My Line.

# Appendix IV

# Memoirs of a Reigning Firefly
### by Jay Hopkins

When I was about to attend the University of Minnesota in the mid–1970s, I wondered if there was a Marx Brothers fan club similar to the Laurel and Hardy group, the Sons of the Desert. I thought about writing to Groucho to see if he'd heard of a fan club but then I remembered Groucho's lawsuit over *The Marx Brothers Scrapbook*. It certainly was not a certainty (try saying that rapidly twenty times) that Groucho would look upon such an inquiry favorably, not with proprietary rights and the like. So, instead, I located the address of Susan Marx, Harpo's widow. Susan knew of no such group, but she *loved* the notion of fans getting together to celebrate the celebrated team and encouraged me to organize such an organization. (Is there an echo in here, or do I perhaps require a broader vocabulary?)

It didn't take long to come up with *The Marx Brotherhood* for a name. I would be the chief officer or Reigning Firefly, named after Groucho's character in *Duck Soup*. (What can I say? The deck was stacked.) Strangely enough, my "credentials" as Reigning Firefly extended to me some kind of shabby authority, or at least a sufficient degree of nerve, to contact and ultimately interview several folks who played key roles in the career of The Marx Brothers, and in the life of Groucho, in particular.

What follows are extracts from interviews with three such people who kindly welcomed me into their homes in Los Angeles: John Guedel, the producer of Groucho's 13-year quiz show *You Bet Your Life*; Nat Perrin, who not only contributed to the scripts of several Marx Brothers films and co-scripted the *Flywheel, Shyster and Flywheel* radio series, but served as Groucho's court-appointed conservator towards the end of the comedian's life, and Erin Fleming, the controversial companion and "manager" of Groucho in his later years.

These interviews were recorded on cassette tape in March of 1979 (Fleming and Guedel) and June of 1984 (Perrin), and have now been unearthed, dusted off, scrubbed down, blow-dried and published here for the first time. As Otis B. Driftwood might add, "From now on, it's every man for himself."

## John Guedel

I met John Guedel at his home in Los Angeles early in the morning—but not early enough, apparently. I showed up at 8 a.m., thinking he couldn't have actually said *6 a.m.* on the phone yesterday. Upon arrival I was greeted with "You were supposed to be here two hours ago!"

Guedel quickly forgave me, however, and welcomed me into his home. After handing me a stack of publicity stills of Groucho from films and the quiz show ("Here, take these! You can keep 'em!"), he obligingly posed for a photograph. Guedel had been uncomfortable with his thinning hairline even when working on the quiz show, and at one time owned a series of "pieces" at various stages of hair growth—not unlike the character of Alan Brady on the old *Dick Van Dyke Show*. "Wait a minute!" he suggested while reaching for a fedora. "I'll give you my Bogie look."

**JH: Was selling the idea of Groucho, as the host of a quiz show, to a sponsor an easy sell?**

JG: I took it to all three networks and they all turned it down. But then I read in the paper that a man named Allen Gellman, who was the head of the Elgin American compact company, was coming out here to buy the Phil Baker show, *Everybody Wins*. He hadn't bought it yet. So I went to the Beverly Hills Hotel.... He remembered the Marx Brothers. He didn't know that Groucho had flopped four times on the radio so he bought the show. Phil Baker fired his agent for putting the article in the paper about coming out "to sign" before it *was* signed.

**JH: You're rather sneaky, aren't you?**

JG: Well, you read the paper! You can get things out of the paper. Agents hardly ever help you at all.

**JH: The show enjoyed a remarkable run from 1947 through 1961. What brought about the cancellation? Was Groucho getting tired of it?**

JG: No, Groucho never tired of it, really. In fact, even after *You Bet Your Life* ended, we tried to revive it as *Tell It to Groucho*, and other barely distinguishable changes in format, including an attempt in Britain. The initial run ended due to timing, really. We started in the top ten. We stayed there all the time, usually in second place, say around 1955–57. NBC kept moving us to a later time and our older audience would write letters telling us that they couldn't stay up that late! So we were trying to get the 8:30 slot on NBC but by the time that slot was available, Lever Brothers, which was one of our sponsors, had purchased that time on CBS. They couldn't put us on opposite themselves! So NBC sold the time to someone else and we were shut out. They didn't have any time for us. By that time, the 10 o'clock time was assigned to another program. The rating was still getting a 39 share which was very good. They don't cancel shows with a 39 share. Anything over 26 or 27 is in pretty good shape. We should have stayed right where we were at 10 o'clock.

**JH: How did the recent re-syndication come about?**

JG: One day in 1973, I got a call from the NBC warehouse in New Jersey. "Mr. Guedel, would you like a set of the Groucho shows for your garage?" I said, what do you mean, a set? He said, "Well, we're destroying them because we need the space." I said how many have you destroyed? He said 15 of them. I said, "What? Are you doing it right this minute?" I said *Stop*! I'm going to talk to New York and make some kind of a deal. I said that if you can't syndicate them, I will. So they put them all together and sent them to me. That's the remaining 235 negatives. The bill was $2,700. I called up Groucho and said "Would you like to go in partners with me as a syndicator?" He said okay. I said, "Well, you owe me $1,350 dollars already as your half of the shipping and it's coming to your house!"

*JH: Weren't you once called "the father of reruns"?*

JG: There are three things that I'm supposed to be known for and all three are terrible! [laughs] All three are *blights on the landscape*! One of them is reruns. We just decided to run *House Party* over again in the summer, the very first summer that they allowed tape. They didn't allow recordings until the fall of 1947. If they hadn't ever allowed recordings, I don't think that we would be sitting here now. I don't think that there would have ever been a Groucho show. Groucho wouldn't be as good on a live show as he would be on a taped show because he was uncontrollable and he'd be right in the middle of something and we'd go off the air because the air time was up. The point is that it would have been a lousy show. We would have been cancelled after the first 13 weeks, there isn't any doubt about it. The second terrible thing that I introduced was the first audience stunt show. I gave a woman the song "Smiles" to sing and after the first line, we'd put an ice cube in her mouth. If we could still understand her by the time she got to the end of the song, she got ten dollars. That's how stunt shows got started, which have been a bane. The third thing that I introduced that became a blight on the landscape was the singing commercial. [Begins singing to the tune of "Polly Wolly Doodle"] *When you're tired and hot and your nerves are shot/your throat is parched and dry/That's when you need a Barley drink/to keep you feeling spry....*

# Nat Perrin

Fate was leading me to Nat Perrin's door.

Well, not exactly. No one was leading me to it, which was the problem. Nat Perrin had, in fact, buzzed me through the security system of his townhouse building but since I had neglected to ask for his door number, it seemed doubtful that I would find his door on the first try. Eternity passed twice as I agonized over which door to select, eventually choosing one randomly on the third floor.

The apologies I had been formulating in my mind instantly disappeared when Nat Perrin greeted me at the door with "How did you know which floor I was on?" Mumbling something about telepathy, I entered his comfortably situated living quarters. Wearing a beige V-neck sweater and loose-fitting slacks, Perrin exuded the contented, casual aura of a comfortable retiree. With his deceptively dour expression, bronze complexion and owlish appearance, he reminded me of the mature Zeppo Marx.

*JH: You were appointed by the court to be the conservator of Groucho Marx in the middle of the highly publicized rift between Arthur Marx and Erin Fleming. By this time, Erin had been displaced by the court. As conservator, what were your duties?*

NP: I was responsible for Groucho's well-being. He was very ill. Unable to take care of himself. About two-thirds of the time he was at home and the rest of the time he was hospitalized. It was up to me to make decisions that the doctors presented. And I made those decisions. Which doctors to use, which ones to change. Who could come into his home, who could not come into his home. I could keep his children away if I wanted to.

*JH: You studied law while I did not. Help me to understand the legal issues at play here.*

NP: There were two litigations. One, to remove Erin Fleming from the position of dominance in his life. The second took place after Groucho died and Arthur charged that Erin had used "undue pressures" to coerce monies from Groucho. I think originally she got herself appointed temporary conservator. But Arthur and the children wanted her removed and they wanted her replaced, preferably by *them*. There could be no agreement in this area but apparently the judge was willing to remove her. That's where I came into the picture. I was originally called by Arthur. He wanted to present my name to the judge. And I was on fairly good terms with Erin. I thought she was crazy—a kook, you know—but I had nothing personally against her. And I just didn't want to come in as an opposition person. I told Arthur that I would only come into it if Erin agreed to it and she called me. Then, I felt that I could come in as genuinely *amicus curiae*. So I came recommended by both sides of the issue. Both sides were difficult in their own particular way. You could deal with the difficulty of the [Marx] side because there was a little more sanity to it. But hers was so unhinged and so emotional that she became very, very difficult for me. After a few months, I asked to be replaced. The judge was very angry with me. One month before Groucho died, then, the judge appointed Arthur's son Andy to replace me as conservator.

**JH: What made your role particularly difficult?**

NP: First of all, she was, to them, an interloper and they wanted her out of the picture. They felt that she was responsible for breaking up the family. And she, of course, wanted to get in closer so that she could be the one holding his hand at his bedside so that he would feel warmer towards *her*. It was a struggle for position, that's what it was! She was a little less reasoning than the other side, but I think essentially they were both struggling for the same thing. I gave them each a time when they could come over to the house. I didn't want anybody coming in the morning and staying all day and sort of staying over. They had their hours. She had her hours. I didn't want any run-ins between his friends and her friends, or him and her, or whatever. I was a traffic cop in the whole thing!

**JH: It must have taken up all of your time.**

NP: Yes, it did. The phone would ring right off the hook! On both sides, and both lawyers, and everybody demanding that I do this and bar her, and what the hell not—you know. She would call me and say that they were trying to poison him. Oh, the craziest accusations! And, oh, maybe they were true but I had no way of knowing. When he died … he left her $150,000, which I thought was very little compared with what I thought he would leave her. I thought it was altogether possible that he would leave her *everything*! Because she had quite a hold on him. But then they undertook to sue her for money they claimed she had gotten from him through undue pressures and through some shenanigans she had stolen the money—the equivalent of stealing from the Estate. This is after Groucho died. This is the second lawsuit—the big lawsuit that was going on more recently. I thought that it would be a hundred to one that she would win that case because she had all the glamour people who only saw the superficial aspects. When she threw a party … they thought that she was a good influence in his life. And in many ways she undoubtedly was. She helped him unbend and start spending money—he was a little slower at spending money. Arthur and his two sisters, through the Bank of America, sued her for money that they felt belonged in the Estate. It had nothing to do with the $150,000 [that Groucho willed to Erin]. Nobody was contesting that. But I didn't want to go to court for either side. I just didn't want to get involved.

*JH: Could you refuse if you were subpoenaed?*

NP: I said, "If I'm subpoenaed you can't count on my friendship." They're not going to subpoena unfriendly witnesses! Anyway, [the Marx children] won the case. They won something like $500,000. I bumped into her lawyer [before the final judgment] and he said, "I don't care if they win. They'll never get a dime." He must have known something. I don't think they've ever gotten a dime.

*JH: I thought it was a very sorry thing to see the trial drag on through the media. It lasted a long time.*

NP: Arthur was stubborn. I think he regrets it. Because I know what those legal bills are. Even if they get the money through a bond, it will have cost them much more.

## Erin Fleming

To declare that Erin Fleming was a controversial figure in the life of Groucho Marx would be an understatement. Nevertheless, I regarded myself as fortunate to be buzzed in through the gates of her modest (in Beverly Hills terms) and attractively furnished home just off of Sunset Boulevard, not far from the Trousdale Estates house at 1083 Hillcrest Road where she had, not long earlier, held sway. I am not here to pass judgment, nor to endorse anything that was reported to me—merely to document a conversation that I experienced in 1979. Our interview began with Erin telling me an anecdote at the expense of Arthur Marx, who had successfully opposed her in court.

EF: I love the story Zeppo told. It's so funny. But of course, he's a Marx Brother. He said the thing that was the matter with Arthur was that Ruth [Arthur's mother] was pregnant 8 months, in the act, and she had to do a dance with Zeppo. They did a mad fandango and she was so fat that he couldn't hang on to her and she flew out of his arms and landed with her zoop up the trombone player or the trombone up her zoop or whatever, and that permanently damaged Arthur's mind. If you knew Zeppo … [hysterical laughter]

*JH: I guess that from now on, this will be known as Zeppo's Zoop Story.*

EF: [laughing] I was talking to Zeppo last night on the phone and Zeppo told me I am in his will. And I said, "You're *not* dying, Zeppo, and if I can't get it out of you when you're alive, I don't want it when you're dead, honey!" [laughs] And that's exactly how I spoke to Groucho. Any talk of a will would just drive me nuts. He would say to me "Guess what I'm leaving you in my will?" I'd say "Please!" and he'd say "I'm leaving you my *luck*." How will I recognize it when I find it? I'm still waiting for it. [laughs]

*JH: It may show up, eventually.*

EF: I hope so, I'm waiting!

*JH: Do you wish to discuss the legal case?*

EF: They [Arthur and The Bank of America] should have gone after the publisher of the Anobile books instead of going after me. Eighty thousand copies had been sold in hard cover up until a certain point. We have testimony and all sorts of things. I mean, that would make sense to me, to go after something where there is money. But, to go after me because the cook said "Oh, that bitch! I just know that she's got millions in Switzerland!" Which was Luella. She has five sets of eyelashes.

**JH: *Describe the staff you oversaw at 1083 Hillcrest Road.***

EF: We had many cooks. Robin was a great beauty and fabulous cook but we couldn't keep Robin because Robin wanted to be in business. She wouldn't want to be stuck in that house. She's not a domestic. She's a free spirit with a college education. Now she has a thriving catering business in Santa Monica. We couldn't possibly pay her what she was worth. Someone like that is like part of the family. When Robin was there I never had to worry. She had a real intelligence. The average cook that wishes to be a domestic in Hollywood is either an itinerant without the papers or they see it as a step towards glamour, and they have varied sorts of problems, and one has to keep a distance from them. We would include them in parties and we were amused by their reaction because people that we didn't think were very important, they would think were tremendously glamorous. Groucho would sometimes nearly faint from laughter over this. We didn't have a huge staff but we always had a cook, and a maid to clean because cooks don't clean. Cooks don't do dishes. So that was the staff and then we had to have nurses around the clock. The afternoon nurse was the chief of nurses and the morning nurse staff was a revolving door. They would just not show up. I must have gone through 200. Better I should fire them than he. He would fire them as they were walking down the street and they would get into their cars and leave him there.

**JH: *It's hard to believe that a nurse would do that.***

EF: Well, you should have met him in the morning, No, he was actually a darling. He was actually a saint. But he was perfectly entitled to his rage. Old men are entitled to their rage. Goddard Lieberson said that to me early on, and it's true. There's a wonderful poem by Dylan Thomas: "Rage, rage, against the dying of the light. Do not go gentle into that good night." That's exactly what he was doing. He was raging against the fact that he was an antique and wanted to be twenty again. Do you have any idea what it is like to be that public of a figure—one *word* that resounds around the world? Without any privacy whatsoever, not even in his own home?

**JH: *Difficult for even a young man, I imagine, but especially for an old man.***

EF: For anyone. For a human being. Especially for a very sensitive man. A man who retreated into his study and read for hours and hours and just wanted some good company and sparkling conversation. And affection.

**JH: *Was that the principal thing that he needed? Affection?***

EF: *Genuine* affection. I don't mean hugging and kissing affection. I mean the kind of affection that is companionship. I wasn't just looking after him—he took care of me, too! It was mutual. I have many problems, I think all young women do, and I shared them with him. I said to him "In my position, I don't think I have any secrets from you at all. I can't think of anything." We'd talk over everything. And share everything. Share disappointments, and his failing health, and trying to, well, to cope with age.

**JH: Not to fight it but to cope with it.**
EF: Yes.

**JH: I imagine the dinner parties helped to keep things light. Would you describe a typical evening's entertainment?**
EF: We would put on little shows after dinner. "Peasie Weasie" was a big number. Bud Cort was in the Peasie Weasie Gang. Also Robyn. That was the beginning of the show we'd do a couple of times a week. I would sing harmony with him. He would sing the top part of the melody. We had a couple of duets. And then whoever was the dinner guest would have to join in. Sammy Davis. Bob Dylan. They were tremendous numbers. Sammy Davis tap danced on and off the table. Jimmy Caan. Elliot Gould was a regular. Elliot would sing various songs from Broadway shows. Groucho had one steadfast rule: No smoking marijuana in the house. But they'd do it in the bathroom. I didn't like to be the policeman, so it was up to Deana, my personal assistant. Every bathroom door had a key that would open it from the outside. And we would just knock and say we're coming in. My number one major problem in that house, with a large group of people, would be sniffing out who was smoking marijuana and kicking their asses out.

**JH: You must have gotten rid of quite a few guests that way.**
EF: No, no, no. They understood. That was the number one, most important, rule. No scandal at Groucho's house. I just didn't want that *National Enquirer* crap going on. It's not that I didn't want it—he didn't want it. I don't wish to sound like I'm speaking for myself when, actually, I was following orders. And they were very well thought out. You know, he talked one way—he used to talk about he and Garson Kanin smoking grass—but he was a very, very, very—"moral" is not the right word, and "ethical" doesn't even begin to cover it … he was healthy in a very clear way. He didn't mind people getting drunk but they wouldn't be invited back for a while. "Straight-laced" is the word. He was much more straight-laced than Zeppo.

**JH: I can imagine.**
EF: Zeppo was a wild man. But *tons* of fun. Groucho was every bit as much fun but much more like the parent of Zeppo. The parent of the Marx Brothers. The one who always made sure that they had what they needed. Groucho, Zeppo, and Gummo had a special bond, of course, that I was never part of. I was Groucho's confidant in many ways but I was excluded from the conversations between the brothers. But then, of course, there was the *code*. The code that Groucho and I had. We could talk without anyone really knowing what was said. That was great fun. Really great fun.

**JH: How did that go?**
EF: So many things came out in court—they were part of the code. When he would give money to George Jessel, for example, he would call up the accountant and the accountant would get the money—it wouldn't be much: two-hundred, three-hundred, or four-hundred dollars. Or sometimes Sheekman or various people requested help. And he wasn't throwing money away; they needed money, you know. And I would go count it out, put it in an envelope. He would later count it and put it in his pocket. In order to tell him that I had done this, I

would say "I laid the doctor." And that meant "I've got the money." Well, can you imagine three cooks testifying in court that I laid the doctor?! It has to be that kind of a code for him because that's the kind of a thing that he'd remember. I'm trying to express to you—I know that you know what I'm talking about—that when two people know each other very, very well, and who understand that yin and yang, they just have a special kind of rapport. And he knew how to handle me. This business about "undue influence," that's love as far as I'm concerned. He unduly influenced me to love him. And I did the best I could.

**JH: Perhaps you can move forward, now that the legal storm has passed.**
    EF: We'll see.

    ***Jay Hopkins**, in addition to interviewing associates of the Marx Brothers, is notorious for being the first American to cross the English Channel on foot and scuba dive to the bottom of Mount Everest. He can be reached at hopkinship@yahoo.com.*

# Appendix V

# The Groucho Marx Theory of Creativity

*by Matthew Coniam*

These final thoughts are offered purely for readers who want them. Though I warned in my previous book about the perils of "taking a joke apart to see how it works" and throughout this one have implicitly counseled against "back-seat" psychological interpretation, the truth is that I find Groucho and his comedy so fascinating that I have found both siren calls irresistible. I have tried to be rigorous in my reasoning, but even if I have failed, the questions I am attempting to get to the bottom of are valid ones in terms of this book's wider points of enquiry: Why was Groucho the comedian he was, as opposed to the comedian he might more easily have been? What influences came to bear on that decision? What is unique about Groucho's comedy? And where does the real man behind the quips factor in all this?

It is customary, I suppose, to ring Bergson's doorbell and run whenever we attempt to put humor on a philosophical footing, but actually *Le Rire* is less helpful here than one might suppose; first because he chose puckishly to write it in French, and second because, even in translation, his project is general; he wants to find the common features of humor in its various forms, whereas what I want to pin down is what makes Groucho *different*. Nonetheless, he gives us an encouraging starting point when he observes that "the comic spirit has a logic of its own, even in its wildest eccentricities. It has a method in its madness. It dreams, I admit, but it conjures up, in its dreams, visions that are at once accepted and understood by the whole of a social group. Can it then fail to throw light for us on the way that human imagination works, and more particularly social, collective and popular imagination?"

The more absurd the humor, the more it needs its own logic. Without it what you have is not comedy, but blancmange. Leo Rosten once jokingly defined Groucho's art as "doing to Reason what Einstein did to Time and Space." In my previous book I used the term "anti-logic" to describe the means by which Groucho's and, especially, Chico's verbal humor is both meaningless and yet, on its own terms, coherent. This is the architectural essential of absurd humor, as Salvador Dali and others so singularly failed to realize. Dali's film idea for the Marxes is a textbook in misunderstanding; unfunny no matter who might enact it but, most importantly, in no way drawing upon the strengths of the Marx Brothers or reflecting the distinctive qualities of their humor in any way.

Elsewhere in this book I suggested that a half-century of the pop-psychoanalytic diagnosing of Groucho has resulted in an essentially fraudulent portrait of his personality, and that viewed through the grown-up prism of evolutionary psychology—rather than from the middle of some Freudian fog—Groucho emerges as we all must: as a human animal, a collision of attributes neither accidental nor pre-destined, nor glibly reducible to the waved wand of morbid influence. This applies equally to his professional gifts as to his personal quirks. It is remarkable how numerously Groucho possessed those characteristics suggested by evolutionary psychologists as conducive to the creative personality: introversion, antisociality, wide range of interests, independence, rebelliousness, tolerance of ambiguity and tendency to melancholy (to say nothing of Jewishness!)

I bring up evolutionary psychology and creativity here for a reason. While working on this book, Groucho has been foremost in my mind at all times of the day and night, to a degree that has sometimes become unwelcome. (I have the kind of brain that lacks an off-switch.) But even I was surprised to find myself reminded of him while reading Sarnoff Mednick's classic 1962 paper *The Associative Basis of Creativity*. This, surely, was a Groucho too far? Yet the more I considered it, the more apposite the connection seemed.

Mednick's idea was that creativity is often associated with the ability to make remote associations between discrete ideas. The strongly creative person, presented with any word or concept, is able to rapidly choose from a range of associations, creating a body of associative connections. From this, further thoughts, concepts and associations (and, potentially, innovations) can then emerge. This associative complexity is the well-spring of creativity. Further, the ability to do so innately and at great speed provides a mechanistic model for the concept of intuitive creative thought, that ability to seemingly "find" rather than build new theories and syntheses in science, new works of music, and ad lib comedy.

Now, clearly, remote association of ideas to produce a comic effect is what Groucho, and his most influential writers (Johnstone, Kaufman, Perelman and all) have always done, and what the screen Groucho does. Puns, and the development of wild chains of association that are developed as if logically extending, but which in fact owe their coherency only to some irrelevant factor such as similarity of sound or emphasis, are all features of Groucho's comic armory that relate directly to Mednick's ideas.

Take a classic Groucho movie line: "Love flies out the door when money comes innuendo." It is the combination of the spuriousness of the association in the context proposed, as against the *obviousness* of the association in purely superficial terms (there is no fair connection between what Groucho says and the comment that prompted it besides the accidental similarity of sound between "innuendo" and "in your window," *but* the aural similarity is, nonetheless, strong and obvious), plus the speed with which Groucho accesses such remote connections and the confidence with which he volunteers them as a valid contribution to the discussion (i.e. as if it conveyed meaning beyond mere associative correlation linguistically) that creates the comedy. (Additional layers—such as the audacity of Groucho performing such associative feats in social contexts that should demand greater restraint and sobriety— add to the humorous effect.)

Without this theoretical model, I would find it hard to account for how we distinguish between a good pun and a bad one, since all are equally—that is to say entirely—meaningless on one level, and likewise explicable on another. Rather, what strikes us as so particularly excellent about, for example, the "innuendo" pun is the remoteness of the "actual" connection being accessed, in inverse relation to the clear "accuracy" of its superficial linguistic justification, plus the dexterity and confidence with which it is retrieved and converted into (again superficially) meaningful-seeming discourse. Whereas "better to have loft and lost than never to have loft at all" is a weaker pun because it is less *resourceful* on these same terms—a vaguer association, and only one syllable, thus "easier" to access. And so we read this as "less clever."

And this is all happening on two levels: this process is what the humor is based in, and thus why we find it amusing, *and* it is what the character on screen is actually *engaged in the act of doing*, and thus why we find *him* amusing, because we imagine him doing in an actual situation what was in fact contrived in a script.

Groucho also seems to embody the distinction between convergent and divergent thought, as formulated by J.P. Guilford. Convergent thought displays great accuracy: the arrival at a single, correct response. Divergent thought, however, displays creativity: the ability to create a range of responses that display imagination and originality. Thus if presented with some unknown object that clearly performs a function, a highly skilled convergent thinker will sum up its properties and conclude its purpose (through "reverse engineering"), but a highly skilled divergent thinker will be able to produce a wide range of hypotheticals, of great variety and invention. Given a commonplace object and asked to display a further use for it, the divergent thinker will produce a range of alternatives in various fields of activity; the convergent thinker will home in on one sensible application of the object. The three most relevant capacities being tested for variation are fluency (the ability to create the widest range of responses), originality (the ability to create the most novel responses) and flexibility (the ability to propose responses of significantly different kinds). If the object is a hammer, a less divergent thinker may come up with various different ways of making use of its essential purpose, which is to hit things. A more divergent thinker, however, will find a wider array of potential uses that are not all dependent on the same essential function, perhaps making use of its shape, or its weight, or some even remoter property. Both forms of response are useful and inventive, but only the latter is truly *creative* in a manner that is analogous to generative creativity in arts and sciences.

As with objects and their function, so with any other associative connection. Divergent thinking of great skill, but developed in tandem with an obvious and invalidating absurdity, is another defining ingredient of Marxian comedy. When Chico proposes that a crime in one house might have been committed by the occupants of the house next door, and his response to being told that there is no such house is that they therefore need to build one, he is enacting a kind of runaway parody of divergent thinking. His aim is to solve a crime and his proposed course of action is clearly insupportable of any such purpose, but because its logical thread remains connected to the original idea he ploughs on regardless, and the humor is created by how *little* he chooses to prioritize against how *much* to ignore, in order to avoid reversing or changing course. Groucho does something similar when he suggests a way to get around the possibility that it may not be permitted to build an opera house in Central Park might be to "do it at night when no one is looking." Again, the merit of a single naïve suggestion for addressing a challenge is presumed to outweigh the multiple grievous violations of logic and practical application it then generates in application.

For both Groucho and Chico it is the co-existence, within their propositions, of a central overriding absurdity and the logical rigor with which they develop the idea, plus their seeming inability to see how totally the former invalidates the latter, that creates the comic effect. This is why their respective processes cannot co-exist, and in their onscreen match-ups Groucho is reduced to a position of normality by the wilder reach of Chico's logic: he is, in effect, out-gunned.

The one interesting occasion when this does not at first appear to happen is, in fact, in the earlier example of the "house next door." Groucho's normal reaction to Chico's absurdity is frustration, sometimes expressing itself in gestures of physical discomfort and even aggression. When he too latches on to the idea of building another house and the two enthusiastically set to drawing up imaginary plans for it, what we are watching is not convergence but capitulation: Groucho has been consumed within Chico's logical processes and is no longer performing autonomously at all. That is why Groucho's response ("Well, now you're talking—what kind of a house do you think we ought to put up?") is as effective a laugh line as Chico's preceding one ("Well, then of course we gotta build one"). We laugh because, just as much as when he reduces Groucho to a shivering wreck of incomprehension or fury, Chico has won again.

Philosophically, this all opens interesting new vistas. Most important of all, it helps suggest a clear intellectual basis to our response to Groucho's comedy. The chief value of Marxian humor as traditionally postulated is emotional: the vicarious release of instinctive behaviors (and reasoning) denied free expression by social convention. This was its appeal to the Surrealists. (They lauded De Sade for the same reason, after all, almost as if to deliberately flag the possibility they may have somewhat missed the point.) Harpo, too, made oft-quoted comments to the same effect, and indeed it's a fair-enough partial reading of his own comedy, but not really the essence of the team as a whole. (Some like to the think of the team as composite parts of a single Freudian personality, with Harpo, obviously, as rampant id.)

This "soft anarchy" reading is ultimately self-consuming, as has been argued by the British existentialist (and recipient of one of the most amusing of all the *Groucho Letters*), Colin Wilson. Freedom of this sort is meaningless unless operating within a wider context of restraint, and relies upon the conformity of others for its existence. As such, as Wilson puts it in the chapter of his *A Criminal History of Mankind* titled "The Disadvantages of Consciousness":

> Humorists who make a virtue of anarchism—the Marx Brothers, Lenny Bruce, Mort Sahl, Spike Milligan—are generally regarded as the comedians of the intellectual, for the man with a sophisticated sense of humor, more daring and therefore funnier than the straightforward clown. (Even T.S. Eliot admired Groucho Marx.) Yet anyone who is slightly over-exposed to this type of humor—say, watching a season of Marx Brothers films on TV—soon becomes aware that its premises will not bear close scrutiny. Refusal to take anything seriously is only funny up to a point; then an odd taste of futility begins to creep in. When Groucho sings "Whatever it is, I'm against it," we only find the sentiment amusing for as long as we fail to think about it. Chaos is refreshing only so long as we can feel that pleasant sense of law and order hovering in the background.

This, in effect, was precisely the dilemma Groucho found himself in as youth culture hero in the 1960s and 1970s: as a rebel-guru in a prevailing climate of rebellion, he surprised himself with his need for the reassurance of an underlying social conservatism, and, in the arts, for aesthetic standards (both moral and structural). And I have come increasingly to the conclusion that what is funny in the Marxes' brushes with authority is something altogether subtler. Their attitude is not one of challenge to the prevailing order, still less an indictment of it, but rather of simple disregard. They are not rejecting societal codes so much as exploiting them for their own ends. As I said in my previous book, "they are forces for good inadvertently, because they are first and solely forces for honesty." Justice, in their purest Paramount form, is never their goal, but an inevitable side-effect of their integrity. They are accidental heroes, oblivious altruists, "bullies who target the strong."

Of course, the Marx Brothers have nothing to contribute to the eternal nature/nurture debate, because while it seems remarkable that one family should produce so many brothers with such pronounced gifts (including instinctive musical talent, mathematical talent and let's not forget Zeppo's inventiveness with engineering and mechanics) the fact that they shared the same genetic inheritance *and* the same developmental environment means there is no way to distinguish between the relevance of either factor. Likewise their Jewishness, though this is a highly relevant factor in creativity studies (the high proportion of Jews in the entertainment field and especially as innovators in comedy is well-known, but recall also their disproportionate presence among Nobel Prize winners). But Jewishness, again, is both a genetic and an environmental endowment, so we come no nearer to knowing which the dog and which the tail. (Personally, I'm a gene man, not because I think the factors usually adjudged environmental are inferior or secondary in their relevance to genetic factors, but because I think in the long run much of what is instinctively placed in the "nurture" column is itself reducible to nature, that is to the outcome of evolved processes. Incidentally, among the many suggested factors contributive to the high creativity rate among Western Jews is the greater than average preponderance of bilingualism in Jewish households, the ability to speak two languages being conducive to the development of remote association skills and thus creativity. It may be recalled here, then, that in addition to English, and however little Hebrew and Yiddish Groucho picked up, he also spoke his mother's native tongue of German with a confidence and dexterity that surprised many who saw him demonstrate it in his later life.)

What Groucho and his brothers give us, therefore, is an experience of a quantitatively different sort to that of any other of the great screen comedians. (Qualitative superiority, of course, is a matter for the individual assessor, though I presume little doubt as to where my personal vote is cast.) Their comedy is satisfying not in spite of its nonsensical and icono-clastic nature, and not because of it (in the simplistic sense perceived by the Surrealists). Rather, in its masterly display of complex associative patterns of language and meaning, it impresses the mind intuitively, so that the experience as perceived is as much an emotional as a cerebral one, somewhat in the manner of great music. The "meaning" of both may ulti-mately be as cold and formal as mathematics, but along the neural pathways of interpretation they travel it is somehow, wonderfully, separated from its meaning-value and diverted into pure transcendence.

# Chapter Notes

Groucho's correspondence, throughout, is from *The Groucho Letters* or *Love, Groucho*, unless otherwise stated. Many of the news reports are syndicated features that appeared under many banners: the one I cite is the one I happened to be looking at. Unless separately indicated, the citing of authors by name below and in the main text should be taken as reference to their respective books (see bibliography).

## Preface

1. *New York Times* (March 8, 1970).

## Introduction

1. *Montreal Gazette* (June 25, 1977).
2. *Warren Times Mirror* (November 9, 1938).
3. Interview with author, 2015.
4. *New York Post* (February 9, 1942).
5. See Diamond: *Gimme a Thrill* (BearManor, 2016).
6. See Coniam: *The Marx Brothers' Lost Film: Getting to the Bottom of a Mystery* (http://www.brentonfilm.com/articles/the-marx-brothers-lost-film-humor-risk-getting-to-the-bottom-of-a-mystery).
7. While it should have been obvious to all that Dumont could not possibly have been the clueless frump Groucho recalled in latterday interviews, the myth has died especially hard, presumably because it's such a great story. Simon Louvish broke the ground superbly in *Monkey Business*, but this writer has been privileged to be party to the researches of Jane Margaret Laight, which will finally present the real, fascinating Miss Daisy Dumont to the world in all her glory. (It is also thanks to Jane's research that I am here able to note, surely for the first time in print, that the middle name Chico gave his daughter Maxine was, believe it or not, Gummo.) Watch this space!
8. The line appears as publicity, among other places, in *Valley Morning Star* (January 2, 1937).
9. Strangely, Woody Allen's claim in *Annie Hall* that it originates in Freud's *Wit and Its Relation to the Unconscious* is untrue—unless I missed it after an entire evening spent plowing through the damned thing.
10. According to the website quoteinvestigator.com, the first known appearance of the club resignation story was in an Erskine Johnson column from October 20, 1949. I've seen it the *St. Petersburg Times* from No-

vember 2 of that year. It then shows up again in 1951, in the *Collier's* articles by Arthur Marx that formed the basis of his biography *Life With Groucho*, and from thence to posterity.
11. Interview with author, 2015.
12. Harry Ritz interviewed in *Esquire* (June 1976).
13. Interview with author, 2015.
14. George Bettinger to author, 2014.
15. MacGillivray.
16. Interview with author, 2015.

## Chapter 1

1. Interview with author, 2015.
2. *Variety* (May 5, 1906).
3. *PM* (January 27, 1946).
4. Contemporary reports on *Twentieth Century* from the Camden, NJ, *Courier-Post* (April 12, 1934), *Lewiston Evening Journal* (August 22, 1934), *Milwaukee Sentinel* (September 6, 1934), *Pittsburgh Press* (August 13, 1934), *Evening News* (April 12, 1934).
5. *Detroit Free Press* (December 18, 1929).
6. I especially enjoy the flavor of their relationship conveyed by a letter in Woollcott's correspondence preparing Harpo for his meeting with Helen Keller, in which he first advises, "If you have it in mind to send flowers, remember that for a blind person one flower that smells like all get-out is better than the most costly bouquet which may be merely something to look at," then adds as post-script: "Come to think of it, Helen would prefer a bottle of bourbon or scotch to a mere bouquet any day" (Kaufman).
7. Bader.
8. Interview with author, 2015.
9. On Benedict: Benedict Burton: *A Social Anthropologist in Britain and Berkeley* (manuscript and audio materials at Department of Anthropology, Berkeley), *Variety* (May 1, 1929), *New York Sun* (June 13, 1933); as press agent: *New York Sun* (August 20, 1934), *Palm Beach Daily News* (March 23, 1937); at RKO and Universal: *Film Bulletin* (July 29, 1939), *Motion Picture Daily* (October 1, 1936), *Variety* (June 11, 1936); and *Room Service: Harrisburg Telegraph* (October 5, 1937). "Sincerest Flattery": *New York Sun* (February 5, 1927). "Birth of a Theatrical Item": *New York Sun* (December 11, 1926). "Press Agents I Have Known": *New Yorker* (March 9, 1929). "My Poor Wife": *Collier's* (December, 1930). For press agents as recur-

ring source of humour, see also *Buffalo Courier-Express* (October 2, 1926) and "A Press Agent to his Favorite Santa Claus" (*New York Sun*, December 24, 1926).

10. "Muscle-Bound" in Groucho Marx Collection, Smithsonian.

11. "Madcap Mary Mooney" in Groucho Marx Collection, Smithsonian. Ken Englund would go on to be a significant comic writer in movies and radio, but at this point he is of additional significance to the Marx Brothers story. On radio, Groucho and Chico had just made the mysterious *Marx Brothers Show*, the pilot (and only) episode of which turns up often on public domain compilations (usually titled "Hollywood Agents"). Almost nothing about the show has hitherto been established, and its stated sponsor, "the Hodgkiss Packing Company" is an obvious dummy. In fact, it was recorded on January 15, 1937 as a sponsor's demo, and by July Groucho and Chico were reportedly in talks with Sinclair Oil Co. in the hopes of it going to full series. MGM were hovering over the project, too: radio producer Bill Bacher, newly attached to the studio as a movie producer but with no assignments forthcoming, offered to produce the series, with MGM's permission, on the understanding that the Marxes would make their next film for Mayer. As we know, an unmatched offer from RKO resulted in stars and studio grumpily parting company, and it is entirely possible that this series was one of the casualties of that process. It is not definite (though very possible) that Englund is the author of the one show that was made, but he was certainly commissioned to write the series, and got as far as penning several prospective scripts, preserved among his papers at the University of California. He would have been working on these scripts at around the same time as he was collaborating with Groucho on *Madcap Mary Mooney*. (*Gloversville and Johnstown Morning Herald*, January 25, 1943; *Long Island Daily Press*, January 16, 1937; *Variety*, August 18, 1937.).

12. Contemporary reports on *The King and the Chorus Girl* from *Milwaukee Sentinel* (April 10, 1937), *Picture Play* (April and June, 1937), *Pittsburgh Post-Gazette* (March 27, 1937), *Pittsburgh Press* (March 6 and 27, 1937), *Spokesman-Review* (April 17, 1937), *Sunday Morning Star* (May 16, 1937), *Sydney Morning Herald* (July 19, 1937).

13. Kennedy.

14. *Valley Morning Star* (January 2, 1937).

15. Mitchell.

## Chapter 2

1. Aborted theatre ideas: *The Groucho Letters*, *Chicago Tribune* (March 2, 1946), *Variety* (20 June and October 24, 1945).

2. Contemporary reports on *Franklin Street* from *Chicago Tribune* (1943), *Milwaukee Journal* (August 9, 1942), *Motion Picture Daily* (September 8, 1942), *Pittsburgh Post-Gazette* (September 7, 1942), *Prescott Evening Courier* (July 22, 1942) and *Variety* (22 July and September 9, 1942).

3. Sherlock Holmes: *Groucho Letters*, Goldstein and *Melbourne Argus* (June 11, 1941).

4. Rosten.

5. Interview with author, 2015.

6. Victory Caravan: Retrospective: Arce, Kanfer, Lahr, Zoglin, *The Groucho Phile*. Contemporary: *Film Daily* (April 27, 1942), *Miami News* (May 1 1942), *Variety* (April 22, 29, May 6, 1942).

7. Depending on who you ask, "Who's Olive?," sometimes known as "The Thorndykes," was written for Groucho either by Manny Manheim or Hal Kanter, though neither were listed among the Caravan's writers, of whom the most likely contenders are Irving Brecher and Ken Englund. (The others were George Kaufman, Moss Hart, Jerome Chodorov, Russel Crouse, Howard Lindsay, Martin Berkeley, Irving Berkeley and Matt Brooks.) A radio version with Dinah Shore is available on CD.

8. *Milwaukee Journal* (January 30, 1944).

9. *Chicago Tribune* (August 6, 1945).

10. *Miami Daily News-Record* (November 24, 1946).

11. Contemporary reports on *Copacabana* from *Chicago Tribune* (October 29, 1946), *Deseret News* (July 2, 1947), St. Petersburg, FL, *Evening Independent* (January 8, 1948), *Film Bulletin* (April 14, 12 and May 26, 1947), *Film Daily* (21 and May 22, 1947), *Kentucky New Era* (January 16, 1948), *Miami News* (January 31, 1947), *Motion Picture Herald* (January 25 and June 28, 1947), *Montreal Gazette* (June 25, 1947), *Motion Picture Daily* (May 2, 16 and 28, June 28, July 1, 16, 22 and 30, 1947), *Pittsburgh Post-Gazette* (November 21, 1947), *Radio-TV Mirror* (February 1954), *Showmen's Trade Review* (August 17, 24 and 31, September 14 and 28, October 5, November 23, December 14, 1946), *Spokane Daily Chronicle* (December 5, 1946), *Spokesman-Review* (October 4, 1947), *Sydney Morning Herald* (November 10, 1947) and *Milwaukee Journal* (November 29, 1946 and May 30, 1947). From the latter, a minority interest footnote that diverted me, at least: "Incidentally, a former Milwaukee player, James Cade, who headed for a Hollywood career last fall, was scheduled for a small part in *Copacabana*. His local friends may have better luck spotting him than this reviewer." Retrospectives: Coslow, MacGillivray.

## Chapter 3

1. Dwan.

2. *Motion Picture Daily* (April 30, 1947).

3. Dick.

4. See Coniam: *Annotated Marx Brothers* for more on various Cowan plans, including biopic, and Cowan generally.

5. Russell.

6. *Toledo Blade* (November 19, 1975).

7. Contemporary reports on *Double Dynamite* from *The Age* (August 22, 1952), *Amarillo Daily News* (December 2, 1947), *Brooklyn Eagle* (October 23, 1948), St. Petersburg, FL, *Evening Independent* (No-

vember 2, 1948), *Evening News* (Pennsylvania) ( July 19, 1948), *Independent Exhibitors Film Bulletin* (March 1, 1948 and October 8, 1951), *Modern Screen* (November, 1951), *Motion Picture Daily* (April 30, 1947), *New York Times* (December 26, 1951), *Ottawa Citizen* (December 1, 1948), *Pittsburgh Post-Gazette* (October 30, 1949, January 21, 1950 and December 25, 1951), *Radio Mirror* (February, 1949), *Screenland* (March, April and November, 1949), *Showmen's Trade Review* (December 18, 1947, February 21, October 30, November 27, December 4 and 25, 1948), *Spokesman-Review* ( January 1, 1952) and *The Times* (San Mateo, California) (December 8, 1947). Marie Behar on Mel Berns and the moustache: interview with author, 2015.

8. In the early forties, as head writer for Milton Berle, he hired Groucho's son Arthur as a gag-man (according to Arce, because he owed Groucho a favor) and later collaborated with him on plays and teleplays. (Their *Everybody Loves Me* is generally taken to be an acidic portrait of Groucho).

9. Groucho Collection, Smithsonian.

10. *Ibid.*

11. *Montreal Gazette* ( July 28, 1951).

12. Contemporary reports on *A Girl in Every Port* from *Albany Democrat-Herald* ( July 13, 1951), *Brooklyn Eagle* (February 28, 1951), *Buffalo Courier-Express* ( June 22, 1951), *Chicago Tribune* (March 19, 1952), *Deseret News* ( July 3, November 23, December 3 and 9, 1951), *Eugene* (OR) *Guard* (September 16, 1951), *Film Bulletin* ( June 18, 1951 and 14 January and February 25, 1952), *Milwaukee Journal* (April 1, 1951), *Montreal Gazette* ( June 23, 1951), *Motion Picture Daily* ( July 11 and December 27, 1951 and February 19 and 26, 1952), *New York Times* (February 14, 1952), *Ottawa Citizen* (May 11, 1951), *Philadelphia Inquirer* (February 21, 1952) *Saratogian* ( July 3, 1951), *Sunday Herald* (March 30, 1952), *Toledo Blade* (February 20, 1951), *Tuscaloosa News* ( June 19, 1951).

13. Early reports claimed the film would star Allan Nixon, Wilson's second husband, but the union was a volatile one and had already cost him a planned role in *My Friend Irma Goes West* (1950), withdrawn during one of their several separations. They had, in fact, divorced in 1952, but this casting was announced afterwards—presumably as a charitable gesture on Wilson's part, but if so, one on which she had second thoughts. (*Hollywood Reporter*, March 19, 1952).

14. Perelman.

## Chapter 4

1. *Variety* (October 29, 1947).

2. *The Mail* (Adelaide) (May 29, 1954).

3. *Buffalo Courier-Express* (February 10, March 31, May 28, 1955), Alex Atkinson: "A Night at the Castle" in *Punch* (issue unknown, 1955).

4. *Buffalo Courier-Express* ( June 8, 1958) and *Tonawanda News* (May 6, 1958).

5. *Milwaukee Journal* (April 1, 1951), *Screenland* (August 1951), *Sydney Morning Herald* (April 12, 1951).

6. *Terre Haute Star* (February 1, 1950).

7. *The News* (Adelaide) (April 15, 1950).

8. *Toledo Blade* (March 2, 1950).

9. Arce.

10. *Desert Sun* (December 1, 1955).

11. *Delta-Democrat Times* (February 1, 1950).

12. *Sunday Gazette-Mail* ( July 17, 1960).

13. All Arthur quotes in this section: *Chicago Tribune* (November 7, 1954).

14. Interview with author, 2015.

15. *Ibid.*

16. *Ibid.*

17. For Groucho, of course, obvious compensation came in the form of a steady supply of free automobiles. And while others on the show weren't treated to quite the same degree of largesse, there were at least generous discounts. Sue Tyler Edwards told me: "During the years my Dad wrote for the show we had several DeSotos. It must have been a pretty good deal because we kept getting them. I remember one weekend we kids decided to surprise Dad and wash our, I think, third new DeSoto. We used the wrong soap, though, some kind of harsh cleanser that took the paint off a good-sized section of the hood. Dad was not particularly into cars, but he never let us touch that one again!"

18. Interview with author, 2016.

19. Groucho quotes on making *Story of Mankind* from *Deseret News* (February 15, 1957), *Lawrence Journal-World* (November 12, 1957), *Toledo Blade* ( January 7, 1957).

20. *St. Petersburg Times* ( June 21, 1956).

21. *Pittsburgh Post-Gazette* (December 27, 1955).

22. *Daily Reporter* (February 7, 1956).

23. *Desert Sun* (December 19, 1961).

24. *Evening Review* ( January 27, 1961).

25. *Ibid.*

26. *Philadelphia Enquirer* (March 3, 1960).

## Chapter 5

1. *Gadsden Times* ( July 17, 1960).

2. Dan Jenkins "Hollywood" syndicated column ( July 31, 1953).

3. Arce.

4. *Chicago Tribune* (February 29, 1960).

5. *Kentucky New Era* (April 22, 1964).

6. Interview with author, 2015.

7. My discussion of *The Mikado* is massively reliant on the specialist knowledge of Marjie Cardwell.

8. *The Groucho Letters.*

9. Kanfer.

10. *Chicago Tribune* (May 16, 1960).

11. *Toledo Blade* (September 27, 1961).

12. *Desert Sun* (October 26, 1961).

13. *Toledo Blade* (September 27, 1961).

14. Arce.

15. *Chicago Tribune* (September 14, 1961).

16. *Pittsburgh Post-Gazette* (May 9, 1962).

17. *The Groucho Letters.*

18. Contemporary reports on *Time for Elizabeth*

from *Chicago Tribune* (October 22, 1946), *Desert Sun* (May 29, 1957), *Film Bulletin* ( Jan 1, 1951), *Knickerbocker News* ( July 7, 1959), *Milwaukee Sentinel* ( July 18, 1948), *Morning Record* (April 27, 1964), *Sarasota Herald-Tribune* (September 2, 1952), *Sunday Herald* (Aug 3, 1958).

19. Kanfer.

20. Arce.

21. *Ibid.*

22. Dwan.

## Chapter 6

1. *Desert Sun* (October 10, 1959). In the same interview Groucho reflects: "Why is it that restaurants are always more beautiful than the people who frequent them?"

2. *Morning Record* (April 27, 1964).

3. *New York Times Book Review* (November 10, 1963).

4. Arce.

5. Sheldon anecdote told me by Steve Cox, author of *Dreaming of Jeannie: TV's Prime Time in a Bottle.* According to actress Marlo Thomas, Groucho also auditioned for the role of her father on the sitcom *That Girl.* This would have been a regular recurring role: very different from the walk-ons. A surprise that he wanted to do such a thing at this point; a bigger surprise that he consented to audition first. No wonder Thomas recalls his being very nervous, and, subsequently, the general feeling of gloom at the realization that he simply wasn't good enough to justify taking the idea further.

6. *Desert Sun* (October 12, 1961).

7. *Kentucky New-Era* (April 22, 1964).

8. *Desert Sun* (December 12, 1964).

9. *Desert Sun* (March 27, 1964).

10. *The Telegraph* (February 24, 1965).

11. *Chicago Tribune* (February 13, 1965).

12. *Deseret News* (April 14, 1965).

13. *Toledo Blade* ( June 11, 1965).

14. Louvish: *Monkey Business.*

15. Kanfer.

16. Interview with Jay Hopkins in *Re: Marx* (Vol. 1, No. 2).

17. *Chicago Tribune* (February 19, 1971).

18. Chandler.

19. Johnson.

20. *Milwaukee Journal* (April 11, 1969).

21. Arce.

22. *New York Times* (March 8, 1970).

23. Marx-Reiner correspondence: Groucho Collection, Smithsonian.

24. *Desert Sun* (December 16, 1958).

25. Groucho Collection, Smithsonian.

26. Baxter.

27. Chandler: *I, Fellini.*

28. *Toledo Blade* (September 3, 1968).

29. *Sarasota Herald-Tribune* (April 30, 1968).

30. *Sarasota Herald-Tribune* (April 30, 1968).

31. Chandler.

32. *New York Times* (March 8, 1970).

33. *Chicago Tribune* (May 21, 1972).

34. *Reading Eagle* (August 20, 1967), Arce, Kanfer.

35. Eden's acting career never did take off, despite the bit-parts Groucho wangled for her in *The Story of Mankind*, *The Mikado* and *Time for Elizabeth*, though she does also show up in tiny or unbilled roles in a handful of other movies. What might have been her biggest break was as Peggy in producer Harold Kennedy's prospective 1959 revival of *The Front Page.* According to the *Desert Sun* ( January 27, 1959) Pat O'Brien was on board to reprise his original role, and Eden beat off a number of rivals (including Mary Beth Hughes) for the part. Sadly, it wasn't until a decade later that Kennedy was able to mount the production, and to considerable success, by which time Eden was no longer performing. She died of cancer at age 53 in 1983.

36. *High Times* (February, 1981).

37. Correspondence with author, 2014.

38. Interview with author, 2014.

39. *Milwaukee Journal* (April 11, 1969).

40. *Daily Reporter* (February 7, 1956).

41. *Gallery Magazine* (November 1973)

42. Des Moines Register ( July 28, 1958).

43. Contemporary reports on *Minnie's Boys* from *The Day* (March 26, 1970), *New York Times* (March 8, 1970), *Pittsburgh Post-Gazette* ( July 14, 1972), *St Petersburg Times* (March 9 and July 20, 1970), *Sarasota Herald-Tribune* ( January 30, 1969), *Sumter Daily Item* ( June 22, 1970). Retrospective: Arce, Kanfer.

44. *Saturday Review* (December 25, 1954).

## Chapter 7

1. *Sarasota Herald-Tribune* (April 4, 1972).

2. *Boca Raton News* ( June 10, 1973).

3. Lahr: *The Diaries of Kenneth Tynan.*

4. *The Hour* ( January 3, 1978), *Yonkers Herald Statesman* (December 31, 1977).

5. Arthur vs. Erin: Kanfer, Norman, Stoliar, *Beaver County Times* (April 21, 1977), *New York Times* (February 6, 1983), *Sydney Morning Herald* (March 30, 1983).

6. *Montreal Gazette* ( June 25, 1977).

7. Contemporary reports on *An Evening with Groucho* from *Canberra Times* (December 6, 1972), *Chicago Tribune* (December 1, 1972), *Desert Sun* (September 11, 15 and 18, 1972), *Long Beach Independent* (November 2, 1972), *Sarasota Herald-Tribune* (February 15, 1972).

8. It remains to be seen what an impartial technical analysis of the audio would conclude as to which proportions of the three shows are used on the disc, presuming the original edit plan has not survived. Indeed, it would be wonderful if all three recordings could be separately released.

9. *Reading Eagle* (November 13, 1972).

10. Interview with author, 2015.

11. Thanks to David McGillivray for making me aware of this oddity, and showing me the poster.

12. Groucho Collection, Smithsonian.

13. All Anobile quotes: interview with author, 2015.

14. Interview with author, 2015.

15. *New York Times* (March 8, 1970).

16. Chandler.

## Afterword

1. With thanks to Marie Behar.

## Appendix II

1. "Talking Man," *The New Yorker*, April 17, 2000.

2. Undated *New York Evening World* clipping in the Smithsonian's Groucho Marx Collection, ca. July 1924.

3. *Variety*, January 14, 1921.

4. *Billboard*, September 23, 1918.

5. It was cheekily advertised as "The Somewhat Original School Act," *Variety*, April 15, 1911.

6. Quoted in Simon Louvish: *Monkey Business: The Lives and Legends of the Marx Brothers*.

7. The photo is in the personal collection of Frank Ferrante. Its date was determined by Paul Wesolowski and Robert Moulton.

8. Both photos are reprinted in Glenn Mitchell, *The Marx Brothers Encyclopedia*. Robert Moulton confirmed the date of the photo shoot.

9. Some of these are reprinted in *The Marx Bros. Scrapbook*.

10. The controversy is reconstructed from Hammond *Herald Tribune* columns in the Groucho Marx Collection.

11. See Robert Florey's interview in *The Marx Bros. Scrapbook*.

12. It's reprinted in *The Marx Bros. Scrapbook*.

13. From a letter quoted in Charlotte Chandler, *Hello, I Must Be Going: Groucho and His Friends*, Chapter Six.

14. See Coniam: *The Annotated Marx Brothers*.

15. The letter, dated February 12, 1942, is in *The Groucho Letters*.

16. See Hector Arce, *Groucho*; or Matthew Coniam, this book in front of you.

17. Reprinted in *The Groucho Phile*.

18. During the *You Bet Your Life* years, Groucho occasionally described himself using this phrase; for example, in "Groucho Marx Begins 9th Year on NBC-TV," *Dally Reporter* (Dover, Ohio), September 19, 1959.

19. See Groucho Marx and Hector Arce: *The Secret Word Is Groucho*.

20. Associated Press, November 16, 1996.

## Appendix III

1. A common mistake made even by those who know the basic facts is to assume that the only episode the cigar line could *possibly* have taken place in was the radio-only episode with Mrs. Story. There's no real evidence to support this assumption, other than the Mrs. Story episode being cited in *The Secret Word Is Groucho*. Since the account offered in the book is highly dubious, we have no way of ruling out the possibility that the line *could* have happened (off-air, of course) in any of the several episodes that featured various overly fertile married couples. Co-director Bernie Smith is the only staff member who always maintained that Groucho said the line, and Smith was the guy in charge of keeping the production log on the contestants—so it's highly likely that he was the one who identified the episode as having been the one with Mrs. Story when he was interviewed for *Secret Word*. There's no sense in my querying Smith's account of the line having happened at all while simultaneously taking his word for it that the line could *only* have taken place in this one radio-only episode. There were several contestants over the years who had far too many children for anyone's good; theoretically, the line *could* have taken place in any of these shows.

2. There's a small chance that some overly trusting folks with poor hearing might have been misled by the witless "re-enactment" perpetrated on LP record by Kermit Schafer (inventor of the term "bloopers"). If you were convinced that was actually Groucho in the Schafer recording, you really need to get your glasses fixed. It's also worth noting that Bernie Smith's daughter Lucinda has confirmed in interviews for the present book that her father never had a copy of the unedited, pre-broadcast recording of the Mrs. Story radio-only episode which has never surfaced (or of any episodes). So that wraps things up with a nice, neat bow: No one has seen *or* heard the line. People just *remember* it!

# Bibliography

As in my previous book, *The Annotated Marx Brothers*, in shaping the historical background to this account of Groucho's career as a solo performer I have made extensive use of contemporary newspapers, periodicals and trade journals; these are accounted for in the Notes and Sources.

In the following list of all books cited and consulted, I have given the exact edition I used: if different, original year of publication is given in parentheses.

Arce, Hector. *Groucho*. New York: Putnam, 1979.

Bacall, Lauren. *By Myself*. London: Coronet, 1980 (1978).

Bader, Robert S. (ed). *Groucho Marx and Other Short Stories and Tall Tales: Selected Writings of Groucho Marx*. London: Faber, 1997 (1993).

Baxter, John. *Fellini*. New York: Fourth Estate, 1993.

Cavett, Dick. *Talk Show*. New York: Henry Holt & Co., 2010.

Chandler, Charlotte. *Hello, I Must Be Going: Groucho and His Friends*. London: Robson, 1979 (1978).

_____. *I, Fellini*. New York: Cooper Square Press, 2001.

Coniam, Matthew. *The Annotated Marx Brothers*. Jefferson, NC: McFarland, 2015.

Coslow, Sam. *Cocktails for Two*. New York: Arlington House, 1977.

Dick, Bernard F. *The Merchant Prince of Poverty Row: Harry Cohn of Columbia Pictures*. Lexington: University Press of Kentucky, 1993.

Dwan, Robert. *As Long As They're Laughing!* Baltimore: Midnight Marquee, 2000.

Eyles, Allen. *The Complete Films of the Marx Brothers*. New York: Citadel Press, 1982.

Goldstein, Malcolm. *George S. Kaufman: His Life, His Theatre*. Oxford University Press, 1980.

Halliwell, Leslie. *Halliwell's Film Guide*. 7th ed., London: Paladin, 1989.

Johnson, Paul. *Brief Lives*. London: Hutchinson, 2010.

Kanfer, Stefan. *Groucho: The Life and Times of Julius Henry Marx*. London: Allen Lane, 2000.

Kaufman, Beatrice, and Joseph Hennessey (eds). *The Letters of Alexander Woollcott*. London: Cassell, 1946.

Kennedy, Matthew. *Joan Blondell: A Life Between Takes*. Jackson: University Press of Mississippi, 2009.

Lahr, John (ed). *The Diaries of Kenneth Tynan*. London: Bloomsbury, 2001.

_____. *Notes on a Cowardly Lion*. Berkeley: University of California Press, 2000 (1969).

Louvish, Simon. *Coffee with Groucho*. London: Duncan Baird, 2007);

_____. *Monkey Business: The Lives and Legends of the Marx Brothers*. London: Faber & Faber, 1999.

MacGillivray, Scott, and Jan MacGillivray. *Gloria Jean: A Little Bit of Heaven*. Nebraska: iUniverse, 2005.

Mark, Arthur. *Life with Groucho*. London: Gollancz, 1954.

Marx, Groucho. *Groucho and Me*. London: Virgin, 1994 (1959).

_____. *The Groucho Letters*. London: Michael Joseph, 1967.

_____. *Memoirs of a Mangy Lover*. London: Mayflower-Dell, 1965 (1963).

Marx, Groucho, and Richard J. Anobile. *The Marx Brothers Scrapbook*. New York: Harper & Row, 1989 (1973).

Marx, Groucho, with Hector Arce. *The Groucho Phile*. New York: Galahad, 1979 (1976).

_____. *The Secret Word Is Groucho*. New York: Berkley-Medallion, 1977 (1976).

Marx Allen, Miriam (ed). *Love, Groucho: Letters from Groucho Marx to His Daughter Miriam*. London: Faber & Faber, 1997 (1992).

Meredith, Scott. *George S. Kaufman and the Algonquin Round Table*. London: Allen & Unwin, 1977.

Mitchell, Glenn. *The Marx Brothers Encyclopaedia*. London: Batsford, 1996.

Norman, Barry. *The Movie Greats*. London: Hodder & Stoughton, 1981.

Perelman, S. J. *The Most of S. J. Perelman*. London: Methuen, 1979 (1959).

Rosten, Leo. *People I Have Loved, Known or Admired*. London: W.H. Allen, 1971.

Russell, Jane. *An Autobiography*. London: Sidgwick & Jackson, 1986.

Stoliar, Steve. *Raised Eyebrows: My Years Inside Groucho's House*. Revised ed. Oklahoma: BearManor, 2011.

Stuart, Gloria. *I Just Kept Hoping*. New York: Little, Brown, 1999.

Wilson, Colin. *A Criminal History of Mankind*. London: Granada, 1984.

Zoglin, Richard. *Hope: Entertainer of the Century*. New York: Simon & Schuster, 2014.

# Index

Page numbers in bold italics indicate pages with illustrations.

Ingram Content Group UK Ltd.
Milton Keynes UK
UKHW032350110623
423083UK00021B/543